THE POWER OF DARKNESS

The Power of Angels, Demons, and Wicked Politicians

"Power without love is reckless and abusive, and love without power is sentimental and anemic. Power at its best is love implementing the demands of justice, and justice at its best is power correcting everything that stands against love."

Dr. Martin Luther King Jr.

MICHAEL RAY LEMONS

ISBN: 979-8-9885303-8-1

Published in United States of America

Published by

DEDICATION

This book is for the brave dreamers fighting against racism, oppression, unfairness, and wrongdoing. We salute the heroes who have sacrificed their freedom or faced major life shifts to challenge a system that too frequently puts others at a disadvantage.

TABLE OF CONTENTS

ABOUT THE AUTHOR

Michael Ray Lemons is an insightful author known for his thought-provoking works that explore complex historical, cultural, and social dynamics. With a keen eye on themes of power, race, and spirituality, Lemons' books challenge readers to look deeper into the forces that shape human history and society.

Trapped Between Two Worlds: The Angel Without Wings – A compelling narrative that delves into themes of faith, inner conflict, and the struggle between light and darkness, exploring the journey of an angel who grapples with their place in a complex, often unforgiving world.

The Esau Effect: Reshaping the World in the Act of War – This work investigates the far-reaching impact of war on global power structures, examining how conflict and the pursuit of dominance have historically reshaped societies, economies, and ideologies.

Cush to Mysterious Babylon: Africa and the Covenant People – Lemons examines the historical and spiritual significance of Africa, connecting ancient civilizations with the biblical "Covenant People" and offering new perspectives on African history's global impact.

Kush to Mysterious Babylon: The History of the Hindu Caste & White Privilege (2nd edition) – This expanded edition provides a deep dive into the Hindu caste system and explores parallels with concepts of race and privilege, shedding light on the intersections of historical power structures and social hierarchy.

The Power of Darkness – In this profound analysis, Lemons uncovers hidden conspiracies and the dark underbelly of American history, highlighting the impact of slavery, capitalism, and geopolitics in shaping the injustices that persist today. This work connects past events with modern social issues, encouraging readers to confront uncomfortable truths about history and power.

Through his books, Michael Ray Lemons invites readers to reconsider mainstream narratives and to reflect on the enduring influence of historical events on today's global society.

ACKNOWLEDGMENT

My deepest thanks go out to those confronting racial disparities in America and dealing with prejudice, unfairness, and oppression. Your stories of fortitude have deeply influenced this book, serving as a potent testament to the pressing call for transformation, comprehension, and compassion. Each story contained herein mirrors your bravery and unspoken realities, steering my educational journey and amplifying voices that are often silenced.

This book is devoted to you—the courageous, the sidelined, and the advocates for justice. It stands as an homage to your unbroken spirit and a rallying cry for a more inclusive, fair society. May it echo as a beacon of optimism and a reminder that we must come together in our quest for equality, ensuring every voice is acknowledged and every story esteemed. Thank you for being the inspiration behind these words and allowing me to carry forward your narratives.

PREFACE

The arrival of White settlers from Europe on the soil of the Americas triggered substantial shifts in the region, including violence. The mass migration to the American frontier quickly became a shared space, and then the clashes, gentrification, and displacement began immediately on the indigenous population. This was accompanied along with kidnapped Africans from across the Atlantic, who were to become the slaves of their captors. The building of America began with the exploitation of abducted men, women, and children, a strategy designed to profit from and optimize the labor of the enslaved, a practice that was instrumental in shaping the society of the New World.

The enslaved individuals became part of a complex system, serving as America's most significant economic asset in a structure deeply embedded in slavery and free labor to benefit whites only. The daily productivity of each person was monitored, and those failing to achieve their set quotas were subjected to physical punishment. The use of the whip and other forms of violence further coerced them into increasing their workload in a shorter time frame. Consequently, the early triumphs and wealth accumulation of global capitalism owe much to the blood, sweat, and suffering of the Indigenous population and African slaves.

The economic engine of capitalism was built from a nightmarish system of terror and violence, founded on the backs of slaves for free labor. This system generated instant millionaires and expansive plantations, particularly in the South. These slave plantations produced raw materials such as cotton, sugar, rice, wheat, and tobacco, which were then exported to the North and countries across Europe. An insidious combination of greed, psychological manipulation, and physical brutality, reinforced by the myth of white superiority, justified this system of forced labor. This not only led to gross injustices but also allowed bystanders to look the other way, thus transforming America into a society blighted by blindness and evil.

The United States, in its past, was torn asunder by a civil war, a conflict rooted in a societal structure that promoted white supremacy and endorsed the enslavement of African Americans. Today, the notion that our nation is slowly evolving into an authoritarian regime doesn't come as much of a surprise. It seems our great nation was constructed on a framework that champions dominance and superiority, closely resembling a caste system.

Yet, there's a silver lining. If we listen closely to the whispers of prophecy, a new era could be just around the corner. If America is indeed the 'Mysterious Babylon,' then those in power may only enjoy their victory momentarily. A change might be closer than we think, promising to be a turning point in our history.

The dynamics of international relations are evolving rapidly, with over 40 countries expressing interest in joining the BRICS group, and 15 have formally joined membership. This emerging alliance, which includes economic powerhouses like China and Russia, has significant implications for Africa, a continent rich in natural resources.

Africa's vast wealth of natural resources has long been a point of interest for global powers. However, the exploitation of these resources often results in the value flowing to the West and East Asia rather than benefiting the African nations themselves. This pattern has historical roots, dating back to conflicts involving Assyrians, Babylonians, Persians, and even the Greco-Roman Empire. Both World Wars also saw African resources playing a crucial role in global geopolitics.

The exploitation of African resources remains a primary method for wealthy nations to influence African states, perpetuating a cycle of dependency and inequality. The rise of the BRICS Alliance marks a potential shift away from reliance on Western powers for Africa, offering a new avenue for partnership.

Top U.S. lawmakers are raising the red flag over the growing clout of the BRICS nations, highlighting that their rise could shake up the current economic order and chip away at the power of the U.S. Dollar. This could mean trouble for the dollar's value. Meanwhile, the U.S. faces criticism for increasing its military presence in Africa, a move seen by some as a way to protect its interests. On the flip side, China is becoming a key ally for many African nations, pouring in investments and creating new trade possibilities. The country is also rolling up its sleeves to build essential infrastructure across the continent, like roads, railways, ports, and energy projects, which are reshaping Africa's landscape.

While some suggest that the BRICS Alliance could precipitate an apocalyptic conflict akin to biblical Armageddon, it warrants a critical and discerning approach, particularly as they imply Africa could become entangled in a geopolitical struggle between Eastern and Western nations. The BRICS Alliance's growth highlights the enduring value of Africa's natural resources in global politics. It is essential to stay attentive to these geopolitical shifts and their possible effects on the future.

INTRODUCTION

The history of America is marked by numerous instances of government involvement in actions that have sparked controversy and debate. These actions, often shrouded in secrecy and political maneuvering, have had significant implications on social equality and peace. It is usually the disadvantaged and marginalized groups that bear the brunt of these actions, finding themselves needing to advocate for their basic rights and freedoms. The impact of these governmental activities continues to shape the socio-political landscape of the nation.

Alabama Prison Labor Lawsuit

A lawsuit has been filed against the State of Alabama in the U.S. District Court for the Middle District of Alabama, drawing comparisons to the post-Civil War "convict leasing system." This system, according to the Equal Justice Initiative, allowed Southern states to "lease" prisoners to private entities such as railways, mines, and plantations for their profit. The prisoners were not paid and were forced to work in hazardous, often lethal conditions.

The defendants in the lawsuit include McDonald's, KFC, Wendy's, and Burger King franchisees, Alabama Governor Kay Ivey,

State Attorney General Steve Marshall, the Alabama Department of Corrections, the Alabama Board of Pardons and Paroles chair, and local government entities like the cities of Troy and Montgomery, Jefferson County, and the Alabama Department of Transportation.

The plaintiffs argue that Alabama profits over $450 million annually from this so-called "forced labor scheme." They claim that since 2018, about 575 private employers and over 100 public employers have profited from the "leased" labor of incarcerated individuals from Alabama prisons.

The lawsuit alleges that the prison labor system in Alabama is equivalent to a 'modern-day form of slavery.' The state is accused of maintaining a racist, exploitative parole system to ensure a steady supply of incarcerated workers for profit. The plaintiffs, current and former prisoners, along with labor unions and a prisoner rights advocacy group, are suing Alabama, fast-food franchisees, and other entities that benefit from this prison labor system. The ten plaintiffs, all of whom are Black, contend that Alabama and private companies have made hundreds of millions of dollars from forced prison labor, which they say violates anti-human trafficking laws, the recently amended Alabama Constitution that prohibits all involuntary servitude as a criminal punishment, and the U.S. Constitution.

The Alabama Department of Corrections (ADOC) has announced a startling development: The warden of Limestone Correctional Facility, Chadwick Crabtree, and his wife Melissa have been taken into custody on drug-related charges. This unexpected turn of events occurred April 20, 2024, when the couple was apprehended at their residence by a coordinated team involving ADOC's own Law Enforcement Services Division, the state's SWAT team, and local sheriff's deputies from Limestone County, all acting on multiple warrants.

Chadwick, with deep roots in Elkmont, Alabama, is not new to the Department of Corrections. His career spans over two decades, during which he has held significant roles, including that of warden at the Birmingham Community Based Facility, a post focusing on the rehabilitation of female inmates. His dedication to the service is reflected on the ADOC website, where he is recognized as a 'Warden III'—the apex of prison officer ranks. This arrest raises many questions about the man who has been a pillar in the correctional community for so long.

Historical Drug Policies and Social Impact

In the 1980s, the legendary investigative reporter Gary Webb of the San Jose Mercury News managed to expose the shroud of secrecy around the crack cocaine crisis and the so-called war on drugs allegedly led by Ronald Reagan. Starting on August 18, 1996, Webb began to unravel the CIA's involvement in drug trafficking in Los Angeles during the 80s. His investigation led him to a drug ring operating in the Bay Area that had been supplying the notorious Crips and Bloods street gangs in Los Angeles with substantial amounts of cocaine for nearly ten years. The profits, running into millions, were allegedly pumped into a Latin American guerrilla army, rumored to have the backing of the US Central Intelligence Agency. Webb's expose showcased how this operation became the missing link between Colombia's cocaine cartels and Los Angeles' black communities, sparking a devastating crack epidemic in urban America and arming LA's gangs with the funds necessary to acquire weapons.

Crack cocaine was not only prevalent in Los Angeles, but it was also widespread among impoverished black and brown communities across the urban centers of America. Its affordability made it accessible to many. Crack was cheap. Politically, crack cocaine was used as a means to undermine black activists who were fighting for equality in the United States. The widespread availability of crack cocaine in the 1980s led to a significant escalation in crime rates. However, it also resulted in more money for the dealers, providing them with a form of power and diminishing their incentive to heed the calls of activists. The ripple effects of this period continue to impact these communities, highlighting the importance of tackling such systemic issues.

Donald Trump and JD Vance are running their 2024 campaign on a platform that could transform America in profound ways. At the heart of their vision is Project 2025, an ambitious initiative backed by the Heritage Foundation and over 100 conservative organizations. Its goal? To reshape the U.S. government from the ground up using a comprehensive policy playbook called the "Mandate for Leadership."

A Threat to the Safety Net. For millions of Americans, Project 2025 spells uncertainty. The initiative proposes deep cuts to social safety net programs that people rely on every day. Imagine losing overtime pay protections, seeing food assistance programs slashed, or watching as early education initiatives like Head Start disappear. For low-income families, the threat of lifetime Medicaid caps could mean putting off essential medical care due to skyrocketing costs.

Rolling Back Civil Rights. Project 2025 also outlines a troubling vision for civil rights in America. It seeks to restrict access to abortion and contraception, roll back protections for LGBTQ+ individuals, and expand religious exemptions that could limit access to healthcare. If implemented, it could erase decades of hard-won progress and create a more divided society.

The Stakes Are High. Project 2025's sheer scope is staggering. Its detailed plans for every federal agency suggest a concerted effort to enact sweeping changes within mere months of a conservative administration taking office. The result could be a country where vulnerable populations are left behind, and civil rights are eroded. As the debate over Project 2025's policies heats up, one thing is clear: the future of American society hangs in the balance.

In a letter expressing concern over a potential Trump victory in the 2024 election, former US Attorney General Loretta Lynch and 40 former DOJ officials thank President Biden and endorse VP Kamala Harris for President, warning of the dangers of a second Trump term. "We enthusiastically join him in endorsing Vice President Kamala Harris as the next President of the United States. Vice President Harris is the best choice to defeat Donald Trump and lead the nation... The stakes could not be higher. Former President Trump poses a grave risk to our country, our global alliances, and the future of democracy. As President, he regularly ignored the rule of law. One of his first acts was to order an unconstitutional Muslim travel ban. His final act was to attempt to stay in power by defying election results and the will of the American people. In between, he appointed extremely conservative Supreme Court justices who reversed longstanding precedents and legal protections: stripping women of reproductive rights, dismantling environmental safeguards, and granting Trump virtual immunity for his 'official acts.'"

These individual stories, while seemingly diverse, underline the systemic injustices and exploitation that persist today, with powerful entities profiteering from the vulnerable. Whether it's a state taking advantage of its prisoners or a government agency allegedly fueling drug trafficking, the fight for justice is ongoing.

Presidential Policies and Racial Prejudices

In the wake of the Nixon administration and the Watergate scandal, President Carter's tenure was seen as a refreshing change.

Known for his anti-war stance, Carter pardoned over 20,000 Vietnam War draft dodgers and lessened the sentences of nearly 600 individuals. In a New York Times piece, Carter criticized America's punitive drug policies, which he believed had caused an explosion in prison populations. "The single greatest cause of prison population growth has been the war on drugs, with the number of people incarcerated for nonviolent drug offenses increasing more than twelvefold," he stated.

However, Carter's policies led to unease among the elite business community, who felt their superiority was under threat. This resistance, coupled with the soaring gas prices of the 1970s, undermined Carter's initiatives, such as expanding the Strategic Petroleum Reserve and creating the Synthetic Fuels Corporation. The Synthetic Fuels Corporation, also known as SFC or the Synfuels Corporation, was formed by the U.S. federal government in 1980. This creation was part of the Energy Security Act (ESA) with the goal of financially supporting the development and building of factories that could commercially manufacture synthetic fuels. Techniques, such as coal gasification, were employed in these plants to produce alternatives to the fossil fuels being imported.

Congress chose to deregulate the energy sector, leading to a spike in gas and oil prices. Misinformation about fuel shortages from Big Oil and OPEC led to panic and long lines at gas stations nationwide. Amidst this turmoil, America faced a hostage crisis and allegations of high-ranking officials manipulating the situation for political gain. Additional factors, such as Carter's demand for human rights and the devaluation of Iran's currency during the Iranian Revolution, further exacerbated the situation.

On August 3rd, 1980, Ronald Reagan made a significant appearance at the Neshoba County Fair, a significant sixteen years after the tragic deaths of Andrew Goodman, James Chaney, and Michael Schwerner. Members of the Ku Klux Klan brutally murdered these individuals during Freedom Summer. During his speech, Reagan promised to "restore the power that properly belongs to states and local governments."

Reagan's rhetoric suggested a desire to revert the country to an era when justice was not synonymous with equality, a time when urban America was vulnerable to conflict. Harmonizing African American society with a system devoid of fairness and without a strong commitment to national unity was challenging. The vision of peace and human rights that President Carter had championed seemed to fade.

Upon Reagan's assumption of the presidency, the change was immediate, marking the beginning of a new era of governance. The rise of the far-right conservative wing within the Republican Party found a voice in Reagan. His administration's policies, particularly regarding drugs, were stringent, even more so than those of Richard Nixon. Long mandatory minimum sentences of 15 years to life, even for first-time nonviolent drug offenses, were introduced shortly after Reagan assumed office.

The simultaneous rise in illegal drugs in inner cities and the cutting of social programs was not a coincidence. During President Johnson's administration, he initiated a "War on Poverty," introducing a suite of domestic social programs focused on education, medical care, inner-city issues, and poverty. The primary objective was to eradicate poverty and racial injustice. However, the Reagan Administration overlooked the progress made by Johnson's administration, favoring limited government instead. It was during the Reagan era that gang members found lucrative opportunities with the influx of crack cocaine, which became widely available, allegedly facilitated by the CIA and other government agencies.

This era was akin to stepping back into a shadowy past, where racist organizations thrived with governmental support.

Institutions tasked with ensuring public safety — the judicial system, law enforcement, and politicians — became entangled in illicit activities. Violence soared in urban communities, corresponding with the rise of new prison facilities nationwide. Nancy Reagan, Ronald Reagan's wife, launched a high-profile anti-drug campaign with the slogan "Just Say No." However, this was happening while illegal drugs were being distributed with the approval of influential figures, with many African Americans becoming scapegoats in a scheme spearheaded by society's elites.

Ronald Reagan was a staunch advocate for states' rights and aimed to dismantle many of the social programs that had emerged from the civil rights era. Within his first two years in office, federal spending on social benefits was cut by over $40 billion across 83 programs. Funding for the Equal Employment Opportunity Commission (EEOC) was also significantly reduced, resulting in approximately 60% fewer cases filed by the EEOC. President Reagan opposed Lyndon Johnson's landmark Civil Rights Act of 1964 and sought to restrict the Voting Rights Act, arguing that these laws infringed on states' rights.

Moreover, Reagan made efforts to undo former President Jimmy Carter's human rights policy. He proposed that the promotion of human rights abroad, particularly in countries like Argentina, El Salvador, and Honduras, as well as various regions in Central and South America, should not be the responsibility of the United States.

The Reagan administration initiated a significant defense buildup and outwardly supported the apartheid government in South Africa. Apartheid was a system of racial segregation that denied basic rights to black people, including citizenship and the right to vote. President Ronald Reagan, along with future Vice President Dick Cheney, who was then a Republican congressman representing Wyoming, were among the staunchest opponents of the Comprehensive Anti-Apartheid Act. This bill proposed stringent sanctions and outlined five preconditions for lifting these sanctions, essentially leading to the end of apartheid in South Africa. This would have also resulted in the release of political prisoners such as Nelson Mandela, then-leader of the African National Congress (ANC).

On September 26, 1986, Reagan vetoed the compromised bill, labeling it "economic warfare." However, the majority of Democrats and Republicans united to override President Reagan's veto on October 2, 1986, demonstrating bipartisan support against apartheid.

The same spirit of hatred and violence that fueled the Klan's efforts to undermine Reconstruction and roll back Black rights in the post-Civil War South lives on in the Heritage Foundation. Some argue that the Heritage Foundation was President Reagan's favorite think tank and that Reagan embodied the ideas and principles it holds dear. Nearly two-thirds of the Heritage Foundation's 2,000 "Mandate for Leadership" recommendations were adopted or attempted by the Reagan administration. This 1,100-page blueprint for the president-elect's transition team outlined a radical vision for reshaping government.

Fast forward to 2024. Donald Trump, the GOP presidential nominee, has sought to distance himself from the Heritage Foundation's latest mandate – a sprawling, 922-page plan to overhaul government that has drawn praise from conservatives. Yet, just as the Klan used violence and intimidation to dismantle African American communities, the Heritage Foundation promoted policies as a weapon to restrict ordinary people's freedoms.

Former President Donald Trump has been under fire for his association with right-wing activist Laura Loomer, known for her anti-Muslim rhetoric and promotion of conspiracy theories. Loomer, who has openly identified as "pro-white nationalist" and "proud

Islamophobe," has been banned from several social media platforms for hate speech violations. Despite this, Trump reportedly considered hiring her for his campaign, sparking backlash from supporters like Rep. Marjorie Taylor Greene. Greene warned that Loomer's extremist views are a "huge problem" that don't align with the MAGA movement and that she lacks the experience to advise a presidential campaign. This criticism comes despite Greene's own history of racially charged statements, with her stating that Loomer's rhetoric crosses a line. Nevertheless, Loomer was spotted accompanying Trump on his plane to the presidential debate against Vice President Kamala Harris in Philadelphia.

Vice President Kamala Harris' campaign argues that Heritage's Project 2025 will still be on the ballot in November, even after the project's director departed. "Project 2025 is on the ballot because Donald Trump is on the ballot. This is his agenda, written by his allies, for Donald Trump to inflict on our country," said Harris campaign manager Julie Chavez Rodriguez. "Hiding the 920-page blueprint from the American people doesn't make it less real – in fact, it should make voters more concerned about what else Trump and his allies are hiding."

In a candid sit-down interview while campaigning, VP candidate Kamala Harris addressed mass incarceration, economic injustice, and institutional racism in America. "We must acknowledge that the American incarceration system is one of our country's greatest public policy failures. The emphasis has been on pushing people out, rather than providing a way back in. This approach has been thoughtless and punitive, a result of wars waged against Americans. Be clear about that. Much of what has led to mass incarceration in America stems from domestic wars. The war on drugs was a war on our own people. That's how it played out."

During a debate with Vice President Kamala Harris, former President Donald Trump made unsubstantiated claims about Haitian immigrants in Springfield, Ohio. He stated, "In Springfield, they're eating dogs. They're eating the cats. They're eating... the pets of the people that live there. And this is what's happening in our country, and it's a shame." Trump's comments came amidst online rumors about an influx of Haitian immigrants in the Ohio city. Harris called Trump "extreme" and laughed at the remark. Moderators noted that city officials have denied the claims as false. The former president's spreading of this baseless and racially charged rumor occurred in front of tens of millions of television viewers.

On September 13, 2024, the city of Springfield, Ohio was disrupted by extremism and threats of violence, highlighting the real-world consequences of conspiracy theories and hateful rhetoric. City Hall was closed due to a bomb threat, and two elementary schools in the Springfield City School District were evacuated.

Days after former President Donald Trump and Vice-Presidential candidate J.D. Vance promoted a baseless conspiracy theory about Haitian immigrants, a group of individuals identifying themselves as Proud Boys marched through the city. They made their affiliation clear by carrying flags and wearing logos associated with the group.

In response to the escalating tensions, Springfield's Mayor Rob Rue made a public plea to national leaders. "Pay attention to what your words are doing to cities like ours," he urged. "We need help, not hate."

The attitudes of American politicians often reflect both public opinion and the systemic prejudices of historical world powers, creating a ripple effect that has impacted the Western world. The Founding Fathers of the United States held beliefs that people of African heritage were inherently inferior and could never equal the intelligence or character of white individuals.

During the 1858 debate between Abraham Lincoln and Stephen Douglas, Lincoln stated, "I am not, nor ever have been, in favor of bringing about in any way the social and political equality of the white and black races. There is a physical difference between the white and black races, which I believe will forever forbid the two races from living together in terms of social and political equality."

Even President Theodore Roosevelt made a bold and prejudiced statement about African Americans: "This perfectly stupid race can never rise. The Negro has been kept down as much by a lack of intellectual development as by anything else." These attitudes from influential figures in America's history have undoubtedly shaped the country's systemic biases and racial dynamics.

Harry Truman, born and raised in Lamar, Missouri, and the grandson of an enslaver, ascended to the presidency, becoming the 33rd President of the United States following Franklin Roosevelt's death. Truman, who self-identified as a bigot and admitted to harboring racial prejudice, was openly critical of the civil rights movement. He referred to Martin Luther King Jr. as a "troublemaker" and expressed that he would not hesitate to remove anyone attempting to stage a sit-in at a store he owned. Truman even used racially derogatory language in personal correspondences, such as a letter to his daughter where he referred to White House servers using a racial slur. In another letter to his wife, Truman expressed his racial prejudice, stating his belief that Black people belonged in Africa, Asians in Asia, and white people in Europe and America.

Truman's presidency is also marked by the infamous decision to use atomic bombs during World War II. He became the first president to authorize the use of an atomic bomb, code-named "Little Boy," which was dropped on Hiroshima, a Japanese city with a population of approximately 350,000, on August 6, 1945. While Hiroshima did host a significant military base, the bomb was not targeted at this facility. Instead, it was dropped in the city center, primarily populated by women, children, and older people.

Three days later, the United States dropped a second nuclear bomb, code-named "Fat Man," on Nagasaki. This plutonium-implosion bomb had a force of 22 kilotons, almost twice as powerful as the uranium bomb dropped on Hiroshima. The explosion instantly killed around 40,000 people. Truman's approval of these bombings remains a controversial aspect of his presidency.

Despite his early prejudices, President Truman underwent a significant transformation that remains one of the most notable in U.S. history. Post World War II, Truman distanced himself from his previous racial biases and made combating racial injustice a political priority. This shift occurred when Truman, appalled by the violence white supremacists inflicted on returning Black veterans, made civil rights a federal priority for the first time since Reconstruction.

In 1948, Truman endorsed a Civil Rights report advocating federal action to end racial discrimination in federal hiring practices and issued an executive order to end segregation in the military. These actions cost Truman the support of many southern whites, making him one of the most unpopular politicians in the United States. However, his transformation underscores the merit of an individual who chooses righteousness over maintaining harmful convictions.

This deep-rooted bigotry in Western history, while seemingly a thing of the past, has left traces that can still be felt today. Albert Einstein once said, "The world will not be destroyed by those who do evil, but by those who watch them without doing anything." Even as recently as Richard Nixon's presidential candidacy, this bias was evident. Nixon positioned himself as the champion of white ethnics and blue-collar workers, expressing frustration with the violence and lawlessness in cities. Privately, Nixon expressed harmful racial stereotypes, using racial slurs in conversations captured on tapes released by the National Archives. In another taped conversation, both Nixon and Secretary of State Henry Kissinger displayed shocking unimportance towards any potential harm towards Jews in the Soviet Union.

These instances underscore the insidious nature of systemic racism and prejudice and the importance of acknowledging and confronting these issues in the pursuit of a more equitable society.

In 1971, President Nixon declared drug abuse as "public enemy number one in the United States" and created the Office of Drug Abuse Law Enforcement (ODALE) to establish joint federal/local task forces to combat the drug trade at the street level. Nixon pushed for mandatory sentencing and no-knock warrants, enforced a stop-and-frisk policy, and placed marijuana in Schedule One (the most restrictive category of drugs), all pending review by a commission that eventually recommended the decriminalization of marijuana for personal use. Despite this recommendation, Nixon disregarded the commission's report, thereby expanding the use of wiretaps and paving the way for zero-tolerance policies on illegal drugs.

In a revealing 1994 interview with journalist Dan Baum for Harper's magazine, John Ehrlichman, who served as Nixon's domestic policy chief, stated that the "War on Drugs" was a political tool designed to target leftist protesters and Black people. Ehrlichman candidly admitted, "The Nixon campaign in 1968, and the Nixon White House after that, had two enemies: the antiwar left and black people."

He continued, "We knew we couldn't make it illegal to be either against the war or blacks, but by getting the public to associate the hippies with marijuana and blacks with heroin and then criminalizing both heavily, we could disrupt those communities. We could arrest their leaders, raid their homes, break up their meetings, and vilify them night after night on the evening news. Did we know we were lying about the drugs? Of course, we did."

Ehrlichman's admission underscores the political manipulation and racial biases underpinning the War on Drugs, highlighting a deeply troubling aspect of U.S. history.

John Edgar Hoover, Director of the Federal Bureau of Investigation (FBI), launched a campaign to link illegal drug use to the rise in crime. The FBI also made efforts to destroy Black leadership in the Civil Rights and Black Freedom Struggle. A counterintelligence program was created to prevent Black militant groups, including the Black Panther Party, from unifying.

According to an FBI memo, the program aimed to prevent the rise of a 'Black Messiah' who could unify and electrify the Black militant movement. Martin Luther King, Jr., Malcolm X, Stokely Carmichael, and Elijah Muhammad were all targeted, but Elijah Muhammad was considered less of a threat due to his age. The FBI's objective, according to a memo, was to "expose, disrupt, misdirect, discredit, or otherwise neutralize" the radical fight for Black rights and Black power structure. Hoover labeled Dr. Martin Luther King as a real contender of a 'Black Messiah' and "The Most Dangerous Negro in America."

As J. Edgar Hoover's reign drew to a close, his secret police had already silenced two of the most powerful voices for racial equality. Malcolm X, the fiery leader of the Organization of Afro-American Unity, and Dr. Martin Luther King Jr., the peaceful head of the Southern Christian Leadership Conference, had both fallen to assassins' bullets. Many others who dared to challenge the unjust Jim Crow laws had either met the same fate or been smeared into irrelevance.

But the most brazen attack was yet to come. In the early hours of December 4, 1969, a team of heavily armed police descended upon a quiet apartment on Chicago's West Side. Inside, Black

Panther leader Fred Hampton lay sleeping beside his pregnant fiancée, Deborah Johnson.

The police burst in, guns blazing. Mark Clark, the young Panther on guard duty, was cut down in a hail of bullets. Despite the pleas of those inside to cease fire, the police sprayed the apartment with at least 90 rounds.

Deborah Johnson later recounted the horror of what came next. From the bedroom, she heard a cop ask, "Is he dead?" Two shots rang out, and another officer callously replied, "He's good and dead now.

"The truth later came to light: Fred Hampton had never even stirred from bed. Drugged by an FBI informant, he was executed in cold blood with two point-blank shots to the head. The police had not come to arrest a dangerous criminal, but to eliminate a threat to their power.

The election of Donald Trump as the 45th President of the United States sparked widespread debate about the potential re-emergence of deep-seated divisions rooted in elitism and racism. The United States was originally founded on a threefold system of governance. The founders designed this system to favor Anglo-Saxon whites through capitalist and socialist structures while simultaneously imposing oppressive systems on people of color.

Donald Trump, who some have described as a purveyor of hate, nevertheless promised to revitalize inner-city neighborhoods for African Americans. However, his campaign slogan, "Make America Great Again," was perceived by some as a call to arms for white supremacists.

The United States has thrived, albeit with a tumultuous and controversial history. The forceful acquisition of land and the exploitation of the indigenous population blemishes its foundations. The tenure and rhetoric of Donald Trump, particularly during his campaign, echo these contentious chapters of history.

At a rally in Vandalia, Ohio, in March 2024, Trump stirred the political landscape with a stark warning. He declared that if his re-election in November 2024 is unsuccessful, the nation might face dire consequences, going as far as to predict a "bloodbath." Addressing an audience in the automotive sector, Trump ramped up his discourse on immigration and foretold the collapse of democracy if he were not to win. He went on to speculate that this election could be the last if he loses.

Moreover, during the start of his campaign in Houston, Texas, Trump referred to the inmates convicted for their actions on January 6th as "hostages" rather than prisoners. He revealed that he might consider granting pardons to some of them should he secure the presidency once more in the upcoming 2024 elections.

In the wake of Trump's election in November 2016, Pulitzer Prize-winning novelist Toni Morrison penned a compelling essay titled "Mourning For Whiteness," which was published in the New Yorker's November 21, 2016 issue. Morrison posits that Trump's victory was driven by the fear of privileged white men faced with a rapidly diversifying country. In her words, "Under slave laws, the necessity for color rankings was obvious, but in America today, post-civil-rights legislation, white people's conviction of their natural superiority is being lost. Rapidly lost."

Morrison further explains that the prospect of a racially diverse America, potentially with another Black President, a predominantly Black Senate, and multiple Black Supreme Court Justices, is a frightening concept for many. She believed that the fear of losing white privilege had driven many Americans to a political platform that equates violence against the defenseless with strength. According to Morrison, these individuals are less angry than they are terrified, with a fear that shakes them to their core.

At a New Hampshire campaign rally, Donald Trump reinforced his anti-immigrant stance, stating that immigrants were " poisoning the blood of our country " - a sentiment that President Joe Biden's campaign has criticized as being eerily similar to Nazi rhetoric. Trump claimed, "They've poisoned mental institutions and prisons all over the world, not just in South America, not just the three or four countries that we typically consider, but they're infiltrating our country from all corners of the world, from Africa, from Asia, they're flooding into our nation." He addressed a large gathering at the Whittemore Center at the University of New Hampshire when he made these remarks. Critics have pointed out that Trump's reference to immigrants as poisoning the blood and as vermin' mirrors language used historically by Adolph Hitler, serving as a veiled signal often used by dictators and authoritarians.

However, on May 30, 2024, a Manhattan jury delivered a groundbreaking verdict in the hush money criminal trial of Donald Trump, convicting the former president on all 34 counts of falsifying business records. This marks a historic moment as Trump becomes the first former U.S. president to be found guilty of a felony. The unanimous decision by the jurors concluded that Trump had indeed falsified business records, specifically to conceal a $130,000 payment to adult film actress Stormy Daniels, aimed at impacting the 2016 presidential election outcome. This verdict brings an abrupt and significant close to the highly publicized and unprecedented New York trial.

The U.S. stands at a pivotal point, wrestling with escalating crises in the Middle East and Ukraine. The Wagner Group, a private military company linked to an associate of Russian leader Vladimir Putin, is suspected of bankrolling Russia's operations in Ukraine. This situation echoes past allegations of the U.S. using funds from its War on Drugs to finance campaigns in Central America during Reagan's presidency secretly.

Yevgeny Prigozhin, a key Putin ally and head of the Wagner Group, was among the casualties in a plane crash near Moscow on August 23, 2023. Known for his ruthless tactics, Prigozhin was accused of financing the Wagner Group's operations by exploiting resources from African countries. The private jet he was traveling in crashed with no survivors reported (New York Times, Reuters).

This unfortunate event occurred just two months after Prigozhin had briefly rebelled against Russia's military leadership in June 2023 (CNN). The reason for the crash is still being examined, but preliminary reports indicate that the private jet wasn't subjected to an external attack (NPR).

In a shocking admission, Putin recently confirmed that Russia is funding the notorious Wagner Group, a shadowy paramilitary organization accused of brutal tactics in Ukraine (Reuters). This revelation has sparked heated debates about the true depth of the Kremlin's financial backing for these mercenaries (Politico). The devastating impact of the 2½-year conflict is staggering: more than one million Ukrainians and Russians have been killed or wounded. This shocking toll will haunt both nations, already grappling with declining populations, for generations to come.

The involvement of groups like the Wagner Group in international conflicts and their alleged funding methods underscore the complex and often opaque nature of geopolitical disputes. Israel is presently spearheading a military offensive in Gaza. This action has led to the demise of over 41,000 Palestinians, including more than 15,000 children, raising concerns about potential human rights violations. Numerous U.S. journalists have faced penalties for criticizing Israel, while Palestinian journalists reporting from Gaza have seen their residences bombed. Palestinians residing in the West Bank, although uninvolved with Hamas, are under occupation by Israeli soldiers. Extremist Israeli settlers are escalating revenge killings and displacing thousands from their homes.

Israel stands accused of recklessly using potent weapons like white phosphorus munitions and massive 2,000-pound bombs in densely populated regions. Tragically, it's often women and children who make up the majority of the victims. Necessities like food, water, and medicine are scarce, adding to the civilian population's distress. Human rights organizations are raising alarm bells, laying blame at the feet of the Israeli government for allegedly weaponizing hunger in their conflict with Gaza. All this while, despite the serious human rights concerns, American weaponry keeps flowing into Israel. This is happening even as the international community recognizes using starvation and dehydration against civilians as a clear breach of war rules.

World Central Kitchen, a humanitarian group led by famed chef José Andrés, has been forced to pause its vital food relief efforts in Gaza after an apparent Israeli strike that killed seven of its workers. Tragically, an incident believed to be an Israeli airstrike on April 1, 2024, resulted in the loss of seven dedicated team members in Deir al-Balah. This organization, known for being a lifeline in the region, had to pause its operations amidst an intense offensive that has pushed countless Palestinians to the edge of hunger. José Andrés, expressed his grief by the events, has vocally opposed the senseless violence and barriers placed on aid groups, along with the use of food as a weapon. The organization, the biggest provider of food aid in Gaza, suspended operations in Gaza, where Israel's offensive has left hundreds of thousands of Palestinians on the brink of starvation. The situation in Gaza remains dire, with many relying on aid to survive.

In the tense days that followed the incident at World Central Kitchen, a chilling event unfolded: a UNICEF aid convoy was directly attacked. As the convoy was about to deliver essential supplies to northern Gaza, shots were fired. This alarming incident was reported by several news agencies, underscoring the extreme dangers that humanitarian workers face. Caught in the midst of chaos, civilians seeking aid were taken by surprise, scrambling to escape the abrupt gunfire. This collaborative mission, involving UNICEF, UNRWA, and other UN agencies, was designed to provide fuel, nutrition, and medical supplies to the people in northern Gaza. The shots originated from the direction of the crossing and were aimed toward civilians, who then fled in the opposite direction.

In a separate incident, the Israeli military admitted to the regrettable killing of three unarmed individuals in Gaza who were shot despite surrendering with a white flag. Despite their visible surrender — shirtless and waving a makeshift white flag — they were fatally shot by Israeli troops. Alarmingly, this universal symbol of surrender seemed to hold no weight with the Israel Defense Forces (IDF) on the outskirts of Gaza City.

In a concerning turn of events, journalist Mohammed Balousha, who brought to light a chilling incident at al-Nasr Children's Hospital in Gaza, was shot and injured. Balousha reported on how hospital staff had to leave four preterm babies behind as they were forced to evacuate without ambulances by Israel. Tragically, the infants' bodies were found decomposed.

The Israeli-Gaza war, which started with an attack on October 7, has claimed the lives of over 116 journalists in the first ten months of the war. This conflict continues to take a heavy toll on those brave enough to report on it.

On January 7, 2024, an Israeli attack targeted a vehicle in Gaza, resulting in the death of two more journalists. Among the deceased was the eldest son of a seasoned Al Jazeera reporter who had previously lost a significant portion of his family in early bombardments.

Journalists Hamza Dahdouh, Mustafa Thuraya, and Hazem Rajab were en route to a task in the southwestern region of Gaza

— a zone presumed to be safe — when a missile detonated their vehicle.

The violence continues to rise. On June 9, 2024, the death toll in Gaza surged as at least 274 people were killed and hundreds injured during an Israeli operation to rescue four hostages. This devastating loss of life follows the deaths of two Palestinian fishermen, who were shot by Israeli troops while fishing off the Gaza coast just days after the hostage rescue. James Elder, spokesperson for the United Nations Children's Agency, witnessed the death of the two fishermen firsthand. His team was attempting to deliver critical food and medical supplies to 10,000 children when they were halted at an Israeli checkpoint.

In a devastating turn, even supposed safe havens have been struck. An airstrike by the Israel Defense Forces hit a school serving as a shelter, killing at least 100 people seeking refuge early on a Saturday morning, according to Gaza's civil defense. This could be one of the deadliest attacks in the 10-month conflict, underscoring the escalating tensions that mediators are struggling to ease.

The humanitarian crisis in Gaza has resulted in a staggering loss of life. U.S. medical experts estimate the death toll to be over 118,000. According to Oxfam International, a non-governmental organization, more than 6,000 women and 11,000 children have been killed – one of the highest child mortality rates in any recent conflict. A new report in the British medical journal Lancet suggests the actual death toll could be as high as 186,000 – roughly 8% of Gaza's population, with many victims still buried under the rubble.

On Tuesday, September 17th, 2024, a shocking escalation rocked the ongoing conflict in Lebanon. Thousands of Taiwan-made pagers carried by Hezbollah forces mysteriously exploded, reportedly in a coordinated attack by Israel. The blasts claimed civilian lives and directly targeted Hezbollah fighters and Iran's envoy to Beirut, marking a bold challenge to the militia's security.

The escalation intensified the very next day. At least 20 people were killed and 450 injured when Hezbollah's walkie-talkies detonated across Lebanon, just 24 hours after the initial pager attacks. These audacious electronic warfare attacks have left thousands reeling in Lebanon, setting the stage for an unpredictable and potentially explosive chapter in the region's longstanding conflict.

The consecutive attacks claimed 37 lives, including those of innocent children. More than 3,000 people were injured, their lives forever altered by the violence. Israeli Defense Minister Yoav Gallant seized the moment to declare that Israel has entered a "new phase in the war" against Hezbollah.

"We are at the start of a new phase in the war — we are allocating resources and forces to the northern arena and our mission is clear: ensuring the safe return of Israel's northern communities to their homes," Gallant stated on Wednesday. "To do so, the security situation must be changed."

A fragile peace has shattered along Israel's northern border. After nearly a year of battling Hamas in Gaza, Israel has set its sights on the militant group Hezbollah. The following Monday, Israel launched airstrikes on hundreds of Hezbollah targets, resulting in over 500 deaths and forcing tens of thousands to flee. The Lebanese Health Ministry confirmed a devastating toll: at least 39 women, two medical personnel, and more than 50 children were among the dead. More than 1,800 people were wounded, making this Lebanon's deadliest day in decades.

The Lebanon-Israel border is a powder keg waiting to explode. Rockets and missiles scream through the skies as Israel and Hezbollah dig in for a long and bloody fight. And in Gaza, a ceasefire with Hamas is nowhere in sight.

The body count is heartbreaking. More than 41,000 Palestinians killed, thousands of them just children. The world watches in horror as the death toll rises. Diplomats race against time to stop the carnage, but every glimmer of hope slips through their fingers. Even the American president points fingers. "Netanyahu is part of the problem," Biden says. The Israeli prime minister shoots back in a Fox News Interview, "There's no deal coming... we're nowhere close." And with that, the killing goes on.

The world watches in horror as children become the innocent victims of escalating violence in Lebanon and Palestine. Save the Children, a global humanitarian organization, issues a desperate plea: an immediate and unconditional ceasefire is the only way to protect these young lives.

"We beg of the world's leaders: use your power and influence to demand respect for international law and justice," the organization urges. "Diplomacy and cooperation are our only hope to end this senseless bloodshed.

"On the ground, the situation is dire. "Today is the deadliest day in months," says Jennifer Moorehead, Country Director for Save the Children. "Imagine families, forced to flee their homes with nothing but the clothes on their backs, their children weeping with fear as the drone of warplanes fills the air. This is the reality we face, minute by minute."

The cross-border exchange of fire was one of the most intense since hostilities erupted last October 2023. Israel issued a stark warning to those in Lebanon: evacuate areas where Hezbollah is stockpiling weapons.

Imagine fleeing your home, not knowing if you'll ever return. This is the terrifying reality for countless civilians caught in the escalating war between Israel and Hezbollah. One official described the scene as "Israeli atrocities," as innocent people are trapped in the crossfire of artillery and missiles. Temporary shelters have sprung up in schools and other facilities, providing a glimmer of safety for about one million displaced individuals. But even finding refuge can be dangerous. The Israel Defense Forces' use of white phosphorus shells has contaminated the ground, making it hazardous for aid workers and impossible for farmers to harvest their crops.

The Israeli government has ordered at least six medical aid missions to leave the Gaza Strip, a move advocacy groups warn could be a "death sentence for thousands of patients." The World Health Organization (WHO) announced the decision on Thursday October 17th, 2024, stating that Israel had informed them via text message without providing a reason.

The ban comes as leaders of Prime Minister Benjamin Netanyahu's Likud Party prepare for a controversial conference promoting the re-establishment of Israeli settlements in Gaza. Critics argue that the move mirrors past patterns of resource exploitation and oppression of the Palestinian people.

The World Health Organization expressed urgent concern over the collapsing healthcare system in Gaza, where malnutrition and disease are rampant. They are pushing for "immediate and sustained access" for medical teams. The region has received no aid, including food, since the Israeli army launched a major ground operation on October 1.

As the conflict intensifies, the world watches anxiously, wondering what's next for this embattled region. Will there be an end to the violence, or will the cycle of fear and displacement continue?

Turkish President Recep Tayyip Erdogan labelled Prime Minister Benjamin Netanyahu as "the butcher of Gaza," suggesting this will define his legacy. UNICEF has urged a lasting ceasefire, stating that indifference to the situations in Gaza and now Lebanon is equivalent to endorsing child killings. The organization warned that additional attacks on civilian population will only lead to further devastation.

In the heart of Africa, Sudan is seized by a chilling civil war that erupted on April 15, 2023, setting the stage for a brutal power struggle. The Sudanese Armed Forces and their nemesis, the Paramilitary Rapid Support Forces, are locked in a fierce battle. The epicenters of this conflict are the bustling capital, Khartoum, and the vast expanse of the Darfur region. In just six tumultuous months, the war has snatched away approximately thousands of innocent lives.

This is not a new ordeal for Sudan. The nation has been wrestling with one of the longest civil wars in history for nearly 22 years. This relentless strife has claimed the lives of an estimated two million people, and many more were forced to flee their homes. The culmination of this prolonged struggle was the birth of a new nation, South Sudan, which declared its independence in July 2011 after splitting from Sudan.

In the midst of this chaos, there are whispers of foreign involvement. The Wagner Group, a shadowy Russian mercenary organization, is rumored to be supplying the Rapid Support Forces with military supplies. They're not alone; Libyan militias and the United Arab Emirates are also believed to be aiding in the war efforts.

The U.S. Department of the Treasury claims that the Wagner Group exploits global insecurity, committing atrocities and criminal acts to extract natural resources and receive payment in illicit gold, especially on the African continent. Russia aims to establish a naval base at Port Sudan on the Red Sea, one of the world's busiest waterways.

Mariam Adam Yaya was forced to flee her village, leaving seven of her children behind, after heavily armed men attacked. "What we went through in Ardamata is horrifying. The Rapid Support Forces killed elderly people and children indiscriminately," she said.

Amira Khamis, a traumatized 46-year-old, said she was targeted due to her Masalit ethnicity and has lost five children. "They systematically kill all the people of dark black color," she said, recovering from her injuries.

Mahamat Nouredine, a 19-year-old who lost four relatives, said the RSF mercilessly targeted the Masalit community. "A group of RSF followed us to a hospital and tried to kill everyone... they laid us on the ground in groups of 20 and fired at us," he said. "Their unspoken goal is to kill people due to their skin color."

Sudan, located in Northeast Africa, is grappling with a severe ethnic conflict. Lighter-skinned or brown-complexioned Africans are perpetrating genocide against those with darker skin. This devastating violence is fueled, in part, by the lingering influence of past colonial powers.

Despite the growing evidence of ethnic cleansing, President Joe Biden has deepened its military ties with the (UAE) United Arab Emirates recognizing the UAE as a defense partner, a key backer of the Rapid Support Forces (RSF) in Sudan. The conflict is fueled by a twisted ideology of racial supremacy, with lighter-skinned Arabs seeking to dominate and destroy darker-skinned Black groups. The world cannot turn a blind eye to the ethnic cleansing in Sudan. It's time for Western powers to take action and hold those responsible accountable. The people of Sudan deserve justice.

The specter of casteism looms large, leaving an indelible mark on societies across the globe. This deeply entrenched system of social stratification once thought to be confined to specific regions, has now spread its roots far and wide. From the vast expanse of Africa to the historic lands of Israel and even the progressive societies of the Western world, the shadow of caste hierarchy is ever-present. It's an issue that continues to shape our world, often in ways that are hidden or unacknowledged, subtly influencing the dynamics of power, privilege, and prejudice.

It's evident in the experiences of Palestinians living in Gaza and the West Bank, the birthplace of Christ, where their skin tone is deemed not light enough to be a part of this power pyramid. The situation is similar for the inhabitants of the African continent, as well as Africans who were forcibly brought across the Atlantic during the slave trade; their darker skin often obscures their humanity in the eyes of others. The idolization of whiteness remains dominant.

In the past, Israel has been inhabited by a variety of groups. Among these were the Caphtorim and Pathrusim, as well as several Balkan groups, including the Philistines. Over time, these Balkan groups merged with the Canaanites, Cainites, and Amorites, resulting in the formation of a collective known as the Tidal of Nations or the Five Kings.

In today's events, it's worth noting that for an extended period, the Israeli government, under the leadership of Benjamin Netanyahu, implemented strategies that divided authority between the Gaza Strip and the West Bank. These maneuvers inadvertently weakened the Palestinian Authority's influence and bolstered the infamous Hamas group, thus obstructing prospects for a two-state solution. This situation has not only generated difficulties for Israel but has also presented significant challenges for past U.S. administrations.

Certain misguided governmental strategies have unintentionally weakened the influence of parents and leaders in city neighborhoods in America. This has, in turn, fueled a surge in violence and drug issues, spreading across both city and country landscapes of America. Interestingly, a notable portion of US citizens seems to prefer a strong-armed rule over a balanced democracy, especially if it slows down the advancement toward equality for people of color.

CHAPTER ONE

Astronomy and Mythology in the Cradle of Civilization

Astronomy compels the soul
to look upwards and
leads us from this world
to another.

———

Plato

So, the great dragon was cast out, that serpent of old called
the Devil and Satan, who deceives the whole world;
he was cast to the earth, and his angels were
cast out with him.

–Revelation 12:9

In its earliest stages, religion, wisdom, and mythology were deeply intertwined with astronomy, profoundly shaping human history. This transformation began in Babylon and spread across the world. Men and women worked together to construct Stonehenge, a magnificent staircase building topped with a temple tower, during the post-Flood era. This structure, built in the ancient Babylonian land of Shinar, was a testament to human pride and rebellion against the Almighty God (Yahweh).

The Tower of Babel and the Dispersion of Nations

The temple tower, or ziggurat, was designed as a sacred sanctuary to welcome spiritual entities descending from the lower heavens. The allure of celestial powers became a cornerstone of people's faith, serving as a source of security and an act of self-glorification. As humanity increasingly communicated with these celestial beings, God the creator intervened to prevent humanity from becoming too entangled with these lesser heavenly entities.

The Bible recounts how, at this point in history, everyone spoke a single language, and a group migrating from the east found a plain in Shinar. They decided to build a stairway to the heavens, the Tower of Babel, as a monument to communicate with these fallen angelic beings and unlock universal secrets. However, the Bible says, 'Now nothing they purpose to do will be withheld from them...So the Lord scattered them abroad from there over the face of all the earth, and they ceased building the city.

From these, the coastland peoples of the Gentiles were separated into their lands, every one according to his language, according to their families, into their nations.

–Genesis 10:5.

So, the lord scattered them abroad over the face of the earth Therefore its name is called Babel, because there the lord confused the language of all the world.

–Genesis 11:8-9

The cradle of civilization emerged in the Land of Ham after the expulsion of these new races of people that the Bible refers to as the Gentiles. This land would give rise to the prolific city-states of the Kushite Kingdom, as highlighted in biblical accounts. The narrative introduces Nimrod, the brave son of Kush and grandson of Ham. Nimrod, a mighty hunter in the eyes of the Lord, established Babel, Erech, Accad, and Calneh in the land of Shinar. From Babylon, he expanded his realm southward into Assyria, building cities like Calah, Nineveh, and Rehoboth Ir in Mesopotamia.

Many scholars suggest that Nimrod's reputation as a renowned hunter of men stems from Babylon's role as a racial tension hotspot, being the first location where the Lord altered racial demographics on a large scale. The Kushites left a spiritual and cultural legacy that permeated the known world. However, many Eurocentric writers have erroneously associated Kush's name with the fallen angel Bel (Beelzebub) to demean his name unfairly.

Nimrod, as Kush's eldest son, often had his name associated with evil due to his resistance against Eurocentrism or foreign invasions into the Afro-Asiatic territory of Kush. It's illogical that the Lord would expel celestial communicators yet permit Nimrod to establish a powerful empire in the Land unless Nimrod was executing the Lord's will. The conventional portrayal of Kush and Nimrod as tyrants is more palatable and less unsettling in the Western world than considering them as protectors of Kushite territory.

The ancient civilization of the Kushites, also known as Ethiopians, included all dark-skinned peoples inhabiting the geographical region stretching from India to Sudan. This region, home to the earliest cultures of Egypt and Mesopotamia, was composed of Eastern and Western Kush. As Herodotus noted, 'the Ethiopians were considered as occupying all south coasts of both Asia and

Africa.' Diodorus Siculus added that 'the Egyptians are colonists sent out by the Ethiopians, Osiris having been the leader of the colony.' Consequently, many historians view ancient Ethiopia as the cradle of humanity.

The first city built post-flood was Kish, now known as Tall al-Uhaimer, in ancient Mesopotamia. Its name is derived from the Biblical Kush, the father of Nimrod. Kush was the eldest son of Ham and grandson of Noah. The region of Tall al-Uhaimer, known as the 'land of Shinar,' is generally identified by most scholars as ancient Sumer. The Hebrew name Kush (or Cush) is associated with present-day Ethiopia, which traces its roots to the ancient Kushite Kingdom. There is no scriptural link or genealogical account to suggest that the dark complexion of the human family is a result of the curses pronounced on Canaan, Kush's brother. Some argue that Kush's descendants are naturally inferior due to Noah's curse on Ham's children. However, there was no curse on the biblical Ham or any curse that resulted in black skin color.

The melanin content of the skin, causing a dark complexion, is advantageous for those living in sunny regions like Africa and less beneficial for people in less sunny areas like Europe. The darker your skin tone, the more melanin protection you have from the sun's ultraviolet rays, which slows the aging process. Notably, Canaan had no Negro offspring; however, Canaan was the forefather of various Canaanite tribes of Palestine known as Pathrusim and Casluhim (Genesis 9:24-25; 10:14). As the Nelson New Bible Illustrated Dictionary clearly states: 'All known people grouped under the name of "Canaanites" (descendants of Canaan) were Caucasoid, not Negroid.

During the late 2nd millennium, under the leadership of Joshua and Caleb, the Israelites occupied and conquered Palestine/Canaan. They were tasked with dislocating the Canaanites from the Promised Land due to their disobedience, greed, and idolatry and dividing it among the twelve tribes. However, many Canaanites remained in the land, which displeased Almighty God.

The Canaanites practiced a polytheistic religion, worshipping many gods, spirits, and demons that possessed god-like powers. They built temples dedicated to Baal, the chief god of fertility and storm. They engaged in sacred prostitution, human sacrifice, and festivals venerating the evergreen tree in honor of pagan deities. Their religious services included male and female prostitutes, statues of pagan gods, singers, altars, and a high priest officiating pagan ceremonies. Rituals, often involving sacrifice, dancing, and sexual orgies, were held on special occasions to maintain good relations with the sacred powers and ward off malignant spirits. The Canaanite religious occult also included divination, astrology, and prophecies from fallen angels or the unseen world.

Despite these practices, many Israelites chose to worship both Canaanite gods and Yahweh, a holy but jealous God. This led to conflict, as exemplified in the Old Testament account of King Saul. Saul disobeyed God's command to destroy everything the Amalekites had, sparing King Agag and the best livestock. As a result, Samuel, God's prophet, declared that Saul had rejected God's word and that God had rejected him as king. The Israelites were to be punished for Saul's disobedience and delivered into the hands of the Philistines. Samuel slayed Agag and left Saul, never to see him again.

After Samuel's death, a substantial Philistine army assembled to wage war against Israel, which caused Saul to cry out to the Lord. Saul learned of a notorious woman in Endor, often referred to as the Witch of Endor, who claimed to have the ability to consult familiar spirits and resurrect the dead. Previously, Saul had sought out mediums and punished wizards who were involved with seductive spirits. According to divine law, Israelites were strictly forbidden from consulting familiar spirits or interacting with celestial powers (1 Samuel 28:8). *"So, Saul disguised himself and put on other clothes, and he went, and two men with him; and they came to the woman by night. And said, please conduct a séance for me, and bring up for me the one I shall name to you."*

Then the woman said, "Whom shall I bring up for you?" And he said, "Bring up Samuel for me." When the woman saw Samuel, she cried out with a loud voice. And the woman spoke to Saul, saying, "Why have you deceived me? For you are Saul!" And the king said to her, "Do not be afraid. What did you see? And the woman said to Saul, "I saw a spirit ascending out of the earth." So, he said to her, "What is his form?" And she said, "An old man is coming up, and he is covered with a mantle." And Saul perceived that it was Samuel, and he stooped with his face to the ground and bowed down

Now Samuel said to Saul, "Why have you disturbed me by bringing me up?" And Saul answered, "I am deeply distressed; for the Philistines make war against me, and God has departed from me and does not answer me anymore, neither by prophets nor by dreams. Therefore, I have called you, that you may reveal to me what I should do.

—1 Samuel 28:11–15

In Genesis, Cain, the eldest son of Adam and Eve, faced a similar fate when he shed the first human blood by killing his brother, Abel. Cain was angered because the Lord found Abel's offering more acceptable than his fruit offering. Envious, Cain committed murder. (Genesis 4:9-11) The Lord questioned Cain, *'Where is Abel, your brother?'* To which Cain replied, *'I do not know. Am I my brother's keeper?'* Then God declared, *'What have you done? The voice of your brother's blood cries out to Me from the ground. So now, you are cursed from the earth, which received your brother's blood from your hand.'*

Cain, who had been a farmer, lost his ability to cultivate the land as punishment for killing Abel. According to Genesis 4:11, God told Cain, *'Now you are under a curse and driven from the ground, which opened its mouth to receive your brother's blood from your hand. When you work the ground, it will no longer yield its crops for you.'* Cain was drained of melanin and became a wanderer in the land of Nod. Over generations, his descendants would relocate to the opposite side of the Balkans, settling around the Caucasus Mountains.

The divide between humanity and Cain's lineage led to a shift from divine grace to seeking guidance from polytheism or demonic spirits. The Bible narrates how Cain was driven from his family and became a 'fugitive and wanderer' on earth, receiving a mark of identity from God.

Cain found sanctuary in the land of Nod, east of Eden. Some scholars propose that Adam was not Cain's father; instead, they suggest that Eve was seduced by Lucifer or another fallen angel, also known as a Nephilim. This union supposedly resulted in a hybrid offspring with both human and fallen angelic traits.

In John 8:43, Jesus (Yeshua Ha'Mashiach in Hebrew) addresses the non-believers in the crowd.

"Why do you not understand My speech? Because you are not able to listen to My word. You are of your father the devil, and desires of your father you want to do. He was a murdered from the beginning and does not stand in truth   and the Epistle to the Hebrews states that "the blood of sprinkling that speaks better things than that of Abel."

–Hebrews 12:24

When the Aryans returned from Europe's mountainous regions, they merged with branches of the Canaanites, Cainites, and Amorites to form the Assyrian Empire. The Bible recounts how the disobedience of the Kushites and Israelites led God to turn His back, resulting in the Hebrew people falling into the hands of the Canaanites. The land of Canaan extended southward to the borders of Egypt along the eastern Nile River, northward toward present-day Lebanon and the coastal parts of Israel and Syria (Phoenicia), and eastward to the Jordan River Valley.

Prophet Daniel identified the Assyrian-conquered Babylon as the first-world Beast System, a governmental/religious system in constant rebellion against God. Similarly, in the book of Revelation, Apostle John refers to Assyria as the first Beast System.

Nimrod's story has been associated with paganism by many biblical and Western scholars. Both biblical and archaeological evidence suggest that Babylon reached its zenith during Nebuchadnezzar's reign. By the 6th century BC, Nebuchadnezzar had swept through the old Kushite territories, looting and burning in a ruthless campaign. However, if we take the Bible at face value, there is nothing explicitly stating that Kush/Cush or Nimrod were involved with fallen angels or idol worship. In fact, Nimrod emerged as the most significant opposition to Indo-European dominance that the world has ever witnessed. Much of the historical accounts of Kush and Nimrod come from the Palace of Ashurbanipal, the Library of Nebo, the Sennacherib Chronicle, and the Epic of Gilgamesh.

These figures were idol worshippers and believed in communication with celestial spirits or sacred gods of the lower heavenly realms. Therefore, it's no surprise they deemed Nimrod a tyrant and labeled Africa's favorite sons as evil. Many generations later, in 721 B.C., Merodach-Baladan, a king from the Chaldean house of Yakin, joined forces with Hezekiah, king of Judah, against

Sennacherib's army to resist Indo-European domination in Mesopotamia. It seems that Kush, Nimrod, and Merodach-Baladan are guilty only of opposing the Aryan (Caucasian) invaders who brought genocide to the Hebrew/Kushite territories.

Mythology and Divine Mandate in Ancient Kush

Many wonder why theologians often associate Bel with the name Kush. This connection stems from an age-old hatred passed down through generations. Genesis in the Bible notes that Kush's descendants included Seba, Havilah, Sabtah, Raamah, Sabtechan, Sheba, and Dan, with Nimrod emerging as a mighty hunter before the Lord. Satan, known for deceit and destruction, blinds people's understanding. But if you search for the Hamites' curse or Kush's expulsion from heaven, you'll find no such references in the Bible.

Kush's territory is recognized as one of the earliest cradles of civilization. According to Genesis, its river, one of the four that watered the Garden of Eden, encircled the entire land. In Matthew Chapter 12, Beelzebub is labeled the ruler of demons—in essence, Bel gave birth to lies.

Nimrod, described as a mighty hunter before the Lord in the Bible, may have been entrusted with the task of expelling recently altered races from Kushite territory by divine command. These new races, awaiting a future Messiah to absolve their sins before reintegration into the global population, were instead tempted by dark forces promising power to those who surrendered. Amidst these celestial exchanges, humankind was beguiled by a forbidden angelic host, leading to the adoption of darker human behaviors. Nimrod's role was thus to purify the land of those who strayed from God, engaging in divination, astrology, and spiritual incantations.

Lucifer, the Prince of Darkness who defiantly refused to bow to Adam, managed to persuade a section of humanity to join him in his battle against Adam's original descendants, the Hebrews. Using his legion of fallen angels, he covertly exerted a supernatural influence to divert mankind from God and ensure their spiritual and physical defeat. This beloved angel of God, who rebelled and led away a third of the heavenly host, is mentioned in Al-Hijr (15:25-41) of the Koran. Here, God commands Satan to bow to mankind, a directive that fuels resentment. The passage reads: 'We created man from dry clay, from black molded loam, and before him Satan from smokeless fire. Your Lord said to the angels, 'I am creating man from dry clay, from black molded loam. When I have fashioned him and breathed of My spirit into him, kneel and prostrate yourselves before him."

From this point forward, the original Hebrew-speaking people became staunch enemies of the fallen angels. Any humans seeking to commune with gods of the lower heavenly realms were expected to harbor a similar animosity towards this original race descended from Adam. By the 18th century BC, post-Ice Age, the Kushite territories encompassed all of Africa, regions along the Aegean Sea, and lands as distant as Central Asia. Crete, located along the Aegean Sea, boasted some of the Mediterranean's most exquisite palaces and administrative buildings. These structures featured advanced aquatic systems consisting of jointed conduits for fresh water and underground drainage systems. The Egyptians, emerging as the Cretans' primary trading partners, engaged in extensive commerce, exchanging goods such as wine, gold, copper, silver, tin, spices, and pearls across Africa and the Mediterranean Coast.

The arrival of the Indo-Europeans sparked a cultural rivalry and revived old conflicts. The Anglo-Saxons, having been isolated in the Balkans and various European mountain regions during the Ice Age, lagged in cultivation and technical knowledge. However, news of fertile lands and wealth spurred tribes to migrate from the Russian hills to territories inhabited by descendants of Ham and Shem, south of Kushite lands and towards present-day Israel. These newcomers constructed towering ziggurats in honor of numerous celestial gods and sculpted images of revered deities. The Indo-Europeans established political and social systems intertwined with various forms of paganism. These systems spread throughout the region, consequently influencing the Hamites and Semitic nations towards idolatry.

The arrival of wealth-seeking newcomers (Caucasians) to Crete, a thriving Mediterranean trade hub, exacerbated existing tensions. This culturally diverse city, home to Egyptians, Ethiopians, and Israelites, had once flourished. However, a massive volcanic eruption on Kalliste Island had devastated Crete. As the Cretans struggled to recover, they began to adopt the idolatrous practices of the Balkan newcomers. These practices centered on astrology, animal rituals, and nature myths, allowing for the rise of fiery serpent deities. Ultimately, these influences took control of the territory, transforming the religious landscape of Crete.

Subsequent volcanic eruptions in Knossos, followed by large tidal waves, devastated much of the Aegean islands in the eastern Mediterranean. The southernmost islands were then invaded by newcomers from the Balkan hills, giving rise to the Greco-Roman city-states. All of humanity shares a collective destiny, yet Satan and his elusive forces hold the power to tempt, test, and punish humankind, exercising control over those who sin. To carry out Satan's schemes and allow the unseen forces of darkness to rule without resistance, the participation of mortal accomplices is necessary.

The United Kingdom of Israel, established in the early 11th century BC following the Exodus from Egypt, divided within a century into the northern Kingdom of Israel and the southern Kingdom of Judah. During this time, the Israelites clashed with newcomers from the European hills who had settled in Canaan. This land, held by the Indo-Aryans since the Exodus era, was reclaimed by the Israelites under Joshua's leadership after Moses' death. Forced into Canaan following their defeat by the Egyptians, the Indo-Aryans migrated down the Nile and allied with other Indo-European tribes.

In the Bible's early sections, these loosely allied Indo-European invaders are referred to as the Sea People, who invaded Crete. Before invading and conquering the Minoan commercial seafaring vessels, the Indo-Europeans primarily used horses for transportation. Upon inheriting commercial ships, the Aryans used these vessels for naval invasions, colonizing territories around the Mediterranean, including the Hittite Empire in present-day Palestine.

After their defeat by the Egyptian navy at the close of the Bronze Age, some of the Sea People, known biblically as the Philistines, settled in Palestine. The ongoing struggle for control of the Plain involved a coalition of Indo-Aryan tribes, which dominated the trade routes linking Israel's commerce with Africa and the Middle East. Joshua and Caleb, while settling in Canaan, rallied a coalition to fight against the Indo-Aryans. Indigenous groups like the Jebusites, Hittites, and Kushites, all ancestrally linked to the Jewish people, supported the Israelites led by Joshua.

This alliance waged war against the Sea People, pursuing them along the road to Beth Horon. According to Joshua 10:10, God intervened, raining large hailstones from heaven and commanding the sun to stand still over Gibeon and the moon to halt in the Valley of Aijalon until the Philistines and other Indo-Aryan tribes were defeated.

However, instead of expelling the Indo-Aryans from the Promised Land, the Israelites maintained the pagan temples and assimilated elements of the Sea People's pagan traditions, invoking God's wrath. The Sea People evolved into the Assyrians, Babylonians, Persians, Greeks, and Romans, who would become leading adversaries in Mesopotamia and, eventually, on the global stage.

When the newcomers conquered Nineveh and overtook Babylon under Nabopolassar, each society had its chief deity in its folklore. The Philistines, who had helped conquer the Minoans of Crete before migrating into Israel, introduced the Greek gods Dagon and Molech, who demanded child sacrifice. The Philistines settled and integrated with the locals in three major Canaanite cities: Gaza, Ashkelon, and Ashdod. In the Valley of Hinnom, the firstborn child would be offered in a fiery ritual to Molech.

The Gehenna, located outside of Jerusalem in the Valley of Hinnom, housed fire-altars where parents sacrificed their children to underworld gods. During these mystical rituals, the evergreen tree became a sacred symbol linking the cosmos, the underworld, and earthly life. Some scholars suggest that Satan used the evergreen tree as a deceptive metaphor in the Garden of Eden. Believed to be a representation of the Tree of Life planted by God in Eden, the earthly evergreen tree was often associated with the eagle-headed god Nisroch and believed to have spiritual wisdom.

Assyrian Conquests and the Cultural Reshaping of the Near East

In Assyrian mythology, the eagle symbolizes strength, courage, and immortality. King Josiah, who rose to power in 628 BC—nearly a hundred years after the Assyrian leader Esarhaddon had first stepped onto Jewish soil—successfully eradicated Assyrian influences from Judah and condemned pagan rituals.

The Assyrians continued to devastate cities and displace inhabitants from Israel and Babylon, compelling thousands of people to move to Africa and other parts of the Kushite territories. A significant number of survivors, fortunate enough to avoid death and displacement from their homelands, found themselves in southern Egypt, specifically in regions like Nubia and Sudan. This area became a new home for many descendants of Jacob and a substantial number of Babylonian natives. The Assyrians maintained the belief that the unseen authority of the Cosmic Order would judge all spared captives. The most skilled among these captives were enslaved and tasked with rebuilding the cities that the Indo-Europeans had demolished.

The rival Assyrians and Babylonians invaded Nineveh, subjecting the local population to forced labor. Sennacherib, the Assyrian king, aspired to conquer the region inhabited by the descendants of Kush, including Nimrod, Havilah, Seba, Sabtah, and Raamah, aiming to unite the Middle Eastern territory under his pagan ideology. In 612 BC, Nineveh succumbed to the invaders, who executed numerous religious and military leaders from the defeated cities. Thousands of natives from Israel, Nineveh, the significant trading port of Tyre, and other Mediterranean cities were taken as prisoners of war by Sennacherib.

In 702 BC, Judah was temporarily saved by the intervention of Ethiopian and Egyptian cavalries. During the reign of King Shabako of the United Kingdom of Ethiopia and Egypt, an effort was made to purge the Coast of Indo-European influence. The Ethiopians faced a dual challenge: battling both a physical enemy and a supernatural force that threatened to spread across Africa and the entire Kushite territory if left unchecked.

With the Aryan influence escalating in Egypt and along the Nile, the worship of Zeus Amun started to permeate the region. Amun became associated with another primary deity, the sun god

Ra (also known as Horus of the Two Horizons), eventually merging to become Amun-Ra. The oracle of Amun was constructed at the Egyptian-Ethiopian border, solidifying Amun as a nationwide deity.

Sennacherib rallied a formidable force against the 25th Dynasty of the Kushites and advanced on Judah. His large infantry, bolstered by cavalry with horse-drawn chariots equipped with long-range bows, was an intimidating sight. The Ethiopians retreated in the face of this onslaught, leaving Judah vulnerable. Sennacherib seized approximately 200,150 people from 46 cities and 20 villages of Judah, forcibly uprooting them along with their valuable possessions and livestock.

Upon arriving at Jerusalem's city wall, Sennacherib boasted of his god, Indra, and his celestial powers. However, in response to Hezekiah's prayers, the Lord intervened, striking down 185,000 Assyrian soldiers. After Jerusalem was saved through divine intervention, the Assyrians retreated to Babylon. This allowed Sennacherib to focus on constructing his administrative palaces in his new capital city, Nineveh. He named his magnificent sanctuary the 'Palace Without Rivals,' also known as the South West Palace.

The South West Palace stood on giant bronze columns shaped like trumpeting lions, their wooden shafts crafted from Lebanese cedar. Glossy alabaster panels adorned the room walls, depicting the king hunting lions on horseback. Human-headed winged bulls were sculpted on the walls, set against lines of blue-glazed bricks. Vivid paintings detailing victorious warriors assaulting rival forces embellished the brightly coated walls.

The Ishtar Temple, honoring the god Ishtar and the celestial powers, sat at the palace's heart. The citadel's visitor rooms displayed portrayals of intimidating warriors and public executions of rebellious fighters. The entire complex was constructed by forced laborers from Babylon, Israel, Judah, and prisoners from along the Nile River.

Sennacherib retained the most talented individuals to work as engineers, artists, and skilled laborers under Assyrian foremen. The Kingdom of Babylon was absorbed into the Assyrian Empire and was named after the pagan chief deity, Ashur.

The Indo-Europeans practiced a polytheistic religion that recognized thousands of sacred gods, each with its sphere of authority. The Indo-Europeans would worship the deity that best aligned with their daily struggles, attempting to appease their chosen deity in each situation.

The Assyrians conquered and maintained territories by eliminating the traditional administrative officials, usually noble citizens based on a hereditary system. They replaced them with a new hierarchy of local population members directly accountable to the king. The Kushites were pioneers in developing and employing iron for diverse agricultural methods and warfare. However, the Assyrians advanced the iron melting technique and added horse-drawn chariots as mobile platforms.

To besiege a town, the Assyrians would build earthworks to cut off supplies and burn fruit trees and crops, forcing inhabitants to either surrender or starve. Known for their brutal tactics, the Assyrians were infamous for mutilating captives by cutting off hands, noses, and ears and even setting them on fire. To further intimidate and insult their enemies, they would sometimes display the skinless bodies of rebellious foes on poles around the towns as war trophies. Anyone who dared to rebel against such oppression would face gruesome death, including the removal of the tongue and gouging of the eyes.

The 2nd Book of Kings records that Sennacherib met his end at the hands of his sons, Adrammelech and Sharezer, while he was worshiping in the temple of Nisroch.

CHAPTER TWO

Empires of Assyria, Babylon, and Persia: Rise and Fall

An empire founded by war has to maintain itself by war.

———

Charles de Montesquieu

Under the leadership of King Ashurbanipal, the grandson of Sennacherib, the Assyrians entered Elam, a fertile region east of the Tigris River named after Shem's eldest son. With the assistance of remnant Indo-Europeans from Babylon and the Parsu tribal group from Persia, the Assyrians invaded Elam and sacked the royal city of Susa.

The Assyrian Conquest and the Fall of Elam

Merodach-Baladan, a Mesopotamian prince who had previously ruled Babylon before the Assyrians' victory, came to the aid of the Elamites. The coalition of Indo-Europeans was also met by a cavalry of Ethiopian troops who supported the Elamites, launching attacks around Babylon and killing the recently installed governor, thereby liberating Ur. While the attacks from the Ethiopians and Merodach-Baladan helped Elam maintain its independence, the Assyrians' brutal tactics instilled fear in Elam's political climate.

Ashurbanipal once again attacked the kingdom of Elam, and after several years of intense combat, he captured the capital city of Susa, causing the central authority to collapse. Ashurbanipal ended the Elamite reign by killing the last king of Elam. The Assyrians then relocated many Elamites to Samaria in northern Israel. To complicate matters further, the Assyrians swapped the Elamites with Jewish citizens of Samaria, relocating them to Elam. The Assyrians, Persians, and Medes divided Elam into separate principalities, which marked the end of Elamite domination in Mesopotamia.

The Assyrian ruler Ashurbanipal took pride in his ruthless atrocities committed during his guerrilla warfare, boasting, 'I tore out the tongues of those whose slanderous mouth had uttered blasphemies against my god Ashur...Susa, the great holy city, the abode of their gods, the seat of their mysteries, I conquered. I entered its palaces, and opened treasuries where gold and silver, goods and wealth...I destroyed the ziggurat of Susa...I devastated the provinces of Elam, and on their lands, I sowed salt' (Ashurbanipal, king of Assyria)

Babylon's grandeur escalated when the Assyrian general Nabopolassar seized the throne with the assistance of the Medes, establishing an independent monarchy separate from Assyrian rule. The kingdom was passed down to his son, Nebuchadnezzar, the greatest king of Babylon, who reconstructed a renowned palace complex into one of the Seven Wonders of the Ancient World.

In Babylon, along the Euphrates River, an official residence was constructed for the king. It featured the famed terraced hanging gardens built to delight the queen. The towering complex, built with impressive technical skills, served both as a city's safeguard and a symbol of authority and intimidation.

During the city's early development, the Babylonians constructed magnificent buildings and ziggurats with glazed brick walls throughout. The sidewalks around the complex were paved with marble stones hauled from the mountains, and the streets were laid with molded bricks. A processional way leading through the Ishtar Gate and Aibur-shabu, a road running between two towering walls over 80 feet high and nearly 50 feet deep at the base, marked the city's main entrance.

Numerous temples were built throughout Babylon to honor their polytheistic deities. One included a large statue of the pagan god Marduk, weighing around 44,000 pounds and made of solid gold, seated on a throne. These structures were built by prisoners of war from Israel, Judah, Elam, and Ethiopia.

The Book of Daniel in the Bible introduces Crown Prince Belshazzar prior to the fall of Babylon. Belshazzar, the biracial grandson of Nebuchadnezzar, ascended to the position of crown prince when his father, Nabonidus, took the throne of Babylon. Belshazzar's mother was Nitocris, the daughter of Nebuchadnezzar. Nitocris's mother was captured from the Kush region during an unsuccessful invasion of Egypt. Nabonidus became king following the short nine-month reign of Laboroarchod.

In 539 BC, the Persian King Cyrus invaded Babylon by ingeniously diverting the flow of the lake that ran through the city walls along the banks of the Euphrates River. The Persian troops marched into the unguarded river gates of the city while Crown Prince Belshazzar and his high-ranking officials were caught up in a feast. As a result, Babylon was captured without a battle. The Babylonians viewed Cyrus as a liberator, and Belshazzar was killed on the very night of the takeover.

The Persian Empire flourished, extending its domain from what is now central Iran down toward the Nile and deep into the Indus Valley. Nabonidus, the former king of Babylon, was taken aback by the speed with which Cyrus conquered the Medes region and the western territories along the Aegean Sea, including Asia Minor.

As Cyrus entered the conquered city of Babylon, he was hailed as the 'Great King' by the multitude of people lining the streets. Darius, the governor of Elam, subsequently arrested Nabonidus.

The Persians, an Indo-European-speaking people also known as Indo-Aryans, originated from the mountainous region of Russia. Various tribes from the Parsua ethnic group settled near the Elamite borders. The Persians would later leverage this proximity to persuade Darius, the governor of Elam and a province of Babylon, to defect.

The Persians unified under the Achaemenid Dynasty, and at the heart of their empire stood their imperial city, Persepolis. This city boasted numerous royal palaces and impressive monuments, overlooking the natural beauty of the fertile plain. However, Persepolis was second in importance to the administrative capital of Susa in the Elam province.

Cyrus applied the wise strategy of using local natives as administrative officials in their city-states. The Hebrew prophet Isaiah prophesied that Cyrus, whom he highly praised, would 'perform the Lord's pleasures' by being anointed as a shepherd. Cyrus declared that the Almighty God 'has given me all the kingdoms of the earth...And commanded me to build Him a house at Jerusalem' (2 Chronicles 36:23).

Cyrus issued a decree allowing the Jews and other people who had been brought to Babylon as forced laborers to return to their homelands. He gained favor among the Jewish people when he allowed the exiles to return to their homeland and encouraged them to rebuild their sacred temples.

Cyrus had gained control of Elam and lands throughout Mesopotamia. In the 5th century, Nehemiah, a descendant of the Jews who were taken captive by the Babylonians and resettled in Elam, was serving as a cupbearer, a trustworthy and significant position, to King Artaxerxes I. When Nehemiah received alarming news about the deteriorating condition of Jerusalem, he sought to convince the king to allow him to oversee the city's rebuilding. Consequently, Nehemiah was appointed governor by the king and escorted by a military entourage to the Holy Land.

Two significant figures, Zerubbabel and Ezra, had returned to Jerusalem under Cyrus's leadership and were assigned to bring about religious and political reforms. Ezra immediately implored the Jews to maintain purity and not provoke the Lord's anger any further by engaging in idolatry and intermarriage with Gentiles. Many Jews had married foreigners, and the children from these unions could not speak Hebrew.

The three men led religious revivals throughout Judah. They expelled prominent priests who had married foreign wives and drove many foreigners out of the nation.

The decline of the Persian Empire was largely due to numerous civil wars among the provinces, which were established for administrative purposes and governed by a satrap or governor. As the empire expanded westward, it absorbed much of the cultures of the surrounding provinces but also caused significant destruction. The Persians created approximately twenty large provinces and established a road system to bolster trade and communication for military and government personnels, allowing messages to be relayed to the king in Susa, the primary capital of the Persian Empire.

The Persians continued their conquests, moving westward throughout Mesopotamia and eastward toward the borders of India. Before long, Persia had subjugated Greek towns along the

Aegean Sea and in Asia Minor. To the West, the Greeks had developed a political society that granted many of its citizens independence and fostered prosperity through industrial trade.

Rebellions and Reforms in the Persian Empire

The revolt of the Persian satrapies paved the way for numerous alliances to form and challenge the king's authority. The spirit of independence and a democratic revolution among the Greek population living in the Persian satrapies fueled these rebellions.

The idea of democratic or individual economic freedom spread throughout the satrapies due to cultural ties with the free Greek cities. This trend, coupled with Persian citizens either fleeing or harboring a spirit of revolt, carried the spark of a superior civilization and created the prospect of a face-off between the two major powers. A religious reformation was also taking place simultaneously in both Persia and Greece.

Darius, I had provided financing for the rebuilding of the Jewish Temple, which had been discontinued some 16 years prior. The Temple in Jerusalem was completed in the 6th year of Darius's reign. Under Darius's rule, the Jews enjoyed a relatively good relationship and a degree of independence with Persia.

Darius built a canal to connect the Red Sea and the Mediterranean and established a network of roads to enhance communication within the empire. While the Persians traditionally worshipped nature deities, including the gods of the heavens, moon, and sun, their religious concepts began to evolve under the influence of Zoroastrianism. The dichotomy of good and evil was central to Zoroastrian teachings, and early Zoroastrian texts began to reflect similarities with the Hebrew concept of a grand hierarchy of angels.

Although Greek religion shared the belief in many gods, it maintained that the cosmos and the planets dictated human life and destiny.

The Persians initiated a series of military campaigns against Greece, with one of the earliest occurring in 490 BC. The Persians sailed across the Aegean Sea with hundreds of supply ships to lead their army in an invasion of the Island of Euboea in an effort to enter the plain of Marathon. The Persians forced their way onto the east side of Attica.

In response, the Greeks joined forces with the Spartans and enlisted both enslaved people and freemen to form a coalition to defeat the Persians at Marathon. However, the Persians were forced to divert their attention to quell an uprising in Egypt, and the death of King Darius I allowed Greece time to build a competitive navy.

A second invasion of Asia Minor began in 480 BC when the Persians decided to cross the Aegean Sea through Macedonia with a massive force of 150,000 troops and nearly 700 naval ships to invade Greece. Artaxerxes, the son of Darius, led this invasion.

The Persian army surged into the abandoned city of Athens. However, the Greeks held off the Persians at Thermopylae, inflicting a devastating blow to the Persian army. The Greeks formed a defensive league of city-states that led to Artaxerxes's navy being defeated at Salamis.

In 424 BC, Artaxerxes was poisoned and killed by the son of his concubine during a great feast while he was intoxicated. His death led to various problems within the empire as the provincial satrapies became more independent, causing serious economic issues.

The Greeks began arriving on the island of Crete around the 20th century BC from the region east of the Caspian Sea in the Balkans. This migration emerged during the height of the Bronze

Age, with the Dorian people migrating into Mycenae and others moving into the Plains of Thessaly, prompting invasions by more Balkan tribes.

A powerful volcanic eruption on the island triggered a devastating tsunami in the capital city of Knossos, which paved the way for Greek-speaking people to move into Crete along the Aegean Sea and Asia Minor. Greek warriors descended into the northern part of Crete in horse-drawn chariots, establishing themselves as masters or recipients of land bestowed by the unseen forces of nature.

The Greeks moved into Crete and destroyed a civilization that had developed more than 2,000 years before their arrival. They burnt royal palaces, institutions, and workplaces that made Minoan decorative materials. The royal city of Knossos, which housed the royal palaces, including the central courtyard with private living quarters for the royal family, was also burnt down. Knossos was a prosperous and beautiful city, considered one of the most magnificent along the Mediterranean before the Greek invasion.

The Greeks destroyed the culture and commercial centers of the thriving Minoan civilization, a course of action they believed was directed by the gods. This aligns with the characteristics of the war god, Indra, as described in the Aryan Bible of the Vedas. Indra, a god of vengeance, is known for causing storms and natural disasters against his adversaries. In the Rig Veda Hymn VI of the Aryan Bible, it is said: 'Indra, great in his power and might, and like Parjanya rich in rain, is magnified...Before his hot displeasure, all the people, all the men, bow down, as rivers bow down to the sea. This power of his shone brightly forth when Indra brought together, like a skin, the worlds of heaven and earth.'

On the eastern side of the Aegean region, in an area that scholar Marija Gimbutas referred to as 'Old Europe,' another group of invaders moved into what is now known as Troy, Ionia, the Island of Kalliste, and other cities along Asia Minor. These invaders then integrated with the locals, forming a loosely confederated group of independent Greek states. Most of the indigenous people were either displaced or reduced to servitude. The glory of the Cretans was passed down through history as the glory of Greco-Roman creativity.

One peculiar attribute of these invaders was their tendency to seize all physical possessions and wisdom from the indigenous people they subdued. However, archaeological excavations have rediscovered much of the Minoans' glory.

The Golden Age of Greek culture was characterized by philosophical creativity, scientific thinking, and efforts to understand the nature of the universe based on relative principles. A significant part of their culture was entertainment that took pride in watching men or animals fight to their death. While Greece was no longer the sole political power in the region, it became the foundational structure upon which imperial Rome was formed.

Rome began as a small agricultural community located at the mouth of the Tiber River on the Palatine and Esquiline Hills. Tradition holds that in 753 BC, Romulus founded Rome after killing his twin brother Remus, becoming the village's first king.

Romulus built a powerful military centered on religious reform that spread across seven hills on the Italian peninsula, all under the control of a king. Over time, conflicts with neighboring tribes led to shifts in Rome's population, military, and political power, tilting it towards the noblest citizens, known as the 'imperium.'

In alliance with the Etruscans to the north and Greek cities southward, the Romans persisted in warfare until 509 BC, when they deposed the final king, Tarquinius Superbus, inaugurating a republic. The republic was divided into two citizen classes: patricians and plebeians. Patricians, high-ranking citizens tracing their roots to Rome's original senate, appointed two judges to preside over their civil disputes. Plebeians, predominantly farmers, elected representatives for legislative duties.

Each province revered a particular god as their patron, with the Romans notably adopting Mithra, the Persian sun god symbolizing loyalty, as their primary deity, second only to Jupiter, the preeminent Roman god. This mirrored Greek mythology, where Zeus reigned supreme. Apollo, Zeus's son, was highly revered as the god of poetry, medicine, light, and healing, while his twin sister Diana was the goddess of fertility.

In the early seventh century BC, Assyrians migrated into Mesopotamia, overtaking the city-states established by Nimrod. Nineveh, one of the world's most ancient and prosperous cities, was conquered by an Indo-European tribal group led by Sennacherib, the Assyrian king. The city succumbed after a two-year siege by Assyrians, Medes, Philistines, and Scythians, who rerouted the Khoser River's flow into the city. This marked the start of the mighty empire's gradual decline, setting off a prophesied war between good and evil, referred to as the "end of days."

This conflict transcends our physical world, occurring in spiritual realms and involving humankind on the physical front. As we decipher the cryptic prophecies of Daniel, as documented in the biblical book bearing his name, we gain insights into future events. Daniel, along with his three companions—Hananiah, Mishael, and Azariah—were tested when captured by the Babylonians. Their resolve was demonstrated as they steadfastly refused to worship the Babylonian pagan gods.

In 605 BC, Daniel was taken captive by King Nebuchadnezzar of Babylon, son of Nabopolassar, during the siege of Jerusalem. The city's cherished Temple was destroyed, and its inhabitants were exiled to Babylon as prisoners of war. Daniel and his three companions were selected to serve in the king's palace, learning the Chaldean language and literature and eventually serving foreign kings. The chief of eunuchs gave them Babylonian names: Belteshazzar (Daniel), Shadrach, Meshach, and Abed-Nego.

When captured, Daniel was barely in his teens. He excelled in learning and wisdom. Due to his extraordinary abilities, he and his friends underwent a three-year training program for the royal administration. Upon examination, the king found their understanding and wisdom far surpassing those of his wise men and astrologers. Daniel was blessed with the ability to interpret dreams.

Prophetic Insights and Imperial Destinies

A year after the Hebrews' exile, King Nebuchadnezzar had a prophetic dream revealing the future of the Gentile kingdoms destined to become world powers. These visions, occurring throughout his life, also foresaw events leading to the Messianic Age when Christ would establish an earthly kingdom. This era, when Gentiles would rule the earth, was referred to by Jeremiah as "the time of Jacob's troubles," with the suggestion that many Gentiles would become hosts for fallen angels. Through metaphorical visions, Daniel was able to predict these future events.

Daniel provided an interpretation of the king's dream, which featured a towering statue composed of various materials. The statue's golden head, silver torso and arms, brass abdomen and thighs, and legs of iron partially combined with clay symbolized a different kingdom. Notably, the silver torso and arms stood for the Persian Empire. This was the second kingdom in the sequence and was deemed less powerful in comparison to Nebuchadnezzar's dominant Assyro-Babylonian Empire.

The third empire, symbolized by the statue's bronze belly, was identified as Greece. Daniel prophesied that this kingdom would succeed Persia and rule with significant authority, but eventually fragment and be divided among four generals worldwide. These divisions of Greece would conquer nations along the Nile and oppress the Jewish people.

The fourth kingdom, emerging from Greece, would surpass all in strength, symbolized by iron. According to Nebuchadnezzar's dream, this empire would shatter and subdue all other nations. Representing the statue's legs, feet, and ten toes of iron mixed with clay, this kingdom would intermingle through marriage but fail to unify, as iron does not mix with clay (Daniel 2:43).

This fourth kingdom divided first, forming the fourth and fifth empires, before eventually splitting into ten sections. By the mid-5th century, the western segment of Old Rome was increasingly threatened by the influx of Germanic tribes known as federates or allies of Rome.

The Germanic tribes laid the foundation for a novel political shift in the West. Many joined the Roman military, while others established independent provinces. German military commanders eventually seized control over the central authority, including the imperial court.

These German provinces evolved into several kingdoms, each under a king. They conquered significant portions of the central authority in Italy, weakening the empire through these internal conflicts. By the 8th century, the Eastern Roman Empire transitioned into the Byzantine Empire. Meanwhile, the German Kingdoms in the West evolved into a Western Islamic society.

In the fifth chapter of Daniel, Belshazzar, the crown prince, hosted a lavish feast for a thousand of his lords, concubines, and wives. The partygoers drank wine from the sacred vessels his grandfather, Nebuchadnezzar, had plundered from the Holy Land. Amidst the celebration, they praised the heathen idols of gold, silver, bronze, iron, wood, and stone while mocking the captive Hebrews and God. The palace was filled with laughter, idolatry, and pleasure.

Suddenly, the festivities were interrupted when a hand appeared and wrote the words "MENE, MENE, TEKEL, and UPHARSIN" on the plastered wall. Terrified, Belshazzar's knees knocked together in fear (Dan. 5:6). He summoned Babylon's astrologers, soothsayers, and wise men, but none could decipher the writing.

The queen then entered the banquet hall and told Belshazzar of a man from Judah with profound wisdom and the ability to interpret dreams. She described Daniel as a possessor of exceptional spiritual knowledge and the ability to solve mysteries, having the Spirit of the Holy God.

When Daniel was presented to the prince, Belshazzar asked, "Are you that Daniel, who is one of the captives from Judah, whom my father, the king, brought from Judah? 'I have heard of You, that the Spirit of God is in you, and that light and understanding and excellent wisdom are found in you'" (Dan. 5:13-14).

Daniel informed the prince that his arrogance against the Lord of Heaven led to the cryptic writing. He explained its meaning: "MENE: God has numbered your kingdom and brought it to an end; TEKEL: You have been weighed in the scales and found wanting; PERES: Your kingdom has been divided and given to the Medes and Persians" (Dan: 5:26-28).

In the seventh chapter, Daniel recounts a night-time vision in which the four winds of heaven stirred the Mediterranean, known as the Great Sea. Daniel observed four massive beasts emerging from the water. The first resembled a lion with eagle wings and stood upright like a man. The second, akin to a bear, held three ribs in its mouth. The third creature, bearing a resemblance to a leopard, had four wings on its back. The peculiar third creature also had four heads and was given authority.

The fourth creature stood apart from the rest, possessing extraordinary strength. With massive teeth, it devoured, crushed, and trampled remnants underfoot. This formidable beast had ten horns, and among them was a smaller horn with human eyes and a mouth uttering grand pronouncements. This little horn grew substantially, uprooting the first three horns.

The Papacy, represented by the little horn, became a potent authority in the Roman Empire through the union of Church and State. This little horn displaced the other three. The Heruli, known for their relentless warfare, including the burning of the sick and elderly, soon fell to the Lombards. The Heruli, Ostrogoths, and Vandals' kingdoms were ultimately extinguished. The Roman Church, likened to potter's clay, governed the Roman Empire for 1260 years.

This worldly system, led by the Papacy, enabled each state of Rome or divided Europe, in their quest for world domination, to commit mass slaughters. African inhabitants, Indigenous peoples of the Americas, and Israelites living in Israel fell victim to these atrocities. The Papacy, as a union of church and state, authorized these horrific acts in the name of religion, resulting in more bloodshed than any other entity on earth.

Daniel was granted a vision of the future judgment of the little horn, which was cast into the fiery flame by the "Ancient of Days." Daniel continued to recount his vision, stating, "The court was seated, and the books were opened. 'I watched then because of the sound of the pompous words which the horn was speaking; I watched till the beast was slain, and its body destroyed and given to the burning flames.' As for the rest of the beasts, they had their dominion taken away, yet their lives were prolonged for some time" (Dan.7:10-11).

Daniel found himself by the bank of the Ulai River, grappling with the meaning of another metaphorical vision about the future of world kingdoms and end-time prophecies. He saw a ram pushing westward, northward, and southward, growing in strength. The ram had two horns, one taller than the other, with the taller one emerging last. From the west, a male goat with a notable horn between its eyes crossed the earth and attacked the ram, breaking its two horns. The ram was powerless, and the goat trampled it. As the male goat grew substantially, four horns emerged, pointing towards the four winds of heaven.

The Angel Gabriel appeared to Daniel to clarify the vision of future events. As the Angel approached, Daniel fell into a deep slumber, but Gabriel helped him stand. Gabriel disclosed that the two-horned ram represented the kings of Media and Persia, while the male goat that attacked the ram symbolized the kingdom of Greece. The large horn between the goat's eyes was the first kingdom of Babylon. The broken horn and the four that rose in its place signified the four kingdoms to emerge from Greece.

Gabriel conveyed to Daniel that unseen forces would aid these pagan nations in their quest for world domination: "He shall even rise against the prince of princes, but he shall be broken without human means...Therefore seal up the vision, for it refers to many days in the future" (Dan. 8:2-26).

Prophet Ezekiel, along with other upper-class citizens and skilled craftsmen, was taken captive during the second invasion of Judah in 597 BC. At the age of 25, during the Babylonian siege of Judah, Ezekiel was exiled. Five years later, he began his prophetic ministry while living among the captives by the Chebar River. In his inaugural vision, Ezekiel saw the heavens open and a whirlwind approaching from the north.

Four flaming angels drove a radiant chariot encircled by a fiery cloud. The angels bore the faces of a man, a lion, an ox, and an eagle. Each peculiar creature had four pairs of wings. Above these angelic forms appeared the likeness of God's Throne. Seated on the throne was Almighty God, surrounded by a luminous aura of fire.

This glorious apparition of the Lord caused Ezekiel to fall face-first to the ground. Ezekiel's visions foretold the judgment of the Hebrews by the Gentile kingdoms and their eventual return to Israel and lands across Mesopotamia. The Lord commanded Ezekiel to stand, and the Spirit helped him to his feet. The Lord declared, "Son of man, I am sending you to the children of Israel, to a rebellious nation that has rebelled against Me... they are impudent and stubborn people...As for them, whether they hear or whether they refuse, for they are a rebellious house, yet they will know that a prophet has been among them" (Ez. 2:3-5).

Ezekiel prophesied that calamity would strike, leading to cannibalism due to severe food and water shortages in Jerusalem. "Pound your fists and stamp your feet, and say, 'Alas, for all the evil abominations of the house of Israel! They shall fall by the sword, by famine, and by pestilence.' He who is far off shall die by pestilence, he who is near shall fall by the sword, and he who remains and is besieged shall die by the famine...Then you shall know that I am the Lord, when their slain are among their idols all around their altars, on every high hill, on all the mountaintops, under every green tree and every thick oak, wherever they offered sweet incense to all their idols" (Ez. 6:11-13). Following the Lord's wrath, the covenant people would be gathered from all corners of the globe to their homeland.

While Daniel and Ezekiel communicated God's message to the Israelites, Prophet Nahum prophesied Judgement on Nineveh. During Nahum's prophetic ministry, he resided in Elkosh, northern Israel. Nineveh, the capital of the Assyrian Empire, was one of the most influential cities of the ancient world. Bigger than its neighboring city, Babylon, Nineveh was one of the oldest and largest cities of antiquity. According to archaeologists, this renowned city was established over 6,000 years ago. Nimrod laid the city's foundations, making it the capital of the Kushite Kingdom.

Earlier prophets were dispatched to Nineveh to herald impending doom and preach about the universal love of Almighty God for all people. Jonah was sent to Nineveh in the 8th century BC, over 150 years before Prophet Nahum. Jonah's mission was to warn the Assyrians to repent from their pagan practices or face the Lord's fierce wrath. The entire city repented, accepting the Lord's grace by renouncing the worship of false gods.

However, by Nahum's time, the people had reverted to their pagan beliefs. Nahum described Nineveh as a city of violence and deceit, stating, "Woe to the bloody city! It is all full of lies and robbery" (Nah.3:1).

In his vision, Nahum narrated how Nineveh, once reliant on the Ethiopians and Egyptians for city defense, saw its Indigenous population led away as prisoners of war by the Assyrian army. As the Assyrians and natives intermingled and adopted the Assyrians' pagan practices, the city eventually fell to foreign power. "The Lord has given a command concerning you: 'Out of the house of your gods I will cut off the carved image and molded image. I will dig your grave, for you are vile'" (Nah. 1:14).

Three years after Nahum's prophecy, the Medes and Babylonians breached the city walls and advanced towards the king's palace. The once magnificent royal residence was left in ruins, trapping many royal citizens. Those who escaped the burning buildings were taken captive, while the sword slew countless others. All of Nineveh's glory was buried beneath the ruins when the brooks of the Tigris flooded the city.

The degradation of the fallen angels, in my view, signifies the supreme adoration of Almighty God. The Holy Bible mentions that the Gentiles made a "covenant with death," suggesting that this pact with evil supersedes all intervening and intermediate spiritual loyalty to Almighty God. To improve the world, loyalty to Almighty God must override all spiritual allegiances to any system of authority.

The belief in a singular, omnipotent entity has always been universal in the Hebrew faith. However, the fallen angels and their earthly allies chose a system of jealousy, pride, and greed to divert people away from Almighty God. A war erupted in Heaven between the Sons of darkness and the Angels of Almighty God before the fall of the rebellious angels. This spiritual battle continues on earth and the lower heavens, with humankind taking sides, aligning with either good or evil.

Without Almighty God, humankind lacks the power to combat Satan and his fallen angels. Lucifer, deprived of his divine power, harbors an obsessive hatred for mankind but is permitted dominion over sinners. Rather than forsaking mankind, the Lord offers us a choice: to choose between good and evil.

CHAPTER THREE

The Biblical and Historical Tapestry of Free Will and Empire

"Nearly all men can stand adversity, but if you want to test a man's character, give him power."

———

Abraham Lincoln

While the Bible contains numerous curses, Satan's power is constrained and must comply with God's Universal Law. Conversely, deception is required to entice mankind into a worldly system of free will.

In the book of Daniel, Rome signifies the final phase of world history dominated by the Gentile ruling system. The Roman government, with its apparent monarch and aristocracy, was comprised of wealthy landowners who were focused on amassing riches and authority. The Roman army started as a group of warriors trying to defend their tribal areas, uniting to fight against neighboring adversaries for control of land and possessions. Rome developed a combined military with foot soldiers and cavalry on horseback. The Romans quickly adopted and improved upon the weaponry techniques and strategies used by their enemies to advance their cause. Rome became the center of the kingdom, and its influence and methods became the archetype for the Western world empire.

The Republic's form of government engaged in brutal warfare to expand Rome's borders into neighboring territories and established a dominant political organization ruled by a senate and two elected consuls. These consuls served as military commanders and political and judicial officials. They were nominated by the Century Assembly (or comitia centuriata). Throughout the Republic's history, only the Century Assembly had the power to declare war and served as the central governing body.

During the transition from republic to empire, the balance of power shifted from the Century Assembly towards the Roman Emperor, the executive branch. The Century Assembly evolved into the assembly of the people, and the powerful Senate was politically weakened.

Ordinary citizens desired a voice in government as a group of ruling-class families, known as patricians, controlled the majority of wealth and political power. The plebeians, a lower class of Roman citizens who managed to amass wealth through trade, formed an assembly to gain power in the Roman government.

Mercenary soldiers were hired to bolster a strong military, utilizing their unique skills for different tactics. By the early 3rd century BC, Rome had established a standing army of four legions, consisting of over 325,000 non-disabled men, in addition to a cavalry of a combined 20,000 men on horseback and chariots.

The Mithridatic Wars: Conflict and Conquest in Asia Minor

The Romans tested their vast military when Mithradates, the king of Pontus, allied with other Greek cities along the Asia Minor Coast to establish a powerful and wealthy empire. Mithradates' army deployed mercenary soldiers in the region to massacre nearly 100,000 Roman citizens throughout Asia Minor and torment captured Roman commanders. The victims included the Roman tax-collecting agents known as publicans and equities who served on jury courts.

In 89 BC, during the First Mithridatic War, Mithradates invaded the Roman province of Pergamum and initiated an attack on Rhodes. This started a five-year war in which many Greek cities rebelled against Roman rule while Sulla was in command of the Roman army. Lucius Cornelius Sulla defeated Mithradates in 86 BC, driving him out of Greece. He imposed a fine on the citizens, equivalent to five years of excessive back tax, and sacked Athens for supporting Mithradates.

Back in Rome, Sulla's successes bolstered his reputation, enabling him to seize dictatorship with absolute authority.

After defeating Mithradates, Sulla used his army to march against Publius Sulpicius Rufus and Gaius Marius. Marius, having been elected consul seven times, had gained significant popularity in Rome while Sulla, once Marius's lieutenant, was at war fighting Mithradates. An envoy was sent to inform Sulla that Marius had replaced him, but Sulla's soldiers stoned the envoy to death and headed towards Rome with five legions. Marius advocated that the soldiers should not look to the Senate for war compensation but to their general, who was responsible for their wages. He sent a large army to stop Sulla's return to Rome. This sparked a civil war on the streets of Rome, with supporters of both Sulla and Marius marching on the Senate and threatening to kill one another. After bitter fighting, Marius fled to Africa while Sulla headed to Greece for another Mithridatic War.

In 83 BC, Lucius Licinius Murena invaded Pontus, alleging that Mithradates posed a threat to Roman territory in Asia Minor. During the First Mithridatic War, Sulla had made an agreement with Mithradates to renounce claims to Greek provinces in Asia Minor, which allowed Sulla to station two legions in the region. Lucius Murena had been left in Asia Minor to oversee the newly captured provinces. Mithradates was allowed to return to Pontus as a friend of Rome and end all hostility. However, when King Nicomedes IV of Bithynia died, hostility erupted again as the Romans took control of the region near Pontus. Mithradates, king of Pontus, invaded Bithynia and drove the Roman army out of the region.

During this period of tension in Rome, there were several slave uprisings. The largest and longest of these began with Spartacus, a Thracian gladiator who fought slaves, prisoners of war, and wild animals for the Romans' amusement. Spartacus and other gladiators were trained to fight condemned criminals who ended up in the arena during officials' inaugurations and other games in Rome.

In 73 BC, Spartacus, along with the Gauls, Castus, and Gannicus, instigated a revolt at Capua that spread throughout Southern Italy. Spartacus assembled a group of enslaved people who stole their masters' weapons and terrorized the rural and mountainous regions of Southern Italy for two years, eventually confronting the army of Cnaeus Pompey. Spartacus and his 70,000 soldiers were defeated in Apulia along the road from Capua.

Rising in popularity, Pompey was granted command of 120,000 soldiers and a naval fleet of 500 ships to annex Bithynia with Pontus after the Roman Senate replaced Licinius Murena with Pompey as general.

In 67 BC, Pompey assumed command and led a series of victories against Pontus in the Third Mithridatic War, which began in 75 BC. The fight over Bithynia was significant due to the region's wealth in silver and gold and its location, which pirates threatened, endangering Rome's food supply from Africa. Mithradates fled the battlefield and sought refuge in a temple when his son Pharnaces turned against him. There, he committed suicide.

The Roman general Pompey finally annexed the region to the Roman Empire, turning it into client provinces. Pompey had Mithradates' many wives, children, and sisters put to death. Rome made a peace agreement with Mithradates' son, Pharnaces, who had opposed the Third Mithridatic War and pledged allegiance to Rome.

When the Third Mithridatic War ended, Rome expanded its borders into the Seleucid Empire, northern Syria, and territory in Armenia. Turning south, Pompey continued his march into Judea, seizing the capital city of Jerusalem. Pompey and his officers killed thousands of Jewish citizens, expelled many other Jews from Jerusalem, and entered the Holy of Holies, the innermost chamber of the Great Temple, where only the High Priest was allowed to enter.

In 62 BC, Pompey, Crassus, and Caesar formed the First Triumvirate, a secret political alliance. With this backing, Julius Caesar won the consul in 59 BC. He used his consulship to pass land and tax-collecting reforms that benefited the Triumvirate. He also secured ratification of his Eastern Settlement, which granted him special command of three provinces of Gaul for five years: Illyricum, Cisalpine, and Transalpine.

Gaul, encompassing modern-day France, Belgium, and parts of the Netherlands, was a significant region in Western Europe and one of Rome's most crucial provinces. While serving as Proconsul, Caesar began an eight-year conquest in 58 BC against

Gallic tribes to expand the Roman Empire across the Rhine River and secure the borders into the British Isles.

The Gallic Wars resulted in a Roman victory that brought portions of Germanic tribes, Belgic, and British territories under Roman control. This territorial gain significantly boosted Caesar's political ambitions. The Gallic Wars gave Caesar fame, military experience, and enough slaves and spoils of war to retain army veterans loyal to him. It is believed that as many as two million men, women, and children lost their lives in Caesar's crusade during the Gallic War.

The Triumvirate members became some of the wealthiest men in the world from the sale of captured enslaved people, spoils of war, and real estate. The commanders were allowed to keep much of the property they acquired.

Crassus, Parthia, and the Shifting Dynamics of Roman Power

Marcus Licinius Crassus was appointed governor of Syria to the east and planned to use his jurisdiction to launch an invasion against the Parthian Empire. Before attacking Parthia, Crassus invaded Jerusalem and seized the temple treasure, then traversed the Mediterranean desert to wage war against Parthia. This resulted in a heavy defeat at the hands of Surena's army, which killed a large number of Roman legions.

The Parthian military was well-equipped with bows and arrows and used camels to resupply their troops. They were able to cut off supplies to Crassus' infantry. The Parthians attacked the Roman garrison with a strong cavalry, fast-moving bowmen, and masses of horse-archers, catching Crassus' troops by surprise. The Roman legions were surrounded, with the Parthians beating loud drums and blaring bells to disorient the Roman soldiers.

The Parthians slaughtered the Roman soldiers, killed Crassus' son, and put his head on a spear for Crassus to see in disgrace. Parthian General Surena attempted to negotiate a truce with Crassus, but he rejected the offer. Crassus and his generals were killed, along with around 30,000 casualties.

Pompey was given the two Spanish provinces and allowed to remain in Rome while commanding his prefectures. Pompey rose through the ranks under the powerful Sulla, who maintained a private army even after his retirement in 79 BC. The Roman legions were more loyal to their commander than the powerful Senate because their pay came from the spoils of war provided by their commander.

Crassus and Pompey joined forces to acquire more land for their army veterans and restore much of the Senate's power lost under former General Sulla. Gaining popularity among the common people, Julius Caesar rose to prominence as a spokesman for the populares (Roman leaders aligned with the people's interests) during his time in political office.

Julius Caesar leveraged his popularity among ordinary Romans and the Italian people when the Senate attempted to persuade the citizens to defend the Republican system in favor of Pompey. As a result, the people chose Caesar as emperor for life.

After Marcus Crassus's death, a civil war broke out that undermined Sulla's constitution, setting in motion a political disorder. The Senate permitted Pompey to station troops to guard the city of Rome. Caesar was furious when he heard the news, and he sent a letter to the Senate proposing that both he and Pompey lay down their command. The offer was rejected in early January 49 BC, and Pompey was allowed to be the sole consul of Rome. Pompey commanded Caesar to resign his command.

In open opposition to Pompey and the Senate decree, Caesar set out to return to Rome. He crossed the Rubicon River with his legions—a violation of the law that prohibited troops from leaving their provinces without the Senate's approval. As he crossed the river, Caesar reportedly uttered the famous phrase "ālea iacta est" ("the die is cast"), symbolizing the point of no return.

The Rubicon River's topography was used as the southern boundary of Cisalpine Gaul and the Roman Republic. Pompey's legions outnumbered Caesar's forces at least three times, putting Caesar in a much weaker position. Pompey believed that Caesar would be short on supplies and exhausted before reaching Rome, but the Senate pressured him to confront Caesar once he crossed the Rubicon River. Pompey ordered his men not to charge but to allow Caesar to advance before attacking.

Rather than pushing forward, Caesar's troops decided to take respite in the highlands near the coastal city of Rubicon. Pompey's strategy involved encircling Caesar's forces, cutting off their supply lines, and forcing them into surrender. Pompey held a significant advantage, enjoying the support of the Senate and an ample supply of resources.

The ensuing battle was marked by fierce combat, as both Caesar and Pompey aimed to gain absolute control over Rome through victory. Additionally, Caesar's foreign allies were actively engaged in the conflict, seeking recognition as legitimate Roman citizens.

The period of the Triumvirate lasted a mere five years before envy and tension within Rome escalated into a civil war. Pompey led the senatorial forces to confront Caesar when he crossed the Rubicon on the northern coast of Italy. Caesar had been granted a five-year extension as the governor of Gaul, but the Roman Senate voted to appoint Pompey as the sole consul in 52 BC, effectively stripping Caesar of his command.

Swiftly advancing towards Rome, Caesar engaged in battles with Pompey's loyal forces along the Rubicon and the Adriatic

Sea, attempting to prevent his rival from reaching the city. Upon his return to Rome, Caesar garnered widespread support and declared himself dictator, defying the Senate. Julius Caesar embarked on a series of political reforms, restoring civil order and forgiving the debts of many Roman citizens.

Pompey, accompanied by seven legions and a significant portion of the Roman Senate, fled Rome and sought refuge in Greece to regroup. Caesar pursued Pompey and his legions into central Greece, where the rivalry culminated in the blood-soaked battleground of Pharsalus. Pompey managed to escape, ultimately finding shelter in Alexandria, Egypt. His fate was sealed when he arrived on Egyptian shores, where he was betrayed and fatally stabbed by King Ptolemy, aided by Lucius Septimius, a former ally of Pompey, and an Egyptian general named Achilles. This ruthless assassination took place in the presence of Pompey's wife.

Upon his arrival in Egypt, Caesar was presented with the severed head of Pompey by Theodotus. Witnessing this gruesome sight, Caesar was moved to tears and extended an olive branch to Pompey's friends and family, offering reconciliation.

Following Pompey's death, the Roman Senate conferred upon Julius Caesar the title of dictator for ten years despite the numerous adversaries he had accumulated while consolidating power in Rome. In a gesture of compassion, Caesar granted Roman citizenship to individuals residing in the provinces. He pardoned many of the republican leaders who had previously opposed him, allowing them to return to the Italian Peninsula.

Caesar was committed to promoting greater equality among the inhabitants of Roman territories. He implemented reforms to extend citizenship to those residing in provinces across North Africa, Gaul, the Balkans, Greece, and Spain. Subsequently, the Senate altered Caesar's title from temporary dictator to emperor for life.

However, in 44 BC, Caesar fell victim to an assassination plot orchestrated by several Roman senators who vehemently opposed his increasing central authority, referring to themselves as the Liberators. This conspiracy was spearheaded by Gaius Cassius Longinus and Marcus Brutus, who fatally stabbed Julius Caesar near the Theatre of Pompey.

In the aftermath of Caesar's assassination, Marcus Antonius, better known as Mark Antony, established an official political alliance with Octavian and Lepidus, giving rise to the Second Triumvirate. Despite professing loyalty to the Senate and aligning himself with Mark Antony, Lepidus was compelled to go into exile, accused of seizing political power.

During Caesar's public funeral, his last will and testament were read aloud. Still, the passionate crowd was so enraged that they set Caesar's body ablaze and instigated riots against the conspirators. This event marked the onset of four years of civil unrest in Rome, as the lower classes of the population were outraged that a select group of nobles had taken the life of Julius Caesar.

By 40 BC, The Roman Empire was divided into eastern and western halves. Mark Antony took control of the East and formed an alliance with Cleopatra VII, the Egyptian Queen. Octavian took control of the west, and in 32 BC, the Senate swore an oath of loyalty to him. They accused Antony of giving away Roman territory to the "whore of the east" by marrying Cleopatra. Mark Antony then began to fight against the Parthian Empire for control of Roman-controlled Judea and Syria.

A final conflict arose during the Second Triumvirate when a civil war broke out between Antony and Cleopatra. In 47 BC, Julius Caesar appointed Antipater, the ruler of Idumea, to be the procurator of all Judea, placing two of his sons, Herod and Phasael, in ruling positions. The Idumeans were of Edomite stock and were enemies of the Jewish people. Shortly after Caesar's death, the Roman Senate named Herod, king of Judea, when Antipater was killed, and his older brother Phasael committed suicide.

Cleopatra convinced Mark Antony to send Herod south to fight the Nabataeans of Arabia (modern-day Jordan), a wealthy port region including Gaza, seeking to gain control of a lucrative trade route through the Mediterranean.

Herod was a ruthless and cunning ruler who went to great lengths to eliminate any potential male heirs to his throne. According to the account in the Gospel of Mark, Herod had John the Baptist arrested. This action was influenced by his wife, Herodias, a menacing stepdaughter, and a concern about John's growing popularity. John the Baptist, a forerunner and cousin of Jesus (known as Yeshua Ha'Mashiach), had publicly condemned Herod's marriage to Herodias because she had previously been married to his brother and had a child with him. John was imprisoned in the fortress of Machaerus and eventually beheaded.

During this era, Rome emerged from the dissolution of Alexander's empire, and a new power struggle erupted, leading to a civil war between Mark Antony and Octavian. Many members of the Senate turned against Mark Antony due to his political alliances with Egypt and his marriage to a foreign queen. By 31 BC, Octavian and the joint forces of Mark Antony and Cleopatra, including naval warfare, clashed on the Ionian Sea near the port city of Actium in northwestern Greece. Octavian's naval fleet was under the command of Marcus Vipsanius Agrippa, and Cleopatra's navy suffered a decisive defeat. Antony and Cleopatra fled to Alexandria, Egypt, pursued by Octavian and his naval forces. Both Mark Antony and Cleopatra took their own lives, and from that moment on, Octavian was portrayed as a god. He eventually assumed the title of Augustus, a name associated with the Father of Rome, within the Senate.

Divine Revelations and Historical Consequences

In the Bible, the Prophet Isaiah is renowned for receiving profound prophetic visions concerning Judah and its capital city, Jerusalem. One of the most memorable of these visions occurred in the year that Uzziah, the king of Judah, passed away. Isaiah found himself in the Temple of the Lord, where he witnessed a majestic vision: "I saw the Lord sitting on a lofty throne, with the train of His robe filling the entire Temple" (Isaiah 6:1).

In his vision, Isaiah saw seraphim, fiery angels, each with six wings, circling the throne. They used two wings to cover their faces, two wings to cover their feet, and two wings for flying. These mysterious angels flew around the throne on which the Lord was seated, singing praises and declaring their devotion to Him. One of these angels cried out: "Holy, holy, holy is the Lord of hosts; the whole earth is full of His glory!" (Isaiah 6:3)

"Then said I, Woe is me! for I am undone; because I am a man of unclean lips, and I dwell in the midst of a people of unclean lips: for mine eyes have seen the King, the Lord of hosts." (Isaiah 6:5).

This verse illustrates Isaiah's response to a powerful and overwhelming vision of God. In the presence of the divine, he is struck by a deep sense of unworthiness and recognizes his sinfulness. Isaiah's experience underscores the awe-inspiring and humbling nature of encountering God in such a direct and profound way.

Following this declaration, another seraph flew to Isaiah with a live coal taken from the altar and touched his lips. The seraph proclaimed to Isaiah: "Behold this has touched your lips; your iniquity is taken away, and your sin purged" (Isaiah 6:7). This encounter symbolized Isaiah's purification and readiness to serve God as His prophet.

Isaiah's prophecies led him to live a symbolic life as a sign to the people. He was required to walk among the Kushites, aka

Ancient Ethiopia, for three years, naked and barefoot, as a warning of their impending doom brought about by the religious idols they had accepted from the Gentiles. Israel and Judah had placed their trust in the Ethiopians and Egyptians for their security against the Assyrians and Babylonians instead of trusting in the Almighty God.

Isaiah's prophecy carried a stark warning to the Kushites that their waters in the sea and river would dry up, and famine would occur as a sign of the Lord's displeasure with their idolatrous lifestyle. The histories of the Kushites and the Jewish people are intertwined, with both groups identified as Hebrews. This description may have been derived from the name Eber, an ancestor of Abraham. This shared identity highlighted the severity of their transgressions and the importance of Isaiah's warnings.

Isaiah's prophecy regarding the Ethiopians (Kushites) came to pass when Sargon, the king of Assyria, attacked the inhabitants in 720 BC. This attack was triggered by a rebellion that broke out in Syria, inspired by the king of Hamath. In response to the revolt, Hoshea, the king of Israel, withheld tribute from Assyria and sought help from the 24th dynasty of the Kushites.

The Assyrians retaliated by laying siege to Samaria, the capital of the Northern Kingdom of Israel, for three years. Eventually, the Assyrians breached the city walls, leading to the fall of the Northern Kingdom of Israel. Many Kushites were taken prisoner, along with the Israelites.

The prophecy is recounted in Isaiah 20:3-5: "Then the Lord said, 'Just as My servant Isaiah has walked naked and barefoot three years for a sign and a wonder against Egypt and Ethiopia, so shall the king of Assyria lead away the Egyptians as prisoners and the Ethiopians as captives, young and old, naked and barefoot, with their buttocks uncovered, to the shame of Egypt. Then they shall be afraid and ashamed of Ethiopia their expectation and Egypt their glory.'" This prophecy underscored the power and sovereignty of God, as well as the consequences of turning away from Him for help and protection.

Throughout the ages, from the era of Assyrian domination to the present time, the Hebrew people have suffered at the hands of various Gentile kingdoms. However, Almighty God used His laws and the visions of prophets to deter people from their sinful ways.

There is, indeed, a profound and invisible spiritual structure in play, guiding humankind either toward Almighty God or toward the path of the evil one, who enthusiastically encourages sin and leads individuals toward darkness. According to the Book of Enoch, Satan is described as having 36 wings with countless eyes and being created out of smokeless fire.

In the book of Genesis, Satan, also known as the Prince of Darkness, was commanded to bow to Adam, who was made out of black sculpted clay. Satan's pride and disobedience to Almighty God led him to be cast down to earth, described metaphorically as falling like a stroke of lightning.

In the 14th chapter of Isaiah, Satan is referred to as "Lucifer, son of the morning." Isaiah warned the Hebrew people to reject the idolatrous traps set by Lucifer, emphasizing the importance of remaining faithful to Almighty God and rejecting the enticements of evil.

In the Book of Enoch, a fascinating journey is described where Raphael, one of the holy angels, led Enoch into the midst of a desert region in the wilderness. Enoch saw a valley with flowing water that irrigated grooves of aromatic trees and plants, all full of fruits. Raphael escorted Enoch over the Red Sea, passing over the angel Zotiel, and led him toward the Garden of Righteousness.

In this garden, Enoch encountered two very large, beautiful, and magnificent trees. These trees had broad, dark green leaves similar to those of the Carob tree and fruits like clusters of grapes, exuding sweet fragrances. Eating from these trees of knowledge granted individuals great wisdom, as Enoch noted: "How beautiful is the tree, and how attractive is its look!"

Raphael, the holy angel accompanying him, explained the significance of these trees: "This is the tree of wisdom, of which your father of old and your mother of old, who were your progenitors, have eaten, and they learned wisdom and their eyes were opened, and they knew that they were naked and they were driven out of the garden." This account mirrors the biblical narrative of Adam and Eve in the Garden of Eden, where eating the forbidden fruit opened their eyes to their nakedness, leading to their expulsion from the garden.

In the Book of Acts, Peter delivers a powerful sermon to the Romans. He proclaims that Almighty God has raised Jesus Christ, the Prince of Life, from the dead - the very one they had killed. He urges them to repent and convert so that their sins may be blotted out and they may experience times of refreshing from the Lord's presence. He foretells the return of Jesus Christ, whom heaven must receive until the times of the restoration of all things, as spoken by all God's holy prophets since the world began (Acts 3:14-21).

Throughout history, many emperors from various regions, including France, Greece, Germany, and America, have failed to restore the Old Roman Empire. However, its tradition continues to permeate the Western world. To some, Rome represents greatness, fascination, and political and economic power. It serves as a reminder that all kingdoms, no matter how mighty, deteriorate over time.

Much of our Western culture and ideas today can indeed be traced back to Roman society. Rome itself was deeply pagan, worshipping false gods whose roots intertwined with those of the Assyrians, Greeks, Babylonians, Persians, and Indo-Aryans from the hills of the Balkans. Their philosophy was based on superstition, polytheistic religion, tyranny, ritual prostitution, idolatry, war, mythology, and fairy tales. All these elements combined to transform Rome into the world's greatest and most admired empire.

The fragmentation of the Roman Empire led to the emergence of new rivals on the world stage, continuing divisions into Eastern and Western blocs, and the rise of individual states. Other great cities faded away, and the network of roads deteriorated. Trade dwindled, and slavery was temporarily abolished.

One of the great provinces, Carthage, often referred to as Rome-in-Africa, experienced its decline. Between 264 BC and 146 BC, Carthage fought three wars with the Roman Empire and nearly conquered Rome during the Second Punic War. Under Hamilcar and Hannibal Barca, the Carthaginians built extensive commercial trading networks that reached into Sicily. Rome, viewing what they perceived as an inferior African nation, attempted to secure a foothold on the island.

However, by 146 BC, Carthage lost all hope of independence. The Romans, fueled by vengeance, enacted a brutal genocide during their occupation. The North African nation of Carthage, which once ruled the western Mediterranean with its exploration of trade and highly sophisticated agricultural-based economy, was brought to its knees.

After the Third Punic War, Carthaginian citizens were oppressed and forbidden from working in agriculture. They were forcibly turned into enslaved people or servitudes under Roman noblemen. The Carthaginians never recovered from this suppression. After the fall of Rome, the nobleman abandoned the city, and Arab invaders eventually overtook it in the seventh century AD. This marked the final decline of a once-great civilization that had stood as a formidable rival to Rome.

The Book of Daniel provides vivid descriptions of a series of beasts, each representing powerful empires. The aggressive behavior of the fourth beast, which conquered all the territory of the third beast, is particularly notable. This fourth beast, often identified as the Roman Empire, is predicted to rule with its beastlike character.

Several nations, including Belgium, the Netherlands, France, Great Britain, Germany, Italy, Portugal, Russia, and Spain, have sought to dominate the seas since the fall of the Roman Empire. Great Britain emerged as the most dominant, until the rise of the United States of America.

Daniel's prophecy foretells that the fourth beast, the Roman Empire, would rule the world in ten segments or divisions until the coming of the Messiah to establish His earthly kingdom. In Daniel's vision, he saw a male goat emerge from the west with ten horns. The horns grew to maturity, and then a little one appeared. This little horn expanded in all four directions, reaching as far as the Holy Land. It exalted itself high up, spoke great things, and cast some of the stars to the ground, trampling them.

This little horn was given an army to oppose the daily sacrifices and cast truth down to the ground. In Daniel's dreams, the little horn from the west grew into a monstrous beast, taking over territories and conducting various sinister activities while continuing to prosper. This vision is often interpreted as a prophecy of a powerful, end-times world empire that will rise before the return of the Messiah.

The fall of the Roman Empire, a kingdom heavily built on slavery, led to a power vacuum, and the European provinces began fighting among themselves for world dominance. This new age, starting around the 15th century, saw the confederation of former Roman cities engage in extensive trade both within and beyond the former empire.

Advancements in navigational techniques allowed fleets to sail across the Mediterranean to North Africa and southward along the coast of West Africa. These expeditions brought back substantial quantities of wheat and olive oil, crucial staples for the European economy.

The Role of Religion in Imperial Expansion

In Spain, the Catholic Church was granted extensive rights to govern certain affairs, and its influence expanded across Western Europe. The Pope had the right to appoint all clerical officers, including bishops, and authorized missionaries to spread the principles of European Christianity.

Ironically, the Catholic Church also became a structure for extending royal power, as it sought to control both governing and religious organizations. The influential Spanish church sent missionaries to spread Christianity from Rome into the African continent. This mission served a dual purpose: it propagated the new Christian religion and also sought to discover sources of wealth for the Spaniards. The intertwining of faith, power, and economic interests played a significant role in shaping both Europe and the regions it interacted with during this period.

Portugal followed suit after Spain in exploring the continents of Africa and Asia, and later the Americas. Their primary objectives were to find food, gold, and enslaved people for trade in the European markets. The Spaniards and the Portuguese replaced enslaved Europeans, who had been captured during the war, with enslaved Africans. They agreed to respect each other's maritime interests as they both sought new trade routes across the Atlantic to the lucrative Spice Islands of Asia. However, Africa soon became the main source of wealth, enabling both nations to grow into powerful colonial powers during the Middle Ages.

In 1494, the Treaty of Tordesillas was signed. This treaty allowed territories newly discovered to the east of an imaginary line in the Atlantic Ocean, extending northward around Africa, to be controlled by Portugal. Simultaneously, the southernmost part of the Atlantic and the eastern region of South America fell under Spanish control. Consequently, Spain claimed the Americas to the west of this imaginary line, and Portugal staked claim to the east and north of the Atlantic.

European fleets transported large numbers of Africans to the shores of the Americas and Europe, where they were forced to work on plantations growing sugarcane, tobacco, and cotton or in mines or serve as domestic servants for white noble families. This marked the beginning of the transatlantic slave trade, a dark and brutal chapter in human history.

The Portuguese established forts along the west coast of Ghana, around the Cape of Good Hope in South Africa, and on Mombasa Island in Kenya. As the Europeans claimed Africa's port cities and built settlements, they began to use religious names for these military and trading posts, such as Fort Jesus, in a blasphemous association of their colonial endeavors with Christ's name.

The late 15th-century discovery of the Americas marked a significant shift in Africa's standing. Once recognized as the wealthiest continent, Africa found itself grappling with widespread poverty. This change was precipitated by a severe population reduction and the plundering of its natural resources, both consequences of the transatlantic slave trade and colonial exploitation. Europeans, viewing these newfound territories as the "New World," believed that divine providence guided their exploratory endeavors and conquests.

Many of today's sermons echo the idea of spreading Christianity throughout the world but often omit the historical context of worldly desires and personal gains that drove much of the colonial era. Bernal Diaz del Castillo, a Spanish conquistador, articulated this stark truth in his eyewitness account, *"The True History of the Conquest of New Spain."* He wrote in detail about the motives of the European conquerors, stating, "to serve God and His Majesty, to give light to those who were in darkness and to grow rich, as all men desire to do."

The Portuguese and Spaniards went on to control the trade routes through the Indian and Atlantic Oceans, enjoying a period of great prosperity at the expense of the lands and peoples they colonized. This history serves as a sobering reminder of the complex and often troubling relationship between religion, power, and colonial expansion.

Ferdinand Magellan, originally from Portugal, and Queen Isabella of Spain, the daughter of King John II of Castile, were married in October 1469. Their union brought two former Roman states under a strong royal administrative system, which focused on the elimination or servitude of all Moorish, Muslim, and Jewish citizens. This was part of a broader European movement towards "racial purity" that was reflected in their colonial policies.

The Spanish monarchy embarked on expeditions through the Aztec Empire in Central and Northern Mexico, subduing much of the territory in less than three years. They launched a campaign against the rural people residing on the Yucatan peninsula, with the aim to bring the entire area from the Gulf of Mexico to the Pacific Ocean, as far as the Guatemalan highlands, under Spanish rule.

The Spaniards committed brutalities against the native populations, including a massacre in Cholula, where many of the natives who had gathered in the town square and refused to pay tribute were slaughtered. Resistance began to rise across the peninsula, but the Spaniards exploited native rivalries, allying with some native groups who were fighting against the Aztec Empire to establish their independent city-states.

This tactical move secured an alliance against the Aztec Empire, providing the Europeans with the opportunity to enter the king's palace. This period marked the beginning of the Spanish colonization of the Americas, which was characterized by exploitation, subjugation, and violent conquests.

Montezuma (Moctezuma), the Aztec ruler, extended a warm welcome to Hernán Cortés, the commander of the Spanish conquest, and his native allies. He offered gifts of gold and silver and invited them to stay in the king's palace. However, Montezuma was taken hostage, and the capital city of Tenochtitlan, along with the towns of Tula, Veracruz, and Tlaxcala, was plundered of its treasures.

The local population, including the Maya, organized a rebellion and drove the Spanish soldiers out of their cities. However, the indigenous population was devastated by infectious diseases such as swine flu, measles, and smallpox, to which they had no immunity. When the Europeans returned several months later with a much larger expedition force, they found a devastated population with many unburied corpses littering the cities.

The Spaniards eventually subdued Mexico and divided the land into administrative divisions, dubbing it "New Spain" and governing it through a viceroy in Lima. In this newly formed Spanish colony, schools were established, and plantations and ranches were set up to raise livestock and grow crops like tobacco, sugar, and cotton for sale in European markets. Sugar, which had been introduced to Europe through missionary journeys, became one of the most lucrative commodities, contributing significantly to the wealth amassed through colonial exploitation.

Portugal made significant inroads into Asia via the Pacific Ocean, establishing a presence in the Spice Islands. They also set up large sugar plantations along the coast of Brazil in South America and on islands in the West Indies. The vast agricultural estates required a large labor force, leading Portugal to transport a significant number of enslaved people out of Africa as the demand for sugar and other goods grew.

Many enslaved people were purchased from local trade merchants or taken as prisoners of war in exchange for goods like whiskey, fabric, and guns. However, the majority were kidnapped from coastal areas of Africa. These regions were ripe targets for pirates and Arab traders who sold captive Africans to the Europeans, a practice that dated back to the Roman era. By 1415, the Portuguese captured Ceuta, a Moorish port city on the Straits of Gibraltar along the North African coast.

CHAPTER FOUR

Dutch Dominance and Religious Reformation: Catalysts of Colonial Expansion

"History is a set of lies agreed upon."

———

Napoleon Bonaparte

In the early 1600s, the Dutch arrived in the Pacific and along the western and eastern coasts of Africa. They launched a series of aggressive campaigns against Portugal to establish their influence over the entire region, only to be challenged by England and France. The Dutch reaped the first fruits of their expansion when they seized a Portuguese fort in the Moluccas and the islands of Ceylon, Melaka, and Java, thereby gaining control of the spice trade.

The Dutch continued their conquest, building settlements along the southern African coast at the Cape of Good Hope and Cape Town. Over the next 50 years, the Dutch built economic success along the Indian Ocean and the African coast with the flood of gold, silver, and spices and the shipment of enslaved people to be sold to plantation owners in the New World. This period marked the height of Dutch colonial exploitation, which mirrored the brutal practices of other European powers.

A significant political event occurred in England in the mid to late 1500s that had profound implications for the country's religious landscape and, subsequently, its colonial pursuits. The Church of England, under King Edward VI, the son of King Henry VIII, initiated a series of reforms that moved the Church away from Roman Catholic doctrines and towards Protestantism.

Religious Shifts and Royal Successions

Edward was the product of King Henry's third marriage to Jane Seymour, who tragically died giving birth to him. Under Edward's reforms, the Church of England broke away from the Roman Catholic doctrine and the authority of the Pope. The changes allowed priests to marry, granted women the right to divorce their unfaithful husbands, and led to the destruction of shrines and images representing specific deities.

However, Edward's reign was short-lived due to his untimely death from an infectious lung disease on April 13, 1553, when he was only fifteen. His half-sister, Mary, the daughter of King Henry and Catherine of Aragon, the Princess of Wales, ascended to the throne. Mary, a staunch Catholic and an enemy of the Protestants sought to restore Roman Catholicism in England. During this period of religious flux, he played a significant role in shaping England's political and cultural identity, impacting its future colonial endeavors.

In 1527, King Henry VIII sought an annulment from his wife, Catherine of Aragon. However, Pope Clement VII refused to annul the marriage. Despite the Pope's refusal, King Henry's Protestant bishops granted him the annulment, allowing him to marry Anne Boleyn, who was ten years younger than Catherine and would become the mother of Elizabeth I.

This move led to the sacking of Rome and the capture of Pope Clement VII by the Emperor of Spain, who was enraged that the Pope had even considered hearing the case. The annulment caused King Henry to split from the Roman Catholic Church and led to his daughter Mary being declared illegitimate. Mary was subsequently barred from the royal palaces.

Catherine of Aragon, the daughter of Queen Isabella I of Castile and King Ferdinand II of Aragon, the joint rulers of Spain and Portugal, spent the remainder of her life at Kimbolton Castle. She died in January 1536, less than three years after her marriage was annulled.

Four months after Catherine's death, King Henry VIII accused Anne Boleyn of adultery, shortly after she had a miscarriage. Found guilty, Anne was sentenced to death by beheading in the Tower of London. Her daughter Elizabeth was only three years old when her mother was executed.

Henry's third wife, Jane Seymour, gave him a son, King Edward VI, the first English monarch raised Protestant. Knowing he was dying, Edward tried to remove his sister Mary from the line of succession due to their religious differences. In his will, he left the crown to Lady Jane Grey, a highly educated woman who spoke English, French, and Latin fluently. Persuaded by John Dudley, Edward changed the order of succession in favor of Jane. However, her reign lasted only nine days.

Lady Jane Grey, the great-granddaughter of Henry VII, was married to Lord Guilford Dudley, the Duke of Northumberland. However, her reign as Queen was short-lived. Jane, Lord Guilford Dudley, and her father were imprisoned in the Tower of London and faced trial for high treason in November 1553. Both Jane and her husband were found guilty, the sentence being either to be burned alive or beheaded, at the Queen's discretion.

The sentence was briefly suspended but was eventually carried out when Jane's father, Henry Grey, the Duke of Suffolk, was found to be supporting Sir Thomas Wyatt's rebellion. On February 12, both Jane and her husband were beheaded, followed by her father two days later in the Tower of London.

Mary I, a devoted Roman Catholic, was crowned Queen of England and Ireland on July 19, 1553. She would later marry Philip II of Spain and restore the jurisdiction of the Bishop of Rome over the churches of England. Through this union, she also became Queen consort of Habsburg Spain. However, Philip eventually deserted his marriage to Mary to return to Spain and claim the Spanish throne. During this period of English history, she witnessed a tumultuous mix of political intrigue, religious conflict, and personal tragedy.

Queen Mary Tudor, also known as Mary I of England, led a brutal campaign against Protestants during her reign, which earned her the infamous nickname "Bloody Mary." Her strong Catholic beliefs made her popular among Catholics, and she took measures to restore Catholicism in England, repealing the religious laws of her brother, Edward VI.

She released Bishop Bonner and Bishop Gardiner, who had been imprisoned in the Tower of London during her father's reign, and restored their bishoprics. Over the next three years, she apprehended nearly three hundred men, women, and children, accusing them of heresy. She rounded up Protestant bishops and burned them at the stake, often placing gunpowder on them to ensure a swift death.

Queen Mary Tudor died on November 17, 1558. Her half-sister, Elizabeth Tudor, an Anglican Protestant, ascended to the throne of England. Elizabeth's reign marked a shift back towards Protestantism, creating further religious and political tensions in the country.

The Dawn of the Transatlantic Slave Trade and European Power Struggles

Sir John Hawkins was the first to establish the Triangular Trade route, which became the primary method for Europeans to transport enslaved people from Africa to the Americas. This route also facilitated the transport of goods such as sugar, tobacco, and cotton from the Americas to Europe, domestic servants to South Asia, and textiles, rum, and beads back to Africa to purchase more captured enslaved people.

Hawkins was backed by wealthy merchants and set sail with three ships across the Atlantic, bound for the Caribbean via West Africa. He returned to England with ships laden with gold, silver, ivory, animal hides, sugar, and enslaved people, all for sale on the European market.

Upon Hawkins's return, Queen Elizabeth, I initially rebuked him, deeming his venture "detestable" and predicting it would "call down vengeance from heaven upon the undertakers." However, when she became aware of the substantial profits to be made, she entered into a partnership with Hawkins.

Hawkins, an English shipbuilder, pirate, and slave trader, was granted permission by Queen Elizabeth to lease the large 700-ton ship Jesus of Lubeck, also known as "The Good Ship Jesus." King Henry VIII had purchased this ship from the Hanseatic League, a commercial alliance between the cities of Hamburg and Lubeck in Germany. Under Queen Elizabeth, the ship was leased to Sir John Hawkins.

Hawkins used his naval expertise to design ships capable of blocking and intercepting Spanish and Portuguese treasure ships returning from Africa and the Americas. This aggressive strategy led to the Spanish banning all British ships from trading in their West Indies colonies. The activities of individuals like Hawkins marked the beginning of England's deep involvement in the transatlantic slave trade, a dark and controversial chapter in the country's history.

British navigators were as skilled as their Dutch counterparts. During this period, European powers were often engaged in disputes among blood relatives over royal powers and their share of the New World. England, the Netherlands, France, Ireland, Spain, and Portugal all arranged marriages within their royal families in a bid to use royal heritage to exercise authority for economic, social, and religious reasons.

On February 1, 1586, Queen Elizabeth I of England signed a death warrant against her cousin, Queen Mary Stuart of Scotland. Mary had sought refuge in England following an uprising in Scotland when she was coerced into marrying Lord Earl Bothwell, the suspected conspirator in the murder of her husband, Henry Stuart, King of Scotland. Accused of treason, Mary spent twenty years in prison before she was executed at Fotheringhay Castle, charged with plotting to kill Queen Elizabeth and claim the English throne.

During this period, a series of dynastic marriages made the House of Habsburg and the House of Bourbon two of the most powerful ruling families in Europe. The Habsburg Dynasty ruled Germany and the Roman Catholic states, while the prominent Bourbon princes led France. These dynasties were often at the center of wars over dynastic expansion and religious reform throughout central Europe, involving most of the Anglo-Saxon nations. This intricate web of family ties, political alliances, and religious conflicts shaped the course of European history during this era.

Shifting Alliances and the Spread of Colonial Ambitions

During the fifteenth and sixteenth centuries, the era of expansion and religious conflicts brought about power struggles across Europe, significantly altering the balance of power. The Dutch desire for independence from Spain played a pivotal role in sparking the Thirty Years War, which resulted in the split of the Burgundian Netherlands into the Spanish Netherlands and the Dutch Republic, also known as the United Provinces. Meanwhile, the Catholic Church extended its influence in Austria and Hungary and began to consolidate its power in the Baltic States.

In Rome, the heart of Catholic Europe, the emperors sought to form alliances with the United Provinces, England, and the Catholic factions of Spain. However, rivalry between the Habsburg and Bourbon emperors caused friction between the German Protestants and Catholics of the Holy Roman Empire, leading to a weakened Germany.

By 1635, Catholic France had signed an alliance to assist Protestant Sweden, marking the beginning of the final stage of the war against Habsburg power. This move was more about France's concern with the growing power of the Habsburgs than it was about religion. The Peace of Westphalia signed in 1648, undermined the Holy Roman Empire's aspiration to spread the Catholic faith throughout the independent states by force.

The treaty allowed German states to practice their religion and conduct their foreign policies, officially ending the Thirty Years' War. However, the French and Spaniards continued to fight until the Bourbon inheritance of Spain in 1659. With the signing of the Treaty of the Pyrenees, which awarded France part of the Spanish Netherlands, territory in western Germany, and a region in northern Spain, France was established as the dominant power on the European continent. The complex interplay of religion, political alliances, and territorial ambitions during this period shaped the geopolitical landscape of Europe for centuries to come.

The death of Queen Elizabeth I in 1603 ended the Tudor dynasty and brought the Stuart line to power, as her cousin James VI of Scotland inherited the English throne. In England, he was known as James I, and his ascension marked the unification of the two nations. He introduced the union as "Great Britain" in his first Parliamentary address.

King James attempted to use his royal power to assert the divine right of kings, a belief accepted by many European nations. However, this notion met with staunch opposition from the English Parliament and the House of Commons. England was in a precarious state at this time, with the recent death of Queen Elizabeth leaving the country in debt and the church playing a significant role in the governance of both Scotland and Ireland.

The tension between the monarchy and the Parliament continued during the reign of King Charles I, who succeeded James I in 1625. Charles' imposition of the Anglican Protestant religious system on the Scottish Presbyterian Church in an attempt to bring it in line with the Church of England sparked a civil war in Great Britain.

Charles' relationship with the Parliament further deteriorated when the Petition of Right was passed, prohibiting the king from enforcing any new tax laws without Parliament's approval. Facing a shortage of money, Charles found ways to collect revenue without Parliament's consent, using royal officials to collect taxes from coastal cities and wealthy landowners, enforcing forestry tax laws, and leveraging forced loans to finance governmental services. This period marked a significant constitutional crisis in England, laying the groundwork for the English Civil War and the eventual execution of Charles I.

Despite the growing tensions, King Charles I relied heavily on what was known as the Personal Rule, or the Eleven Years' Tyranny, from 1629 to 1640. During this period, he ruled without summoning Parliament, leading to a significant lack of Parliamentary tax revenue and a consequential financial strain. This became a significant problem when a Scottish army invaded England, and Charles found himself unable to pay English troops to fight against the invasion.

Starting in 1638, King Charles attempted to impose reforms on the Scottish political and religious systems. He demanded loyalty to the crown and declared Anglican Catholicism as the only approved form of religion, sparking a series of conflicts between England and the Church of Scotland known as the Bishops' Wars.

In the first Bishops' War, the King launched an ambitious military campaign against the Covenanters, a Scottish Presbyterian movement that opposed his religious changes. However, the campaign ended inconclusively with the Pacification of Berwick treaty, which was an agreement between the Kingdom of England and the Kingdom of Scotland. In response, the Covenanters raised an army and overruled the Scottish Parliament, setting off the Wars of the Three Kingdoms. This series of conflicts, which included the English Civil War, the Scottish Civil War, and the Irish Confederate Wars, was largely centered around opposition to Anglicanism and its upholding of Roman Catholic heritage. These wars marked a tumultuous period in British history, demonstrating the deep religious and political divides that existed within and between the kingdoms.

The Covenanters were a Scottish Presbyterian group that bound themselves to uphold the Presbyterian doctrine as the sole religion of Scotland. In 1640, King Charles I launched a second campaign against the Scots with his Royalist forces. Still, the Covenanters countered with an aggressive offensive under General

Leslie in what came to be known as "The Second Bishops' War." This conflict led to the summoning of the Long Parliament to ratify the Treaty of London in August 1641, which subsequently sparked the Irish Rebellion two months later as Irish forces attempted to seize control of the English government in Ireland.

A power struggle ensued between the Long Parliamentarians and the supporters of King Charles, known as the Royalists, splitting the governing body of England and leading to the First Civil War. On August 22, 1642, King Charles raised the Royal Banner at Nottingham to rally loyal troops. However, when he arrived at the seaport of Hull to seize ammunition for the war, the new governor, Sir John Hotham, refused to grant the Royalists access to the stored arsenal. Hotham insisted that the town gates would remain closed and their arsenals would not be surrendered without parliamentary authority.

In 1643, the Scottish government and the Covenanters agreed to provide troops to fight against the Royalists, creating a tactical advantage for the English Parliament with the signing of the Solemn League. The subsequent Scottish invasion in 1644, followed by the Covenant and Ireland, marked a turning point in England's First Civil War. These entities became allies with the English Parliament. King Charles could no longer raise enough revenue to support a substantial Royalist force, leaving him to counter with a small number of mercenary soldiers.

In 1645, in the midst of the civil unrest, the Parliament created the New Model Army, led by Sir Thomas Fairfax, with Oliver Cromwell as Lieutenant General. This army represented a significant shift from the traditional English military structure. The New Model Army was comprised of soldiers who were liable for service anywhere in the country, including Scotland and Ireland, rather than being tied to a single region. Selection was based on an individual's ability to fight rather than their family heritage or societal wealth. Many officers from existing units became ordinary soldiers or were discharged.

The soldiers in the New Model Army were trained to surprise the enemy with swift tactics and were open to new ideas to improve fighting methods. Many of the soldiers, veterans, and draftees alike held deep religious convictions and brought with them a shared belief in establishing a Commonwealth, which included direct military rule. Some were fighting for democracy and a desire for constitutional guarantees against Charles's royalist government.

Oliver Cromwell, who had started his military career as a cavalry troop leader at the indecisive Battle of Edgehill in October 1642, had risen to the rank of Lieutenant General by the time of the Battle of Marston Moor in July 1644. At the same time, many Puritans, who had begun the Great Migration to the New World, returned to England to fight against Charles's monarchy. By 1649, King Charles I was put on trial for treason and executed based on an ancient Roman law, given that the British constitution did not provide for the trial of a king.

While Britain was embroiled in this bloody internal struggle, Spain, the Netherlands, and Portugal were exploring the New World in pursuit of wealth. Catholic missionaries spread across the newly established Spanish colonies in the New World, converting and baptizing thousands of Indigenous people in an effort to "Christianize" the population of the Americas. The Dutch East India Company set up settlements at the Cape of Good Hope in southern Africa, while the Portuguese built forts on both the western and eastern coasts of Africa to capitalize on the slave trade and their quest for gold. Armed with steel crossbows, muzzle-loaded firearms, cannons, and a variety of archery and spear weapons, the Europeans subdued the Indigenous populations, whom they derogatorily referred to as "savages."

Over time, the brutal and uncompromising strategies employed by European slave traders to maintain a constant supply of enslaved people for their newly formed plantations had devastating effects on the African continent. African chiefs raised concerns about the depopulation of their territories, but their complaints fell on deaf ears. The population in the coastal regions of Africa declined dramatically, and warfare increased. The Indigenous populations in the Americas faced a similar fate.

In Hispaniola alone, the Taino population plummeted from a million to less than fifty thousand within the first ten years following Columbus's landing. The Spaniards exploited the island's inhabitants, forcing them to work in mines to extract gold and silver or pay tribute to Spanish administrators.

While the Europeans claimed to be bringing the "heathens" to God and introducing them to the civilized world under the sovereignty of the Catholic Church, both Africa and the Americas had thriving civilizations long before the arrival of the European settlers. This indoctrination was more of a psychological bondage imposed on the inhabitants of these continents.

The true intent behind the Europeans' actions was perhaps best summarized by a Dutch slave trader, who remarked, "From us, they have learned strife, quarreling, drunkenness, trickery, theft, unbridled desire for what is not one's own, misdeeds unknown to them before, and the accursed lust for gold." This brutal chapter of history laid bare the devastating impacts of the European colonial expansion, which was driven by greed and a disregard for the lives and cultures of the Indigenous populations.

Queen Isabella of Spain declared that the Indigenous populations encountered in the New World would be referred to as "Indians" and considered her subjects. This gave Spaniards the right to use the inhabitants as laborers. Commodities from the New World and Africa, such as sugar, cotton, dyes, spices, potatoes, coffee, corn, tobacco, and livestock hides, became essential to the European economy.

By the end of the 16th century, the Spaniards had established a colony on the Island of Cebu, the only Spanish colony in Asia. This colony was used for trade across the Pacific Ocean and was named the Philippines in honor of King Philip II of Spain.

In the early 17th century, as the Great Migration to the New World was underway, an English fleet set sail for North America. Back in Europe, religious strife, class warfare, and severe depression due to lost wages in the textile industry created a strong desire for a new beginning. The prospect of gold, silver, farmland, and untold wealth resonated deeply with Europeans, leading many to leave the Old World in search of hope in the New World. Initially, the lack of religious conflict in the New World was seen as a positive aspect of this new territory.

However, it wasn't long before Europeans began imposing their religious beliefs on the Indigenous populations and using these differences as a justification for land seizures, genocide, and exploitation. This marked the beginning of an era of colonialism that would have profound and lasting impacts on the Indigenous populations of the Americas, forever changing the course of their history.

By 1689, the War of the League of Augsburg, often referred to as the War of the Grand Alliance after England and Scotland joined the League, had begun against King Louis XIV of France, who sought to expand his empire's borders. The main objective of the League was to defend the territory of the Holy Roman Empire, including the German-controlled Rhineland Palatinate and the Alsace region, from French expansionism. This conflict, known as the Nine Years' War against France in Europe, was referred to as King William's War in the American colonies.

Colonial Rivalries and the Reshaping of North American Territories

Great Britain was financially strained due to a shortage of gold and silver and a loss of agricultural productivity, which led to high inflation. These factors, along with France's territorial ambitions, made France one of the most powerful nations in Europe. Conflicts between the Great Powers in Europe led to warfare on three continents: the Americas, Africa, and Australia.

In the Americas, the French were viewed as less threatening than the British and were somewhat more respectful of Native American territories. This led the Native Americans to ally themselves with the French in the conflict known as the French and Indian War, a series of battles between France and England in North America that lasted for seven years. This conflict, part of the larger Seven Years' War, resulted in the French being expelled from Canada and the Native Americans losing the majority of their land in North America.

While England, the Netherlands, France, and Spain had been rivals in Europe for centuries, the wealth from natural resources and land in the New World sparked new rivalries in the colonies. England sought to extend its borders further west, threatening the French living along the Mississippi and Ohio River Valley. In response, the French and Native Americans decided to attack before England could finish building forts in western Pennsylvania and the Virginia colony. Spain joined the war on the French side.

The war ended in 1763, leaving Great Britain in control of all territory east of the Mississippi River. Additionally, Britain gained control of Florida from Spain, further expanding its influence in the Americas. This marked a significant shift in the balance of power in the New World, with Britain emerging as the dominant colonial power.

Much like the legendary city of Babylon in its heyday, European settlers crossed the Atlantic with a sense of divine purpose and established their own governments in the New World, ruling with impunity despite the stark differences between their societies and those of the Indigenous peoples. Many of these settlers, particularly the Puritans, envisioned a covenant with God, tracing back to the original sin of Adam and Eve and the subsequent promise of redemption through the teachings of Jesus Christ in the New Testament.

However, this dream of religious freedom and supremacy, coupled with a quest for wealth, led to a horrific genocide of the Indigenous peoples and provided a twisted justification for the institution of slavery, based on a biased, man-made interpretation of God's will for humanity.

The pilgrims, originally bound for the Colony at Jamestown, Virginia, were forced by violent storms to anchor at the Bay of Cape Cod, near present-day Provincetown, Massachusetts. They were sanctioned by the London Company, which had royal approval from King James I to establish colonial settlements in the New World.

As settlers arrived daily from Europe, predominantly England, they inhabited what would become the thirteen colonies. Most of the Native populations had either been killed in conflicts or had migrated westward. The London Company established settlements near the James River on the Virginia Coast, acquiring large tracts of land in North America, including territory in Canada. The Plymouth Company was granted exclusive rights to settle in New England and Maine, in the hope that the colonists would discover gold and other raw materials to send back to England. This period marked the beginning of a significant shift in the demographics and power dynamics of the New World.

Upon landing, the settlers gathered together and pledged to honor both God and the King of Great Britain, declaring the site to be named Jamestown. Shortly thereafter, people began to arrive from England, Germany, France, Scotland, Spain, Sweden, and Ireland to settle in the colonies of the New World. Each European nation sought to control as much of colonial America as possible, viewing it as an opportunity for economic, political, and social expansion.

Spain had already claimed a large part of South America, and many religious groups, viewing the Indigenous peoples as subhuman, sought to spread their faith throughout the New World. Some groups, like the Puritans, attempted to impose their beliefs on others, even to the point of killing or incarcerating those who violated Puritan laws.

In 1604, King James I of England commissioned 47 scholars of the Church of England to translate the Bible. Completed in 1611, this translation, known as the Authorized Version or King James Bible, was sourced from Greek for the New Testament, Hebrew and Aramaic for the Old Testament, and Greek and Latin for the Apocrypha. The Authorized Version of the King James Bible became the most published Bible translation in the world and the standard version used by both Anglican and Protestant churches.

This translation also had a direct impact on the nation of Ethiopia when the Authorized Version decided to substitute "Kush" or "Cush" with "Ethiopia." The Bible confirms that the ancient land of Kush was near or associated with the Garden of Eden and the four riverheads of Paradise. One of these rivers was the famous Pishon, which along with the Euphrates, "skirts the whole land of Havilah, where there is gold. And the gold of that land is good. Bdellium and onyx stones are there. The name of the second river is Gihon; it is the one which goes around the whole land of Kush." This translation influenced perceptions of these regions and their historical and scriptural contexts.

When he was king, King Charles II of England granted a substantial amount of land to William Penn, a Quaker religious leader, to settle a debt. This land came to be known as Pennsylvania, a region rich in farmland, timber, fur, and raw materials. The Quakers, known for their pacifist beliefs, respected the Indigenous peoples and refused to engage in warfare against them. While Quakers faced persecution and imprisonment in other colonies, Pennsylvania became a relative haven where they could worship without fear of persecution.

However, following the French and Indian War, Great Britain underwent significant changes. The war had depleted the British treasury, prompting the English Parliament to attempt to impose unpopular taxes on the American colonies to cover the costs of maintaining soldiers and British administrators there.

In 1764, Britain introduced the Sugar Act, which heavily taxed non-British sugar and molasses sales and required colonists to provide housing and food for British soldiers. The following year, the British Parliament passed the Stamp Act of 1765. This act required colonists to purchase stamps for legal documents, playing cards, newspapers, marriage licenses, calendars, and various daily transactions to demonstrate that a tax had been paid on these items.

The colonists were deeply dissatisfied with the new tax laws. In response, many organized protest groups and boycotted British goods to resist the imperial tax and trade policies. This growing resistance marked the start of escalating tensions between the American colonies and Great Britain, laying the groundwork for the eventual outbreak of the American Revolution.

As the American colonies resisted British rule, a parallel struggle for independence was taking place on the island of Hispaniola, now home to Haiti and the Dominican Republic. Haitians were fighting for freedom from French colonial control, just as the Americans were battling the British. Both turned to France as a potential ally against their common enemies.

The French and Indian War had reshaped the global power dynamic. Although Great Britain emerged as the dominant industrial power, Hispaniola remained the most prosperous slave colony in the Western Hemisphere. Yet, it was also a fiercely contested territory, scarred by the rivalries of European colonial powers.

On February 4, 1794, France's ratification of emancipation abolished slavery and armed Haitians to fight against Spanish and British forces vying for control of Hispaniola. Led by Toussaint Louverture, grandson of an African chief, former slaves united to defeat the British and Spanish armies. This victory brought both Haiti and the neighboring Spanish colony of Santo Domingo together under a single rule on the island of Hispaniola.

Meanwhile, France regained control of its lost western Louisiana territory amidst these renewed conflicts, culminating in the signing of the Treaty of San Ildefonso in October 1800. These events marked significant milestones in the struggle for independence and freedom in the Americas and the Caribbean, setting the stage for future revolutions and the reshaping of colonial power dynamics.

The Haitian Revolution and Its Global Impact on Colonial Dynamics

Despite their victories over the British and Spanish, Napoleon Bonaparte, the French Emperor, betrayed France's earlier promise and passed a new constitution reinstating slavery in the former colony. In response, Toussaint Louverture boldly declared himself governor for life of all Hispaniola in 1801. Under his leadership, he fortified Haiti's defenses, built a strong military, and forged trade agreements with newly independent nations, including Great Britain and the United States. The Haitian Revolution thus secured Haiti's place as the second independent nation in the Americas, following the United States' lead in 1783.

However, the news of the slave revolt was met with apprehension by American political leaders, many of whom were slaveholders themselves. In an attempt to suppress the revolt, they provided support to the white population of Saint Domingue. Many white refugees from Haiti settled in Baltimore, Philadelphia, and New York with the help of the French government. Meanwhile, both the United States and British governments pursued policies to isolate Haiti and cut off trade relations with the new state.

In 1802, Toussaint was captured under deceitful circumstances in Cap-Francais when he boarded a French ship to sign a peace agreement. He was deported to the Fort de Joux prison in the Jura Mountains. Despite his capture, the Haitian Revolution continued under his lieutenant, Jean-Jacques Dessalines.

The conflict ended in November 1803 with the defeat of the French at the Battle of Vertieres, driving the Europeans off the island and establishing Haiti as the first independent nation of African heritage in Latin America. This left an encouraging legacy throughout the Western world. While France recognized Haitian independence in 1825, the United States did not officially acknowledge Haiti as a sovereign nation until 1862, under the administration of President Abraham Lincoln.

Despite the revolutionary changes in Haiti, the colonial powers were not finished with their attempts to exert control over the island. The fertile plantations of Haiti, cultivated by former enslaved laborers, produced great quantities of sugar, tobacco, cotton, and coffee — commodities in high demand in Europe and the United States. During this era, Haiti was possibly the richest colony in the world, with sugar plantations producing tons of sugar annually.

Many religious groups, including the Puritans and Quakers, espoused the virtues of hard work. However, in Europe, they enjoyed the privilege of having enslaved people perform manual labor. Many Europeans sought to pan for gold, silver, furs, and precious minerals, leaving the arduous work to the enslaved people.

The promise of freedom to enslaved people during the American Revolutionary War against Great Britain, coupled with the success story of Haiti, played a significant role in propelling the United States toward its own Civil War. The French colony of Saint Domingue (the western third of the island of Hispaniola), along with Spanish Santo Domingo, housed over a million African slaves working on plantations before the Haitian Revolution. These tropical Caribbean islands produced nearly 200,000 tons of sugar annually, along with profitable crops of tobacco, rice, and other commodities.

Each plantation often featured a mansion complete with a music room, a ballroom, a library, a grand dining room, a kitchen, a stable, and numerous guest rooms for friends and acquaintances. The contrast between the wealth of the plantation owners and the harsh conditions endured by slavery further underscored the stark disparities and injustices of the colonial era.

The Haitian Revolution, a thirteen-year struggle, ended slavery but left deep divisions in its wake. The mixed-race mulatto population, descended from French colonists and African slave women, felt their interests overlooked. As the educated sons and daughters of French fathers, mulattos had risen in status under colonial rule, identifying more with their European heritage than their African roots. This created a rift within the newly liberated society. Further straining relations, the French government imposed a monopoly on Saint-Domingue's trade, much like Britain's earlier policies towards the American colonies – a key spark for both revolutions.

In the Caribbean, the French and Spanish established a racial hierarchy rooted in colorism. At the bottom were Africans and Creole slaves. Mixed-race mulattos, often freed at birth or able to earn their freedom, held a higher status, even gaining full citizenship. Yet, despite their African roots, many mulattos came to resent enslaved Africans and sometimes even owned slaves themselves. To white business owners and merchants, the French-speaking mulattos and Creoles represented an economic threat, potentially undermining the livelihoods of the white working class.

After the Haitian Revolutionary War and the removal of Europeans, with the exception of the Polish, from Haitian soil, the mulattos became the elite in Haiti's social and economic development. In 1806, Dessalines was murdered, sparking a civil war between the mixed-race mulattos, led by Alexander Petion, and Henry Christophe. This conflict divided Haiti into two nations.

Despite the United States' similar history to Haiti, it joined France, Great Britain, and Spain in refusing to recognize Haitian independence. It demanded that Haiti compensate white plantation owners for their lost colony. This high ransom burdened the Haitian government well into the 20th century, with warships positioned offshore, awaiting a moment of weakness to intervene. This reveals how the legacy of colonialism and racial hierarchies continued to shape Haiti's path long after its revolution.

The Western perception of Black people has been warped by a complex web of damaging myths, rooted in centuries of inherited biases, harmful stereotypes, and systemic racism. Many Europeans, influenced by dehumanizing beliefs, viewed non-white individuals as less than fully human. When Europeans first arrived in Africa in the 15th century, they encountered thriving civilizations: prosperous economies, fertile lands, and well-educated, elegantly dressed people. The stark contrast between African wealth and superiority and European prejudices fueled both admiration and resentment.

For centuries, powerful nations like England, France, Spain, Portugal, and Rome—even dating back to the Assyrians—were aware of Africa's advanced societies. Yet, they propagated a false narrative of racial superiority, nobility, and material wealth, fueled by greed. Recognizing the vast resources of Africa and the Americas, these European powers sought to exploit them, giving rise to New World interests.

Such interests in the New World fueled racial prejudice based on envy and greed, significantly hindering economic development on the African continent. Instead of seeking reconciliation or recompense for these injustices, the residue of hatred has perpetuated through generations, often justified by the assertion that divine power has granted the white race global dominance.

This warped mindset has twisted humanity's potential for righteousness into a ruthless struggle for power, breeding oppressive nations. Charles Darwin's theory of natural selection, proposed amidst global upheaval, suggested that adaptations favoring survival benefit individuals best-equipped to compete. However, the concept of "survival of the fittest" has been repeatedly misused to justify systemic oppression and inequality, fueling a vicious cycle of prejudice and injustice.

CHAPTER FIVE

Social Darwinism and the Dynamics of Spiritual Warfare in History

"Injustice anywhere is a threat to justice everywhere."

———

Martin Luther King Jr.

The concept of Social Darwinism, a delusion of Darwin's theory of evolution, has often been used to justify a hierarchical structure of society, placing certain groups as superior and others as inferior. This has often resulted in indigenous peoples across various continents being labeled as lesser or weaker races, reinforcing systemic inequalities.

This hierarchy system, according to some interpretations, gives power to Lucifer and his rebellious angels over the worldly system, reflecting a belief in spiritual warfare and the struggle between good and evil.

During the reign of Emperor Domitian, the Apostle John was exiled to the island of Patmos, off the coast of the Aegean Sea in Asia Minor. It is here that, according to Christian belief, John received a series of symbolic visions from the Lord. These visions make up the Book of Revelation in the New Testament of the Bible.

Eschatological Visions and the Imperial Scramble for Africa

The Book of Revelation warns humanity about the severe consequences of choosing to follow Satan's temporary schemes and reveals God's wisdom and plans for the future. It affirms the belief that God rules over both the spiritual and physical world and will deal with humanity according to their actions, particularly those that are sinful. This serves as a reminder of the spiritual consequences that accompany the choices made in the physical world.

In Christian eschatology, the return of Jesus Christ, known as Yeshua Ha'Mashiach in Hebrew, is prophesied to occur during the great battle of Armageddon. This event will mark the end of the worldly system, a system believed to have been established under the authority of Satan and his unseen spiritual rulers who rebelled against Almighty God.

In the Book of Revelation, the Apostle John describes his first vision of Jesus Christ as "One like the Son of Man," with hair like wool and eyes like flaming fire. His feet resembled fine brass as if they had been burned in a furnace, and a sharp double-edged sword emerged from His mouth.

The vision is interpreted as a prophecy of Christ's return to judge humanity and establish His divine government on earth. In Revelation 1:7-15, it is written, "Behold, He is coming with clouds, and every eye will see Him, even they who pierced Him. And all the tribes of the earth will mourn because of Him." This passage emphasizes the universal recognition of Christ's return and the profound impact it will have on all of humanity, marking a pivotal moment in Christian eschatology.

In the late 19th century, European powers renewed their scramble for Africa, seeking to carve up the continent. The British set their sights on North Africa, particularly Egypt, in a bid to counter French expansion. Before long, the British government declared a protectorate over Egypt and turned its attention to Sudan, then the largest country in Africa. This ancient land, known as the biblical Punt and the heart of the Old Kingdom of Kush, lay east of the Red Sea.

In Sudan's capital, Khartoum, the White and Blue Nile rivers converge, flowing northward through Sudan's arid deserts. The British employed a divide-and-conquer approach, placing Sudan under joint Egyptian-British administration. This arrangement fostered a class system favoring Arab Muslims in the north, sowing seeds of cultural tension and violence with their Christian counterparts in the south. The slave trade, exacerbated by Sudan's division, further fractured the nation's social and familial bonds, undermining any potential for unity against European colonizers.

In 1881, Muhammad Ahmad, a Sudanese Islamic religious leader who proclaimed himself the Mahdi (Guided One), led a campaign against the growing military and economic presence of the Europeans. With support from some Egyptian nationalists, he sought to prepare the way for the second coming of the Prophet Isa, the long-awaited redeemer. Muhammad Ahmad's goal was not only to expel the oppressive Western-leaning Anglo-Egyptian authorities in the north but also to replace the whole of Sudan with a strict Islamic government. This marked another significant chapter in the complex history of colonial resistance in Africa.

In February 1884, British General Charles George Gordon led a combined force of Egyptians and loyal Sudanese troops to evacuate non-Sudanese from the capital city and defend it against an invasion by the Mahdists, followers of Muhammad Ahmad. The

Mahdists besieged Khartoum, cutting off its food and supplies. After a ten-month siege, an estimated 50,000 Mahdists broke through the city walls, killing Gordon and thousands of the Anglo-Egyptian garrison.

In January 1885, Muhammad Ahmad seized control of Sudan, establishing his capital in the Nile-side village of Omdurman and briefly extending Sudanese borders into Ethiopia. However, his rule was short-lived; Muhammad Ahmad died unexpectedly on June 22, 1885, just six months after the fall of Khartoum. Abdullah al-Taaisha, the Mahdi's chief deputy and an Ansar general, succeeded him as leader of the Mahdist state as the new Khalifa. Abdullah al-Taaisha bolstered the military by establishing ammunition workshops. Yet, his tenure was equally brief. In 1898, a British-led force commanded by Lord Kitchener hunted down his forces, the Mahdists, at the Battle of Omdurman, delivering a final defeat at the Battle of Umm Diwaykarat.

The Europeans determined to claim Sudan, returned with overwhelming firepower: machine guns, modern rifles, and heavy artillery. The Mahdist forces stood little chance. By 1899, Sudan had been proclaimed a condominium under British-Egyptian authority, ending any semblance of independence.

In the aftermath of their victory, the British prioritized developing the economy and infrastructure of northern Sudan, while European powers largely isolated the south from trade, education, and basic healthcare. Over the next three decades, European colonial powers carved up the African continent, laying the groundwork for future global conflicts. The southern region was left economically and politically underdeveloped, with limited access to education and dominated by an Islamic ruling class.

The imposition of Anglo-Egyptian rule disrupted Sudan's tribal cohesion, prompting many to flee to neighboring countries like Ethiopia, Egypt, Kenya, and Uganda to escape European domination. This mass displacement strained the refugees' ability to sustain themselves, leading to widespread famine, disease, and malnutrition.

Colorism, or discrimination based on skin tone, further exacerbated divisions. The cultural preference for lighter complexions prevented unity between darker-skinned Africans and the lighter-skinned Arabs in the north, a divide that would continue to stoke conflict into the present day.

Certain regions along the southern borders and the Western Upper Nile were consolidated with the French West Africa Empire until 1960 when they became part of the independent state of Mali. Many of today's civil conflicts across Africa can be traced back to the aggressive tactics used by European powers across the continent.

King Leopold's Congo and the Birth of Lumumba's Legacy

Meanwhile, King Leopold II of Belgium was racing against the British, French, and Portuguese for control of the wealth of the Congo in Central Africa. The coastal area of the Congo had been a region for slave trading since the early 15th century. However, the interior of the Congo, with its wealth and diverse tribal groups, was largely unknown to European explorers.

On December 17, 1865, Leopold II was crowned King of the Belgians in Brussels. Soon after his coronation, Leopold, often referred to as the Butcher of Congo, became fascinated with exploring Central Africa following reports of vast amounts of raw materials that could be exploited for wealth. Private European and American corporations hired explorers to discover the source of the Nile River and their exploits were widely reported in newspapers, fueling further interest in the continent's resources.

King Leopold II of Belgium took a keen interest in the re-nowned explorer Henry Stanley, offering him a substantial sum to establish a colony in the Congo. Leopold and Stanley hatched a secret plan to colonize Central Africa as the king's personal fief-dom, making Leopold the sole ruler of the Congo. They set about deceiving the major European powers while establishing a system of forced labor to build the king's empire.

Though Belgium was a small nation, it faced stiff competition from Britain, France, and Germany for control of the Congo. Undeterred, Leopold promised to allow all European nations to trade freely in the region. He assured the European powers that his intentions were purely humanitarian, claiming he sought to educate the Congolese. Leopold launched a savvy public relations campaign to persuade Europe that the Congo should fall under the King of Belgium's benevolent control.

The Berlin Conference granted Leopold permission to treat the Congo as a neutral zone, with the stated intent to spread Christian values, advance scientific knowledge, and eradicate the slave trade. Leopold created the International Association for the Exploration of Congo to promote his false humanitarian and missionary work, all while building a forced labor system in the Congo.

Leopold established Boma as the capital city on the north bank of the Congo River and divided the region into 14 administrative districts, naming the new colony the Congo Free State. In 1891, he declared that all natural resources in the Congo belonged to the Congo Free State. Leopold personally became incredibly wealthy from extracting resources such as gold, diamonds, copper, tin, cobalt, rubber, and ivory from the Congo, obtained through violent coercion. He colonized the Congo, establishing large plantations producing cotton, palm oil, coffee, rubber, and kwanga and exploiting the region's enormous freshwater river basins.

Across the Congo, Congolese people, including small children, were forced to meet quotas of rubber to be given to Leopold's state agents. African men who resisted were often killed or hung in public view by Leopold's soldiers. This brutal regime of exploitation and violence marked a dark chapter in the history of the Congo under King Leopold II's rule.

Leopold II constructed an extensive network of roads and railways. He took advantage of the Congo's waterways to extract and transport vast quantities of raw materials from the Congo Free State for sale on the European market. Entire Congolese farming villages were razed to make way for lucrative rubber plantations for the Belgian markets. This devastation brought food shortages to the people of Congo, who could no longer cultivate their food or generate income for themselves. Instead, they were forced to work on farms and in mines to produce revenue for the Europeans.

Those who refused to work or failed to meet the minimal quotas often faced horrific punishment, including amputation of a hand, enforced by the Force Publique army. This army was composed of rival tribal groups and Africans trained from a young age to carry out brutal missions for Leopold's ruthless regime. Well-armed agents of the Congo Free State enforced these cruel labor laws. The Force Publique would often hunt down and round up rebels who had escaped and fled into the wilderness.

When found hiding in the forest, Congolese people, including women and children, were brutally murdered, and their headless bodies were displayed on poles in the form of a cross as a warning to others who might consider disobeying orders. It's estimated that between 10 to 15 million people died during the 23 brutal years of Leopold's rule over the Congo, with many more lives lost due to starvation, lack of medical treatment, and vulnerability to new diseases introduced to African soil.

These psychological tactics by the Europeans were not new to the African region. This form of Western sorcery, characterized by dehumanization and oppression, can be traced back to the first European encounters with people of African origin. Some argue that the roots of these tactics can be traced even further back to ancient texts like the Vedas, which claim to contain celestial knowledge from fallen angels or gods from the lower heavens.

The Western phenomenon involved steering Africans away from their faith and giving absolute power to the new white Anglo-Saxon rulers. These new masters then instituted divisions based on ethnicity, culture, and skin tone with the intent of defeating and subjugating the so-called weaker groups. Congolese historian Dr. Isidore Ndaywel E Nziem estimates the death toll during Leopold's era to be around thirteen million, which accounted for about half of the population during the Congo Free State genocide.

In the early 1900s, rivalry over colonial expansion and economic interests in Africa intensified, leading to conflicts among European nations. Elder Dempster Company, one of the UK's largest shipping companies with a fleet of over 500 ships, held a contract with King Leopold to transport ammunition and other weapons into the Congo. The ships returned from the Congo Free State carrying tons of rubber, palm oil, gold, copper, ivory, and timber to be sold on the European market. It was this wealth and the resources of the Congo that enabled Leopold to finance massive building projects and pull Belgium out of a financial deficit.

By 1908, the Belgian government annexed the Congo Free State, renaming it the Belgian Congo and removing Leopold as its sole ruler. However, the growing demand for rubber in the early 20th century kept the Congo Free State among the top African nations producing the commodity. As the colonial powers of Europe were partitioning the African continent, Belgium and the colony of the Congo Free State were seen as a buffer, hoping to remain neutral from armed conflicts.

Finally, on June 30, 1960, Patrice Emery Lumumba, a Congolese leader of the MNC Party, became the first democratically elected Prime Minister of the Republic of the Congo, marking its independence from Belgium. At Lumumba's ceremony in the Parliament Building, King Baudouin of Belgium praised the work of Leopold II, a statement that was considered a tremendous insult to Lumumba and the people of the Congo. In response, Lumumba delivered a defiant speech confronting the atrocities of Belgian colonial rule, marking a significant moment in the Congo's journey towards independence and self-governance.

Prime Minister Lumumba's response to King Baudouin presented a stark contrast to the narrative propagated by the Belgian authorities. He addressed his fellow Congolese, saluting them as victorious fighters for independence and urging them to remember June 30, 1960, as a date forever engraved in their hearts. Lumumba emphasized the struggle for independence, a battle filled with tears, fire, and blood, and declared that no Congolese would ever forget the hardships of the eighty years of colonial rule.

Lumumba spoke of the suffering under forced labor, the inadequate pay that led to hunger, poor clothing, inadequate housing, and the inability to care for their children. He lamented the abuses, insults, and blows endured simply because they were 'Africans.' He reminded his people of the shootings that killed many and the merciless imprisonments of those who resisted the regime of injustice, oppression, and exploitation.

However, Lumumba also assured his people that this was in the past. The future of the beloved country was in the hands of its people. He touted the capabilities of the black man working in liberty and vowed to make the Congo the pride of Africa. He acknowledged the agreement with Belgium, which was prepared to offer aid and friendship, emphasizing that their cooperation would benefit both countries.

Lumumba also urged his people to respect the life and property of their fellow citizens and foreigners living in their country. He asserted that those who misbehaved would be expelled, while those who conducted themselves well should be left in peace. He called upon all Congolese to work towards creating a national economy and ensuring their economic independence.

Prime Minister Patrice Lumumba's powerful speech concluded with a stirring call to honor those who fought for the nation's liberation and a celebration of Congo's newfound independence and sovereignty. His final words - "Eternal glory to the fighters for national liberation! Long live independence and African unity! Long live the independent and sovereign Congo!" - encapsulated the resilient spirit of the Congolese people and their hope for a free and thriving nation. These words continue to resonate as a poignant reminder of Congo's journey towards self-determination and autonomy.

Patrice Lumumba's passionate stand against Western imperialism, embodied in his powerful speech, is believed to have led to his downfall. Allegedly, the governments of Belgium, Great Britain, and the United States conspired to remove Lumumba from power. The Central Intelligence Agency (CIA), with authorization from President Dwight D. Eisenhower, established a covert operation known as Project Wizard aimed at removing Lumumba from office. Lumumba's speech was severely criticized by Western governments, and the Belgian authorities actively participated in a coup organized by Colonel Joseph Mobutu, which resulted in Lumumba's arrest. Lumumba was later executed by a firing squad, an act carried out by Belgian and Katangan authorities. His death was mourned globally, with Malcolm X calling Lumumba "the greatest Black man who ever walked the African continent."

Today, the Democratic Republic of Congo is believed to be the world's wealthiest country regarding natural resources, with untapped mineral wealth potentially worth as much as 24 trillion US dollars. However, the country is still reeling from Africa's deadliest war since World War II, which has claimed nearly six million lives since 1998. Ongoing sporadic violence has plunged the Congo into a humanitarian crisis, with nearly half of its victims being children and around 50,000 Congolese perishing each month.

The Shadow of Empire: Colonial Legacies and the Seeds of Conflict

Picture this: It's the late 1800s, and the scramble for Africa is in full swing. Germany, hungry for its piece of the colonial pie, sets its sights on the region that is now Namibia. But this isn't a peaceful takeover. The Germans arrive on the heels of a devastating genocide that's left deep scars.

The Germans wasted no time making their mark. They build forts and trading posts, their eyes fixed on the glittering diamonds of the Zambezi region and the fertile banks of the Orange River. White settlers flood in, their hands grasping for the rich land. But this land isn't empty. The Herero people, Namibia's indigenous tribe, have called this home for generations.

The clash is inevitable. The settlers seize the land, forcing the Herero off their ancestral grounds. Starvation and suffering sweep through the native population. This is the dark history of Germany's colonization of Namibia, a tale of greed, violence, and the enduring struggle of a people fighting to hold on to their homeland.

During World War I, the area became a battleground between European powers vying for its natural resources, such as diamonds, gold, copper, and lead. Namibia and Congo's importance extended into World War II because both nations were rich in uranium, a crucial resource for the atomic bombs dropped on Hiroshima and Nagasaki, Japan.

The assassination of Archduke Francis Ferdinand, heir to the Austro-Hungarian throne, and his wife, Duchess Sophia, on June 28, 1914, in Sarajevo, Bosnia, by the Black Hand, a Serbian terrorist group, marked a significant turning point that led to the outbreak of World War I. The neutrality of Belgium came to an end when Germany, after issuing an ultimatum to Belgium in early August demanding passage through Belgian territory, decided to invade western France.

The great powers of Europe had been feuding over territories in Austria, Africa, and the Middle East, and clashes intensified as they sought to expand their political and economic interests globally. Difficult living conditions and ethnic cleansing of Armenians by the new Turkish government led the Armenians to side with Russia. Germany, Austria-Hungary, Italy, and the Turkish government formed a pact, becoming the Central Powers.

By the turn of the 19th century, nearly all of Africa and the Middle East were under the authority of the European powers, including Israel and Palestine. What the Bible once described as a land flowing with milk and honey became a horrific scene of slaughter, fueled by European imperialism and linked to social Darwinism. This theory, which stresses the right of superior individuals and nations to rule, led to a shift towards genocide and cruelty.

Great Britain, France, Belgium, and Russia were all bound by alliances, treaties, or private agreements. A territorial dispute between the Austro-Hungarian Empire and the Serbs, who sought to create an independent state, caused friction between Russia and Germany, who were also bound by treaties to protect their interests. The Germans believed that allowing Serbia to extend its borders after the Balkan Wars of 1912-13 towards the Adriatic Sea would increase Russia's influence due to the high population of Slavs within the Austro-Hungarian Empire. Russia was determined to support the Serbian government's bid to become an independent Slavic state in the Balkans and break away from the empire. The assassination of Archduke Francis Ferdinand and his wife, Duchess Sophia, became the final event that led to World War I.

As World War I progressed, the United States could no longer remain neutral due to Germany's submarine attacks on Great Britain. German U-boats threatened Great Britain's naval defenses, and the Central Powers used this opportunity to bomb London and other parts of England, showcasing Germany's technical superiority in night fighting. The United States Congress voted to declare war on Germany on April 6, 1917, providing the Allied Powers with a strategic and psychological advantage. The Great War caused over six thousand deaths each day, amounting to twenty million casualties over the course of the war. The devastation of World War I concluded on November 11, 1918, when Germany signed an armistice to end the fighting. The death toll from the war is estimated to range from eight to ten million.

The post-World War I era saw a surge in racial tensions across the United States, particularly in African American communities. The summer and early fall of 1919, infamously known as the Red Summer, were marked by race riots in over thirty cities. White mobs attacked African Americans, fueled by competition for jobs, as veterans returned home from the war. From Washington D.C. to rural Arkansas and Chicago's South Side, the end of the European conflict sparked clashes and violence that shook the nation.

In Elaine, Arkansas, a sharecropper's meeting demanding fair pay turned deadly. A white mob, intent on disrupting the gathering, attacked the church where it was being held. The ensuing racial violence claimed the lives of five white men and over a hundred African Americans. The mob rampaged through the black community, torching homes and churches and killing anyone they encountered.

Chicago suffered the deadliest rioting of the Red Summer. More than 1,000 homes were set ablaze, leaving countless people homeless. In a shocking incident, an African American teenager drowned in Lake Michigan after white youths pelted him with stones for crossing an unofficial racial boundary on a Chicago beach. Though the white attackers were culpable, the police arrested a black man for allegedly inciting the violence. Across the country, African Americans were hunted down by white mobs and lynched or burned alive in horrific displays of racial terror. The Red Summer of 1919 remains a grim chapter in America's history, a stark reminder of the deep-seated racial tensions that have long plagued the nation.

The notion that supposedly superior European civilization granted whites the right to dominate globally resonated with many white Americans, fostering deep-seated prejudice against darker-skinned people. This bias transcended U.S. borders, taking root in numerous European nations. As the favoritism for lighter complexions intensified, it became a defining factor in economic opportunities, cementing a skin-color-based social hierarchy.

In the United States, by 1930, the "one-drop rule" - a socio-legal principle of racial classification that deemed any person with even one African ancestor as 'Negro' - was no longer officially the law of the land. However, the implications of this rule still had a profound effect on society. Individuals of mixed-race unions or those with lighter complexions often found themselves absorbed into the upper class. Thus, skin tone became the strongest psychological barrier determining the success of African Americans.

This "pigmentocracy" or colorism created a social hierarchy within the African American community and further perpetuated racial inequality worldwide. White Americans took advantage of this divide by perpetuating hatred within racially mixed communities, using the one-drop rule as a tool of division and control.

The widespread delusion that European features equated to higher social status relegated darker-skinned African Americans to the bottom of the social hierarchy, intensifying the discrimination they faced. The return of black veterans from World War I stoked white fears that African Americans would no longer accept their assigned inferiority.

In the post-World War I era, colorism was wielded to divide the black community, and deception was used to maintain control, conditioning neighborhoods to turn against each other. Low-income black neighborhoods, often derogatorily labeled and lacking basic infrastructure like running water, sewage, and electricity, were hindered in neglected conditions. This period remains a grim chapter in America's struggle with racial relations and inequality.

In Daniel 7, the 'little horn' vision is often seen as a symbol of the Antichrist's rise. This figure, with human eyes and a mouth spewing arrogance, embodies deceit and boastfulness. The Antichrist, with his captivating voice and apparent miracles, is said to lead many astray, seducing them to follow Satan and his cronies.

"I watched then because of the sound of the pompous words which the horn was speaking; I watched till the beast was slain, and its body destroyed and given to the burning flame," the ultimate fate of this beast (often interpreted as the Antichrist or his worldly system) is destruction.

2 Thessalonians 2:9-10 sheds further light, stating, "The coming of the lawless one is according to the working of Satan, with all power, signs, and lying wonders, and with all unrighteous

deception among those who perish, because they did not receive the love of the truth, that they might be saved." This highlights the Antichrist's deceptive nature, as he operates under Satan's influence, wielding power and performing false miracles to deceive those who reject the truth.

According to these interpretations, the Antichrist's primary goal is to sow deception and turn people from God's love. This struggle is envisioned as a global conflict, with the Antichrist's influence infiltrating regions worldwide, from Africa and the Middle East to Europe and the United States. This belief underscores the concept of spiritual warfare, emphasizing the importance of discernment and truth adherence amidst deceptive forces.

In 2 Thessalonians 2:11, the Apostle Paul indeed warns about a time when God will send a "strong delusion" to those who choose not to believe the truth but instead find pleasure in unrighteousness. This passage is often interpreted as a prophecy about the end times when people will be led into deception by the Antichrist, an entity associated with Satan.

According to this scripture, those who reject the truth and take pleasure in unrighteousness will be susceptible to this delusion, leading them to believe what is false or, as the verse states, "the lie." In many interpretations, this lie refers to the deceitful promises and allure of the Antichrist.

This verse highlights the importance of steadfast faith and adherence to the truth to defend against such deception. It underscores the potential spiritual dangers of materialism and unrighteousness and the need for vigilance in maintaining one's faith and righteousness. It serves as a reminder that those who choose to ignore the truth and indulge in unrighteousness may be led astray.

In the aftermath of the Civil War, defeated Southern states enacted the Black Codes, laws designed to restrict the freedoms of newly emancipated African Americans and control their movements and labor. Essentially a system of vagrancy laws, the Black Codes allowed authorities to arrest formerly enslaved people and force them into low-wage, involuntary labor.

The Black Codes aimed to uphold white supremacy, regulating African American life across most Southern states and undermining the freedoms granted by the Emancipation Proclamation and, later, the slavery-abolishing Thirteenth Amendment.

Central to the Black Codes were vagrancy statutes. These laws empowered police to arrest individuals on mere suspicion of criminal activity or lack of permanent residence. Those unable to pay imposed fines often faced hard labor for local governments or private employers.

Enforcement was often brutal and biased. Local groups rounded up African Americans, forcing them into contract work. Some laws taxed unmarried black women, while certain railroads refused to sell black people tickets, effectively trapping them in towns and condemning them to peonage.

The Black Codes remain a grim reminder of the lengths some went to preserve racial hierarchies and deny African Americans their hard-won rights and freedoms in the Civil War's wake.

From the Civil War to World War II, Southern whites exploited vagrancy laws to maintain racial hierarchies and access a cheap African American labor force. State legislatures and local authorities passed broadly worded laws targeting minor offenses, aiming to control African American migration through intimidation and incarceration.

The prison system became a lucrative industry, with prisoners leased to work off fines. The revenue generated by these court practices economically destabilized black communities, as African American men faced disproportionate incarceration due to racial bias.

The societal impact was profound. Black families grew more vulnerable, with single-parent households proliferating. Government aid often became necessary for healthcare access and basic living standards. This contributed to a widening racial wealth gap rooted in inequality.

The United States currently has the world's highest incarceration rate, with African Americans disproportionately represented on every state's inmate rolls. Southern states lead the nation in incarceration, with Louisiana, Mississippi, and Alabama topping the list.

In 1995, Alabama reintroduced chain gangs, where prisoners refusing to work were chained to a hitching post. The U.S. Supreme Court deemed this practice "cruelly and wantonly inflicting pain" in 2002. U.S. District Judge Myron Thompson called the overcrowded conditions at Alabama's sole women's prison, Julia Tutwiler, a "ticking time bomb," highlighting the severe issues plaguing the U.S. prison system.

CHAPTER SIX

The Impact of Global Conflicts on Theological Prophecies

"The only thing necessary for the triumph of evil is for good men to do nothing."

———

Edmund Burke

The Book of Joel contains prophecies about end times, including the great battle of Armageddon. An influential figure, the Antichrist, will attempt to impose a mark of allegiance to a beastly system, restricting commerce to those who refuse to worship the Beast or accept the mark. Revelation also foretells this final clash of good and evil.

Joel 2 vividly describes this battle: "Blow the trumpet in Zion, sound an alarm in My holy mountain! For it is at hand: A Day of darkness and gloominess, a day of clouds and thick darkness. A people come, great and strong like those who have never been, nor will there ever be any such after them. A fire devours before them, and behind them, a flame burns. The land is like the Garden of Eden before them and behind them a desolate wilderness." This passage paints a picture of a powerful army advancing with destructive force, leaving desolation in its wake. The prophecy foretells a day of darkness, signaling great upheaval. The contrast between the Garden of Eden and the desolate wilderness suggests a dramatic, devastating transformation of the land.

These biblical passages are often interpreted symbolically, reflecting spiritual realities and future events. While interpretations may vary, they generally point towards a time of significant spiritual conflict and the importance of faithfulness and vigilance in such times.

The Book of Revelation contains passages some interpret as referencing a socio-economic system tied to the "mark of the Beast." This mark is often seen as a symbol of allegiance to a worldly power or deceptive system. However, interpretations of these passages vary widely among religious traditions and individuals.

The Impact of Geopolitical and Spiritual Conflicts

Some draw parallels between the Revelation system and historical or contemporary socio-economic structures shaped by race, religion, and ethnicity. The Indo-European caste system comes to mind, illustrating how societal structures and economic privileges have sometimes been molded by discrimination and diverse hierarchies.

In many historical contexts, including the colonial era, lighter skin often correlated with social and economic superiority. White Anglo-Saxon settlers, for example, were often granted exclusive market privileges, amassing wealth and power based on race.

Natural resources like gold, silver, diamonds, and agricultural commodities held little global market value unless controlled or traded by the dominant culture. Resources were often seized from indigenous populations in the Americas, Australia, and Africa, furthering the interests of white Anglo-Saxon settlers. This reflects a history of exploitation and racial inequality that has shaped global socio-economic structures.

The prophets of old warned against self-centeredness, arrogance, and greed, seeing these as catalysts for war and corruption. They called for humility, justice, and righteousness. Yet, many societies, particularly those driven by colonial and imperial ambitions, have acted otherwise.

In reality, the global economy was built on violent conflicts and exploitations, notably the colonization of Africa, establishing a financial system that marginalized people of African heritage. This perspective highlights the lasting impact of colonial powers' actions on global economic structures.

The Prophet Joel foretold a Day of Judgment, when the looted Hebrew treasures would become a curse for the Gentiles. He urged repentance and prophesied divine retribution against Antichrist ideology endorsers. These proclamations serve as a call for righteousness, justice, and a warning against self-centered acts and systems.

*"The sun shall be turned into darkness, and the moon into blood,
before the coming of the great and awesome day of the Lord.
And it shall come to pass that whoever calls on
the name of the Lord shall be saved."*

*"On account of My people, My heritage Israel, whom they have
scattered among the nations; they have also divided up my land.
They have cast lots for My people and have paid a boy for a harlot
Swiftly and speedily I will return your retaliation upon your head;
Because you have taken My silver and My gold, and carried into
your temples My prized possessions."*

—Joel 2:31–3:5

In 1948, the United Nations General Assembly adopted a resolution to partition Palestine into two independent states in the aftermath of World War II. This decision sparked controversy and conflict, laying the groundwork for enduring regional tensions.

The more significant portion of the partitioned Palestinian territory was allocated to the creation of the State of Israel, claimed by migrating Jewish settlers citing historical ties. The smaller region was designated for the Arab population, the native Palestinians. This arrangement drew parallels to South African apartheid.

Many Palestinians were displaced from their homes, with their displacement often justified by perceived Jewish cultural superiority. Powerful Western nations, remnants of the old Roman Empire, and the United States saw this partition as a chance to expand their influence in the West Bank and intervene in the affairs of Arab countries and the newly established State of Israel.

May 14, 1948, marks a significant turning point in Middle Eastern history. On this day, the newly declared State of Israel was invaded by an Arab coalition, including Egypt, Jordan, Syria, and Iraqi forces. This marked the start of the 1948 Arab-Israeli War, a major regional conflict.

The Arab forces launched an attack on Israeli forces and were able to cut off the Negev region from the rest of Israel. The Negev was a significant part of the territory allocated to Israel by the United Nations in the 1947 Partition Plan for Palestine.

This war marked the beginning of a series of conflicts between Israel and its Arab neighbors, which have continued in various forms to the present day. The geopolitical landscape of the Middle East has been significantly shaped by these conflicts, creating a complex situation with deep historical roots and significant implications for international relations.

The establishment of the State of Israel in 1948 led to significant demographic changes in the region. Approximately 700,000 Palestinian Arabs fled or were expelled from their homes during this period, an event known in Arabic as the Nakba, or "catastrophe." At the same time, many European Jewish refugees migrated to Israel, further changing the region's demographics.

The settlers viewed Israel as the ancestral homeland of all Jews worldwide. This perspective, however, is rooted in a complex and contested history, and interpretations of it vary widely. Some argue that this viewpoint is based more on a secular political agenda rather than historical or scientific evidence.

Historical research indicates that the region now known as Israel/Palestine has been occupied by various groups over the centuries, including the Philistines, Assyrians, Persians, and Romans. These groups were often in conflict with the Indigenous people who lived there.

The tale of Israel's past is a fascinating mosaic of events and cultures. The truth, however, often remains shrouded in mystery. Israel's history is marked by invasions from various Balkan groups, including the Philistines, who intermingled with

Canaanites, Cainites, and Amorites to form the Tidal of Nations or the Five Kings. This amalgamation of cultures eventually led to the emergence of the Assyrian Empire.

The Book of Genesis tells us about the Caphtorim and Pathrusim, known as the Hyksos in Egypt, who ignited the Aegean islands with bloodshed, particularly Crete, before migrating to Israel, Judah, and Egypt. A fierce rivalry for control of the plain ensued, with a coalition of Aryan tribes conquering Negeb, a crucial connection point for Israel's trade routes with Arabia (a Middle Eastern territory).

Indigenous Kushites also inhabited Israel and Judah (Judea). Another group, the Children of Jacob, or Israelites, migrated from Egypt, adhering to the Hebrew faith and a Covenant with the Creator. According to the Book of Joshua, these descendants of Jacob joined forces with various Kushite tribes suffering under the oppression of the Balkan invaders.

Under the leadership of Joshua, a united force launched a surprise attack on the Philistine invaders. The scriptures recount a miraculous event where the Lord commanded the sun to stand still and the moon's shadow to block daylight until the invaders were defeated. This marked the beginning of a new chapter in history.

The Israelites and native Kushites decided to coexist with the settlers but adopted certain customs from the Balkan invaders. Over time, this practice evolved into a caste hierarchy that is prevalent in Israel and the Western world today. Today, Palestinians aren't considered light enough, and people with Afrocentric features are deemed too dark to be a part of this power structure.

It's worth noting that these interpretations are complex and controversial, and opinions differ widely among historians, archaeologists, and geneticists. The region's history is multifaceted and deeply intertwined with cultural, religious, and political narratives.

On October 7, 2023, there was an unprecedented escalation in conflict as Hamas fighters infiltrated Israeli territory using motorized hang gliders, marking the first known use of this tactic. They launched ground attacks, opened gunfire, and abducted Israeli soldiers and civilians.

Footage from Israeli social media revealed armed Hamas paragliders crossing Israel's southern border from the Gaza Strip immediately after a rocket attack on the country. Upon crossing the heavily fortified border, the masked terrorists landed on motorized dune buggies attached to large sails.

As per The Times of Israel, an IDF spokesperson confirmed the infiltration from "land, sea, and air." The two-seater paragliders, in a seated trike configuration, had the rear occupant piloting the aircraft while the armed front passenger was poised for quick disembarkation and assault on the landing zone. The single-seater paragliders featured an engine and propeller directly mounted on the pilot's back.

In the wake of an unprecedented attack by Gaza-based militant group Hamas, Israeli Prime Minister Benjamin Netanyahu declared war against them, announcing to his stunned nation, "Citizens of Israel, we are at war. The enemy will pay an unprecedented price."

This escalation in the ongoing Israel-Palestine conflict has precipitated a humanitarian crisis of "epic proportions" in the Gaza Strip, as described by the United Nations. Residents grapple with food and electricity shortages, compounded by the constant threat of injury or death from Israeli airstrikes.

In response to the escalating crisis, U.S. President Joe Biden has called on Prime Minister Netanyahu to expedite the delivery of humanitarian aid to Gaza, even as the region continues to be pummeled by airstrikes. The situation has been likened to a holocaust for the Palestinian people, with Israel warning of a protracted war with Hamas.

Aid agencies have characterized the civilian toll in Gaza as catastrophic. Thousands of people have stormed United Nations warehouses in their desperate search for food and basic supplies.

In Jericka Duncan's poignant story on CBS News, titled "For Palestinian and Israeli Americans, the unimaginable is now a reality," the heartbreaking reality of the conflict in the Middle East comes to life through the words of Kasem, a Palestinian American who shares his deeply personal perspective. Kasem's words serve as a powerful testament to the devastating toll this long-standing conflict has taken on innocent lives in Gaza. He emphasizes that every household in Gaza bears the scars of loss, with children, fathers, and cousins being taken away by the violence. His words resonate with the universal truth that suffering is not confined to one side of the conflict; it touches both Palestinians and Israelis alike.

Kasem's profound empathy is evident as he expresses his anger at the ongoing bloodshed and loss of innocent lives, regardless of their nationality. He yearns for a peaceful resolution that would spare the lives of countless children who are caught in the crossfire. Kasem's emotional turmoil reflects the deep-seated desire for peace and reconciliation among Palestinian and Israeli Americans, echoing the sentiments of countless individuals who yearn for an end to the cycle of violence in the region. Through Kasem's perspective, Duncan's story highlights the urgent need for dialogue and diplomacy to bring an end to the suffering of innocent civilians and pave the way for a more hopeful future in the region.

In its early years, Israel maintained a close relationship with the Apartheid South African government led by Jan Smuts, a fervent advocate of racial segregation, white minority rule, and Jewish nationalism, or Zionism. Smuts, a key figure during the First World War, led South Africa's white-controlled armies against German-controlled South-West Africa and commanded the British Army in East Africa.

Israel held a position of esteem within South Africa, particularly for its Apartheid system of government. Apartheid South Africa was one of the 33 nations that supported the 1947 UN partition resolution of Palestine. Post-Second World War, the white minority regime of South Africa emerged as one of Israel's critical military and economic allies.

Allegedly, the two nations collaborated on nuclear weapons development, with the Israeli Air Force believed to have deployed the first modern drone technology in combat against Angola and Syria starting in 1981. The South African government's 1976 yearbook noted a commonality between the two nations, stating: "Israel and South Africa have one thing above all else in common: they are both situated in a predominantly hostile world inhabited by dark peoples."

Contemporary Advocacy and Historical Echoes of Racial Justice

Presidential candidate Cornel West publicly advocated for Palestinian rights on October 28, 2023, during a march in downtown Los Angeles. The event drew thousands of supporters, reflecting the growing concern over the escalating conflict in Gaza. A video of West's potent criticism of Israel's strikes on Gaza, which he referred to as a "genocidal attack," has attracted significant attention, amassing approximately 1 million views on social media platforms.

The humanitarian crisis in Gaza is deepening as continuous Israeli strikes have resulted in fuel and energy shortages, critically affecting the functioning of essential medical facilities. Despite the recent public outcry in America, calling for the Biden administration to demand a ceasefire, the President has yet to take action. However, Israel has conceded to daily four-hour humanitarian pauses in the northern Gaza region.

At the rally, Dr. Cornel West delivered a passionate speech in support of Palestine. He argued, "Being sympathetic to the Palestinians and Palestinian children does not mean you harbor hatred towards others. The loss of life, including 10,000 individuals and 4,000 children, is a tragedy. It is not logical to suggest that because you love Palestinians, you despise someone else."

West went on to clarify, "We do not despise our Jewish brothers and sisters. What we abhor is the brutal Israeli occupation and the harsh siege on Gaza. In response to these overwhelming atrocities, the least we can demand is a ceasefire."

He criticized Washington's response to the crisis, saying, "Yet, we have these individuals in Washington, D.C., suggesting a 'humanitarian pause' instead of a ceasefire. I urge you to wake up, recognize the humanity of the Palestinians, and address the situation with the seriousness it demands."

West concluded his speech with a strong critique of American foreign policy, "It's outrageous that the American government had the audacity to veto a humanitarian pause while our Palestinian brothers and sisters are under attack. We must introspect - what kind of nation are we? What kind of people are we?"

The chilling memory of the horrific event at Charleston's Emanuel African Methodist Episcopal Church is a grim reminder of the persistent battle against racial violence and extremism in America, too. This incident, set against a backdrop of global upheaval due to demographic and social changes, shook the world. A gunman's rampage ended the lives of nine innocent souls, including Reverend Clementa Pinckney, the church's pastor and a South Carolina state senator.

Reverend Pinckney was more than just a spiritual guide; he was a beacon of hope for many. Elected to the state legislature at the tender age of 23, he dedicated his life to serving his community and championing change. His unwavering commitment to preaching and community service was a testament to his dedication to uplifting his congregation and advocating for change.

The unsettling act of terror by Dylann Storm Roof paints a grim picture of the violence endured by black communities in America. Roof, a 21-year-old white man, insidiously infiltrated the largely black congregation, mirroring the betrayal of Judas Iscariot in the Bible. He spent over an hour in the midst of the worshippers before launching a barrage of gunfire. The fact that he used a weapon purchased with money given to him for his 21st birthday is particularly haunting, underlining the ease of gun access. Roof's premeditated actions were reportedly planned over six months, underscoring the pressing need to address not just domestic terrorism but also the root causes that foster such hatred and extremism in today's America. This tragic event is a stark reminder of the urgent need for comprehensive strategies to combat racial violence, gun control, and the protection of places of worship in the United States.

The Emanuel AME Church, co-founded by Morris Brown and Denmark Vesey (Telemaque), has a history marked by racial conflict. Vesey and supporters planned a slave uprising in Charleston, South Carolina, seeking liberation and refuge in Haiti. Authorities learned of the plan through slave informants, leading to Vesey and 36 others being secretly tried and hanged on July 2, 1822. The church was destroyed, and black congregations were banned in South Carolina.

Founded during slavery, Emanuel AME served as both a place of worship and refuge from racism in Charleston.

Black churches, particularly in the South, faced racist attacks during the civil rights era. White supremacists viewed them as threats and racial prejudice persisted in the South. The Jim Crow era saw the burning of churches, homes, and businesses and the adoption of black codes. The justice system contributed to systemic racism, with beatings and torture as penalties for disobedience. Public beatings and lynchings were the preferred tools of supremacist groups.

In the early 1960s, black churches in the South were frequently firebombed to intimidate civil rights protesters. Dwight Eisenhower's 1960 Civil Rights Act introduced penalties for those obstructing voter registration or voting attempts. In 1957, Congress established the United States Commission on Civil Rights to protect citizens' civil rights at all government levels, angering white supremacists who perceived federal interference in state matters.

The Civil Rights Act of 1957 was the first civil rights legislation passed since Reconstruction. It followed increased violence against African Americans after the 1954 Brown v. Board of Education decision, argued successfully by Thurgood Marshall, whom Lyndon Johnson later nominated as the first black Supreme Court Justice. This legislation aimed to address voter disenfranchisement through practices like literacy tests and poll taxes that had affected many African Americans.

In 1963, Dr. Martin Luther King Jr. organized peaceful mass demonstrations in Birmingham, Alabama. Bull Connor, the city's Commissioner of Public Safety, responded with police dogs and fire hoses. This event garnered widespread attention, making civil rights a global issue. The same year, the March on Washington drew approximately 250,000 participants in a nonviolent protest advocating for African American civil rights and economic equality.

Dr. King first gained national recognition in 1955 when he and other civil rights activists were arrested for leading a boycott of the Montgomery, Alabama, transportation system, which enforced racial segregation on buses, requiring nonwhites to give up their seats to whites and sit at the back.

In May 1961, John Lewis and other Freedom Riders, both black and white, were beaten with baseball bats, hammers, and chains when their bus arrived downtown in Montgomery, Alabama. After the senseless attack, more protesters joined the freedom riders throughout the south. "Burn them alive," as firebombs were thrown into the buses, one protester remembered. The mob shouted, "Fry the goddamn niggers." Chaos spread throughout the South, including religious institutions, which became the headquarters of some of the protests. On September 15, 1963, four members of the Ku Klux Klan planted at least 15 sticks of dynamite attached to a timing device beneath the front steps of the 16th Street Baptist Church in Birmingham, killing four innocent girls.

President Lyndon Johnson forwarded the civil rights bill to Capitol Hill for enactment into law. Dr. King and Malcolm X met there to observe the Senate debate on the bill. The primary opposition to the bill came from Senators Strom Thurmond and Richard Russell. Russell declared, "We will resist any measure or movement that could lead to social equality, racial mixing, and blending in our states."

The Civil Rights Act was signed into law on July 2, 1964. It prohibited discrimination in public places and empowered the federal government to take legal action against states that discriminated against women and minorities, ensuring equal opportunities for all.

On 7 March 1965, SCLC colleague Hosea Williams and John Lewis, Chairman of the Student Nonviolent Coordinating Committee (SNCC), were teargas and beaten by state troopers on an unsuccessful attempt to cross the Edmund Pettus Bridge on a march from Selma to the state capitol in Montgomery known as "Bloody Sunday." It became a national outrage when John Lewis was televised saying, "I don't see how President Johnson can send troops to Vietnam—I don't see how he can send troops to the Congo—I don't see how he can send troops to Africa and can't send troops to Selma."

On August 6, 1965, President Lyndon Johnson signed into law The Voting Rights Act, which aimed to overcome legal barriers at the state and local levels that prevented African Americans from exercising their right to vote under the 15th Amendment. While others advocated for equality by "any means necessary," Dr. King used Bible stories to help end segregation and injustice. Using Moses's story in Exodus, Dr. King inspired his followers to the long-lasting struggles they were to endure through non-violence in their campaign for freedom and brought unity to the civil rights movement. Dr. King used his fiery sermons to expose the truth of racism and discrimination, which helped shape some of our most fundamental values through principles of love and forgiveness.

In his 'Letter from the Birmingham Jail,' Dr. Martin Luther King Jr. expressed gratitude for the role of the Negro church in integrating nonviolence into the struggle for equality under the law. His leadership led to the enactment of two pivotal legislations in American history - the Civil Rights Act and the Voting Rights Act. Dr. King's influence was recognized when Time Magazine named him 'Man of the Year' in its January 1964 issue. Further, on December 10, 1964, in Oslo, Norway, he received the Nobel Peace Prize for his nonviolent resistance and leadership of the Civil Rights movement in America, becoming the youngest recipient of the award at 35.

In addition to the civil rights movement, global conflicts significantly influenced the cultural and political trends of the era, often referred to as a classical Jungian nightmare cycle or the Swinging Sixties. This period saw numerous laws and reforms enacted to eradicate inequality and injustice nationwide. Dr. King, increasingly disturbed by America's involvement in the Vietnam War, delivered a groundbreaking speech titled 'Beyond Vietnam: A Time to Break Silence' to an audience of 3,000 at Riverside Church on April 4, 1967.

He expressed his concerns that the war was devastating the hopes of the marginalized at home, sending young men crippled by societal injustice to secure liberties in Southeast Asia that were denied to them in their own country. Dr. King asserted a strong link between the fight against domestic civil injustices and the protest against violent, dominating foreign policies. Despite criticism questioning his motives and the wisdom of his path, he remained resolute, stating, "Why are you speaking about the war, Dr. King? Why are you joining the voices of dissent? Peace and civil rights don't mix. Aren't you hurting the cause of your people?"

Dr. King ardently connected his sermons and speeches to ongoing events. He once remarked, "Given the unfortunate misunderstandings that persist, I find it crucial to clearly and succinctly express why I am convinced that the journey from Dexter Avenue Baptist Church — my initial pastoral assignment in Montgomery, Alabama — leads unambiguously to this pulpit tonight. I stand before you this evening to fervently appeal to the nation I hold dear. This discourse is not directed at Hanoi or the National Liberation Front. It is not targeted at China or Russia. It is not an effort to ignore the complexity of the situation or the necessity for a group solution to the Vietnam catastrophe. Nor is it an endeavor to portray North Vietnam or the National Liberation Front as models of virtues or to disregard the part they must play in effectively resolving the issue. Even though they might have legitimate reasons to doubt the sincerity of the United States, life and history compellingly demonstrate that disputes can never be settled without mutual trust and compromise."

Dr. King made it clear that his intention was not to address Hanoi or the National Liberation Front but rather to communicate directly with the American populace.

"As a clergyman, I deem it appropriate to subject Vietnam to my moral examination, given the seven significant reasons that impel me to do so. The battle in Vietnam and the social struggle we have been engaging in, in America bear a striking resemblance. There was a flicker of hope for the destitute, regardless of race, through the poverty alleviation program. However, the intensification in Vietnam obliterated this initiative, redirecting resources to a war that acted like a damaging vortex. I increasingly perceived the war as a foe of the impoverished and felt driven to challenge it in that light.

Beyond annihilating the hopes of the domestic poor, the war's atrocities disproportionately propelled their sons, brothers, and husbands into battlefields to perish, far removed from the freedoms they were denied at home. Negro and white boys were seen dying together on television screens, a stark contradiction to a country that couldn't accommodate them in the same educational institutions. They were seen setting alight huts in a poverty-stricken village while they could barely coexist on the same street back home. I couldn't maintain my silence against such brutal exploitation of people with low incomes.

To those who question my involvement in the peace movement because of my position as a civil rights leader, I reply: when the Southern Christian Leadership Conference was established in 1957, our motto was 'To save the soul of America.' We held the belief that our vision shouldn't be confined to specific rights for black people but rather that America could never attain true freedom until the descendants of its slaves were entirely emancipated. Essentially, we concurred with Langston Hughes, the African American poet of Harlem, who had earlier penned:"

O, yes, I say it plainly, America never was America to me, And yet I swear this oath – America will be!"

Dr. King proceeded to argue his position, infusing his beacon of nonviolence into the civil rights movement:

"The luxury of harboring the god of hate or kneeling before the shrine of retribution is no longer a cost we can bear. History's oceans are rendered tempestuous by the incessantly surging waves of hatred. The landscape of history is strewn with the debris of nations and individuals who chose to tread this self-destructive path of loathing. As Arnold Toynbee rightly states: love is the ultimate force that makes for the saving choice of life and good against the damning choice of death and evil. Therefore, the first hope in our inventory must be the hope that love is going to have the last word."

Despite Dr. King's strong stance against the Vietnam War, many black newspapers and allies, including the NAACP, distanced themselves from him, considering his merging of civil rights and the anti-war movement a tactical error. President Lyndon B. Johnson, enraged by what he saw as ingratitude, demanded that King soften his criticism of the war.

Undeterred, Dr. King chose to amplify his voice, intending to pressure Congress to reconsider its foreign policy in order to address domestic issues. He advocated for an economic bill of rights, assuring employment for all willing to work. "We are spending all of this money for death and destruction and not nearly enough money for life and constructive development," King argued. In response, President Johnson, from his Oval Office, reportedly questioned, "What is that goddamn nigger preacher trying to do to me?"

On April 30, 1967, Dr. King further solidified his stance, starting his sermon at the Riverside Church on "Why I Am Opposed to the War."

In his sermon, Dr. King urged America to confront the tragic truth of the Vietnam War. He stated, "The time has come for America to hear the truth about this tragic war. Rationalizations and the incessant search for scapegoats close our eyes to our sins.

Superficial patriotism is no longer enough; living with untruth equates to spiritual slavery. True freedom comes from knowing the truth, as Jesus said, 'Ye shall know the truth, and the truth shall set you free.'"

King made his anti-war stance clear, saying, "The hottest places in hell are reserved for those who maintain their neutrality in times of moral crisis. Silence becomes betrayal."

He called for a return to humility and justice, warning that arrogance could lead to the downfall of America's power. He declared, "Let us go out this morning with determination. I have not lost faith. I'm not in despair because I know there is a moral order." He invoked the words of Carlyle, Bryant, and Lowell, asserting the inevitability of truth and justice.

King shared a vision of a world united in peace, a symphony of brotherhood where justice and righteousness were abundant. He envisioned a day when the words of the old Negro spiritual, "Free at last! Free at last! Thank God Almighty, we're free at last!" would resonate globally, signaling an era of peace.

Dr. King gave America a prophetic warning in his final year: choose life or face slow demise. His campaign shifted to expose racism and exploitative conditions fostered by the economic policies of the United States and Great Britain. He recognized the revolutionary age they lived in, one that would significantly alter human history. His last address before his assassination to the Southern Christian Leadership Council in Atlanta, Georgia, on August 16, 1967. *Where Do We Go From Here: Chaos or Community?*

"In assault after assault, we caused the sagging walls of segregation to come tumbling down... Ten years ago, Black people seemed almost invisible to the larger society, and the facts of their harsh lives were unknown to the majority of the nation. But today, civil rights are a dominating issue in every state, crowding the pages of the press and the daily conversation of white Americans. In this decade of change, the black race stood up and confronted his oppressor. He faced the bullies and the guns, and the dogs and the tear gas. He put himself squarely before the vicious mobs, moved with strength and dignity toward them, and decisively defeated."

"During this era, the entire edifice of segregation was profoundly shaken. And so, we still have a long way to go before reaching the promised land of freedom. Yes, we have left the dusty soils of Egypt, and we have crossed the Red Sea that had for years been hardened by a long and piercing winter of massive resistance, but before we reach the majestic shores of the Promised Land, there will still be gigantic mountains of opposition ahead and prodigious hilltops of injustice. (Yes, that's right) We still need some Paul Revere of conscience to alert every hamlet and every village of America that revolution is still at hand. Yes, we need a chart; we need a compass; indeed, we need some North Star to guide us into a future shrouded with impenetrable uncertainties."

Assessing Dr. King's Vision for Racial Equity and Social Reform

"Now, to answer the question, "Where do we go from here?" which is our theme, we must first honestly recognize where we are now. When the Constitution was written, a strange formula to determine taxes and representation declared that the Negro was 60 percent of a person. Today, another curious formula declares that he is 50 percent of a person. Of the good things in life, the Negro has approximately one-half those of whites. Of the bad things of life, he has twice those of whites. Thus, half of all Negroes live in substandard housing. And Negroes have half the income of whites. When we view the negative experiences of life, the Negro has a double share. There are twice as many unemployed."

"Even semantics have conspired to make that which is black seem ugly and degrading. In Roget's Thesaurus, there are 120 synonyms for blackness, and at least 60 are offensive, such as blot, soot, grim, devil, and foul. And there are some 134 synonyms for whiteness, and all are favorable, expressed in such words as purity, cleanliness, chastity, and innocence. A white lie is better than a black lie. The most degenerate member of a family is a "black sheep." Ossie Davis has suggested that maybe the English language should be reconstructed so that teachers will not be forced to teach the Negro child 60 ways to despise himself, and thereby perpetuate his false sense of inferiority and the white child 134 ways to adore himself, and thereby perpetuate his false sense of superiority."

Dr. King asserted that unity among all Americans, regardless of race, is essential to combat poverty and foster civil rights, thereby establishing equal opportunities for all. He expressed his disappointment in both the Republican and Democratic parties, criticizing their perceived betrayal of the black community. He pinpointed Southern Dixiecrats and conservative northern Republicans for undermining liberal civil rights legislation.

Post-World War II, the Truman Administration and Congress enacted the Atlantic Pact, the Arm Pact, and the Marshall Plan, a European recovery program. This $13 billion initiative removed trade barriers, stimulated economies, rebuilt infrastructure, and provided significant food aid to devastated European nations and Japan. The Marshall Plan restored Europe's economic structure while overlooking Africa's needs. In 1951, it was succeeded by the Mutual Security Plan, which continued Europe's financial aid.

Following the Civil Rights Acts, Dr. King and other influential figures rallied for a powerful stand against racism, poverty, and social inequality. Dr. King, undeterred by geographical limits, vowed to shape his destiny amidst a world where people of color were still grappling with the harsh realities of colonization and slavery. He shone a spotlight on the deeply ingrained racism that plagued America and the world, drawing a parallel with W.E.B. Dubois's earlier words on the 'color-line' issue.

Dr. King didn't shy away from criticizing the United States for its seeming prioritization of rebuilding Western Europe over tackling the pressing issues within its black communities. He painted a grim picture of the potential fall of Western civilization if racism continued to be ignored, stating, "Racism can well be that corrosive evil that will bring down the curtain on Western civilization."

He further issued a stern warning, "If Western civilization does not now respond constructively to the challenge of eliminating racism, some future historian will have to say that a great civilization died because it lacked the moral courage to overcome racism."

Across the globe, black and brown individuals in former European colonies in the West Indies, Latin America, and Africa were subjected to the same pervasive prejudice that black Americans faced. Dr. King, despite his satisfaction with the Civil Rights Act, was a vocal opponent of the Vietnam War in 1967. He saw racism, economic exploitation, and militarism as intertwined "triple evils." He described the Vietnam War as a racist conflict, with African Americans disproportionately drafted and more likely to face combat.

Dr. King also criticized the Marshall Plan, believing it exploited resources for European interests. He argued that funds spent on war were wasted in Vietnam's killing fields and perpetuated suffering in Latin America through Western exploitation.

Stokely Carmichael, a rising civil rights leader who once followed King's nonviolent approach, became disillusioned.

Carmichael, who was once a member of the Nonviolent Action Group and the Student Nonviolent Coordinating Committee (SNCC), joined the militant Black Panther Party. He found nonviolence ineffective against the persistent violence and humiliation from white supremacists and law enforcement.

In 1966, civil rights activist James Meredith embarked on a solo March Against Fear from Memphis to Jackson, covering 220 miles, to challenge the persistent racism in Mississippi. Meredith, the first African American to enroll at the University of Mississippi, aimed to boost black voter registration. His march gained more protesters due to media coverage after he was shot by a white supremacist on the second day of his walk.

Carmichael, who had ascended to the position of chairman of the SNCC, gave his famous "Black Power" speech, advocating for the essential need for black political and economic influence. The catchphrase "Black Power" echoed around the world, serving as a symbol of resistance against European colonial rule in Africa and a rallying point for worldwide black solidarity. King considered "Black Power" to be an "unfortunate choice of words," while Carmichael contended, "When you mention black power, you're referring to establishing a movement that will obliterate everything that Western civilization has engineered." Despite the U.S. House of Representatives' condemnation of the speech, the term "Black Power" resonated among the audience. The day before the march made its way to Jackson, Meredith made a comeback, walking side by side with Dr. King and other leaders.

Eventually, Dr. King acknowledged the psychological allure of "Black Power" for those who had been long oppressed under white dominance, appreciating its significance to those who were conditioned to perceive the color black as derogatory. Stokely Carmichael, who had been detained twenty-seven times for nonviolent protests and had suffered abuse in prison, emerged as an emblem of this transformation. He welcomed militancy and self-determination, relocating to West Africa in 1969 and adopting the name Kwame Ture in homage to African socialist leaders.

The rise of black militancy during the 1960s and early 1970s was a response to the persistent police brutality, white supremacist groups, and government corruption that African American communities faced. Amidst ongoing disenfranchisement and systemic racism, the Black Liberation Struggle aimed to dismantle the Jim Crow system, foster racial pride, and establish black political and cultural institutions to protect black collective interests and resist American global imperialism. The Black Panther Party, founded by Huey P. Newton and Bobby Seale, set up community social programs, educational initiatives, free breakfast programs for children, and community health clinics.

Though the Black Power movement arose from the Civil Rights Movement, many young African Americans deemed the latter too conventional and sought a quicker path to genuine racial equality. Dr. King, a fervent champion of racial harmony and nonviolence, began to acknowledge the significance of black identity in his later years. The Civil Rights Movement and Black Power represented the primary ideologies fueling the widespread battles against inequality. The Black Power movement had a profound influence, fostering racial pride, enhancing self-confidence in black communities, and promoting self-reliance through unity and self-determination.

Nonetheless, Black Nationalism and black separatism stirred tension among mainstream Civil Rights Movement leaders, who perceived Black Nationalism as a veiled form of black supremacy. Critics contended that suggesting inherent unity or cultures based on race was inherently racist. However, the movement indisputably played a pivotal role in inspiring African Americans to form a legitimate political force for social and economic self-reliance.

In the final stages of his life, Dr. King grappled with deep depression and heartache. His distress over the political climate, the Vietnam War, death threats, and Middle East turmoil cast a shadow over his message of "redeeming the soul of America." Despite the opposition and chaos, he remained committed to being a "drum major for peace."

A month before his assassination, King delivered a soul-searching sermon at the Ebenezer Baptist Church in Atlanta, Georgia, titled "Unfulfilled Dreams." Drawing from the book of Kings, he compared life to Schubert's "Unfinished Symphony," expressing the struggle of striving to complete unfinishable tasks. Despite his attempts to promote compassion, love, and forgiveness, his dreams remained unfulfilled, burdened by the moral contradictions of a government that sought to undermine his peace-promoting efforts.

The FBI had accused King of inciting riots, labeling him "the most dangerous and effective Negro leader in the country." His sermon reflected his internal struggle, comparing his trials to those of the biblical David. He acknowledged the agony of unfulfilled dreams, a reality he shared with his congregation.

While the Black Militants and the Civil Rights Movement shared commonalities, the militants did not subscribe to King's vision of spiritual salvation for all races. They believed in violence and segregation as the means to achieve self-respect and real equality. This principle of "black power" threatened to divide the civil rights movement and alienate white supporters. King argued against any form of racial supremacy, stating, "A doctrine of black supremacy is as evil as a doctrine of white supremacy."

King addressed the threats on his life, saying, "If physical death is the price that I must pay to free my white brothers and sisters from a permanent death of the spirit, then nothing can be more redemptive." He envisioned a spiritually reborn America that recognized the worth of all men, casting aside the racism that hindered its democratic growth. His dream was to eradicate segregation through principles of forgiveness, faith, love, and brotherhood. Like Martin Luther, the Protestant reformer who challenged the Roman Catholic Church, King fought for the common people, and their messages forever altered the course of history.

In an interview with reporter Eleanor Fischer, Malcolm X articulated the difference between segregation and separation, advocating for the establishment of a separate black territory within America. He commented on Martin Luther King Jr.'s efforts, arguing that King was "disarming the black people of America of their natural right." Malcolm X believed that if the government could not secure justice for black people, it was time for black people to secure it themselves.

In the 1950s, Reverend Billy Graham, alongside Dr. King, preached at events in the South, espousing the Gospel as a tool to end racial segregation. During a revival in Jackson, Mississippi, Graham demanded the removal of ropes separating black and white sections. When the usher refused, Graham did it himself, stating, "There is no scriptural basis for segregation." However, Graham's commitment to dismantling segregation was called into question when he reportedly accepted segregation at some of his crusades and declined to march alongside King or other civil rights activists.

In his book Billy Graham and the Rise of the Republican South, Steven P. Miller quotes Graham as saying, "If the law says that I cannot march or I cannot demonstrate, I ought not to march and I ought not to demonstrate." Graham saw racism as a "problem of the heart" solvable through Christian conversion. In contrast, King and other civil rights activists emphasized the need for systemic change.

CHAPTER SEVEN

Memphis 1968: The Strike That Rallied a Nation

"Change does not roll in on the wheels of inevitability, but comes through continuous struggle."

———

Martin Luther King Jr.

In 1968, the tragic deaths of Robert Walker and Echol Cole in Memphis due to a malfunctioning compression unit compelled Dr. King to address human rights violations and working-class injustices. The city of Memphis offered the families of Walker and Cole one month's salary and $500 toward burial expenses but no insurance or workers' compensation. These deaths sparked the 1968 Sanitation Workers' Strike, which brought King to support the workers in his final march before his assassination. Newly elected Mayor Loeb declared the strike illegal and threatened to replace the strikers, stating, "This is not New York, and nothing will be gained by ignoring our law." Referring to the 1966 New York City transit strike and New York City sanitation strike from

February 2 through February 10, 1968, 7,000 sanitation workers went on strike, which settled with a large pay increase.

Echoes of New York: The Memphis Sanitation Strike Begins

Two days after the end of the New York City 1968 strike, approximately 1300 black sanitation workers in Memphis walked off the job in protest. The strike evolved into a significant civil rights struggle, garnering national media attention and attracting prominent civil rights leaders and the NAACP. The strikers joined the American Federation of State, County, and Municipal Employees (AFSCME) Local 1733, adopting the slogan "I Am A Man." Local ministers formed Community on the Move for Equality (COME) under the leadership of King's longtime ally, local minister James Lawson.

Meanwhile, in the wake of the tragic deaths of Robert Walker and Echol Cole, Dr. King returned to the pulpit at Ebenezer Baptist Church in Atlanta, Georgia. Two months before his assassination, he delivered a sermon titled "The Drum Major Instinct." In it, he explored the basic human desire for recognition, importance, and to be first — an instinct he warned could lead to tragic prejudices.

Dr. King shared the biblical story of two brothers, James and John, sons of Zebedee, whom Jesus nicknamed "sons of thunder." Their mother asked Jesus if her sons could sit in glory at his right and left hands. Similarly, Peter asked in Matthew 19:27, "See, we have left all and followed You. Therefore, what shall we have?" Dr. King referred to the disciples' self-ambition as the "drum major instinct."

Jesus responded to these ambitions with a call to servitude: "But so shall it not be among you: but whosoever will be great among you, shall be your servant: and whosoever of you will be the chiefest, shall be servant of all."

Like many Hebrews, James and John dreamed of a forthcoming king who would free Jerusalem and establish his righteous kingdom on Mount Zion. They saw Jesus as this king and envisioned the day when he would reign supreme as the new king of Israel. Their request to Jesus reflected this dream: "Now, when you establish your kingdom, let us sit on the right hand and the other on the left hand of your throne."

In his sermon, Dr. King explored the concept of the "drum major instinct," the basic human desire for recognition, importance, and superiority. He cited Alfred Adler's psychoanalytic theory that this quest for recognition and distinction is the basic drive of human life, superseding even Freud's argument of sex as the dominant impulse.

King shared a conversation with some white wardens during his time in the Birmingham jail. Despite their insistence on the rightness of segregation, King pointed out their shared economic struggles with black people and how they were unknowingly supporting their oppressors due to the blinding effects of prejudice.

King turned the sermon back to Jesus's teachings. He highlighted Jesus's response to James and John's request for seats on his right and left when his kingdom was established. Instead of condemning their ambitions, Jesus redirected them, saying, "You want to be important. You want to be significant. Well, you ought to be. But I want you to be first in love. I want you to be first in moral excellence. I want you to be first in generosity."

King expressed this was a new norm of greatness —greatness defined by service to others. Dr. King spoke of a man, born into obscurity, who never sought worldly accomplishments or recognition yet became the most influential figure in human history — Jesus Christ. Despite never writing a book, holding an office, starting a family, owning a house, visiting a big city, or traveling far from his birthplace, Jesus's impact on the world eclipsed that of all armies, navies, parliaments, and kings combined. His greatness was in his service and love, a lesson King believed was vital for all to learn.

Despite his personal struggles, Dr. King was committed to elevating nonviolence and pushing for an Economic Bill of Rights for the nation's poor. He and other civil rights leaders organized a multiracial force to march on Washington, D.C., engaging in nonviolent civil defiance to demand economic justice. The Poor People's Campaign sought to unite people of all races under the shared experience of hardship and to persuade the Johnson Administration and Congress to prioritize a $30 billion anti-poverty package focused on job creation, healthcare, and decent housing. King believed it was time to shift from "reform" to "revolution," moving from an era of civil rights to an era of human rights.

On April 3, 1968, King traveled to Memphis, Tennessee, to support striking sanitation workers, temporarily shifting his focus from the Poor People's Campaign. Despite battling a migraine and fatigue, he was called upon to address a crowd at Bishop Charles J. Mason Temple on a stormy evening. Initially, King had asked Ralph Abernathy and Jesse Jackson to speak on his behalf so he could rest and prepare for his upcoming sermon titled "Why America May Go to Hell." However, the crowd's insistence on hearing from King led to Abernathy's call to "Room 306," prompting King to cut his rest short and address the audience.

Despite the storm warning, Dr. King was grateful to see the large crowd gathered to hear him speak, a testament to their determination. He remarked on the state of the nation, the turmoil, and the global uprising of people demanding freedom, whether in Johannesburg, Nairobi, Accra, New York, Atlanta, Jackson, or Memphis. He expressed his joy at witnessing these historical developments and gratitude for being in Memphis....

"The nation is sick. Trouble is in the land; confusion all around... Something is happening in our world. The masses of people are rising up. And wherever they are assembled today, whether they are in Johannesburg, South Africa; Nairobi, Kenya; Accra, Ghana; New York City; Atlanta, Georgia; Jackson, Mississippi; or Memphis, Tennessee -- the cry is always the same: "We want to be free..."

If something isn't done, and done in a hurry, to bring the colored peoples of the world out of their long years of poverty, their long years of hurt and neglect, the whole world is doomed. Now, I'm just happy that God has allowed me to live in this period to see what is unfolding. And I'm happy that He's allowed me to be in Memphis.

"Secondly, let us keep the issues where they are. The issue is injustice. The issue is Memphis's refusal to be fair and honest in its dealings with its public servants, who happen to be sanitation workers.

And then I got into Memphis. And some began to say the threats or talk about the threats that were out. What would happen to me from some of our sick white brothers?

Well, I am still determining what will happen now. We've got some difficult days ahead. But it doesn't matter to me now because I've been to the mountaintop. Like anybody, I would like to live a long life. Longevity has its place. But I'm not concerned about that now. I want to do God's will. And He's allowed me to go up to the mountain. And I've looked over. And I've seen the Promised Land. I may not get there with you. But I want you to know tonight that we, as a people, will get to the promised land. And so, I'm happy tonight. I'm not worried about anything. I do not fear any man! My eyes have seen the glory of the coming of the Lord."

On the evening of April 3, 1968, the day before his assassination, Dr. King savored a soul food dinner at the home of Rev. Samuel (Bill) and Gwen Kyles before a mass meeting with the SCLC. In his final days, King began advocating for "the power of economic withdrawal" as a means of strengthening black institutions and empowerment. He proclaimed at Bishop Charles Temple, "Up to now, only the garbage men have been feeling pain. Now we must kind of redistribute that pain."

King's last conversations revealed a shift in his perspective on integration. In a discussion with Harry Belafonte, King expressed a troubling realization: "You know, we fought long and hard for integration as we should have...But I tell you, Harry, I've come to a realization that deeply troubles me. I've realized that I think we may be integrating into a burning house." In his speech "Beyond Vietnam," King further emphasized his evolving viewpoint, stating, "I am convinced that if we are to get on to the right side of the world revolution, we as a nation must undergo a radical revolution of values." His words hinted at the need for fundamental changes in societal attitudes and structures beyond merely integrating into existing systems.

A year had passed since King's Vietnam speech, and his tireless fight against injustice, racism, poverty, and war had not waned. On the evening of Thursday, April 4, 1968, King stepped out onto the balcony of room 306 at the Lorraine Motel in Memphis. He leaned over the rails shortly after 6 p.m., conversing with Jesse Jackson and musician Ben Branch, who was scheduled to perform that night. King requested that Branch play 'Precious Lord, Take My Hand' at the meeting. It was at this moment that a single 30.06 bullet, fired from a Remington Model 760, rang out.

The bullet pierced King's right cheek, shattering his jaw and several vertebrae as it descended towards his spinal cord. Abernathy reported that the bullet's force twisted King's body, causing him to fall diagonally backward. King lay unconscious on the balcony, a profusion of blood spilling from the severe facial wound. He was rushed to St. Joseph's Hospital, where he was pronounced dead at 7:05 p.m. on April 4, 1968. The 39-year-old civil rights leader and revolutionary thinker, described by Abernathy as "the most peaceful warrior of the 20th Century," had fought his final battle.

Following the news of Dr. Martin Luther King Jr.'s assassination, riots erupted in at least 110 cities across the United States. Looting and arson swept across the nation mere hours after the civil rights leader's death. In Atlanta, Governor Lester Maddox refused to lower the State flag to half-staff and declined to allow Dr. King's body to lie in state at the capitol building. Instead, he commanded state employees to turn their backs on the more than 200,000 mourners and stationed 160 state troopers around the State Capital. Maddox instructed the troopers to "shoot them down and stack them up" should protestors attempt to enter the building. However, he later consented to lower the flag when Lyndon Johnson mandated it federally.

A Nation in Turmoil: The Immediate Aftermath of Dr. King's Assassination

Before his tenure as governor, Lester Maddox was an Atlanta restaurant owner and fervent segregationist. He brazenly violated the newly enacted federal Civil Rights Act by refusing to serve three black Georgia Tech students. Maddox, the owner of the "Pickrick Cafeteria," a restaurant on Hemphill Avenue in Atlanta, Georgia, made it clear that black people would not be served in his establishment. In the summer of 1964, when three black Georgia Tech students attempted to purchase chicken from his restaurant, Maddox brandished a pistol at them, uttering: "You no good dirty devils! You dirty Communists!"

Violence erupted on the West side of Chicago, spreading over a 28-block stretch along West Madison Street. The most significant damage occurred between Roosevelt Road on the South side and the Lawndale and Austin neighborhoods on the West Side, with additional damage reported on Chicago Avenue to the North. Rioters smashed windows, looted stores, and set buildings ablaze. President Lyndon Johnson dispatched 5,000 troops to the city, bolstered by additional forces from the Illinois National Guard, focusing primarily on the city's West and South Sides, where the majority of the rioting and looting had taken place. Mayor Richard J. Daley ordered the police "to shoot to kill any arsonist or anyone with a Molotov cocktail in his hand." Notably, gang members from the Blackstone Rangers and the East Side Disciples helped protect the South Side ghetto from further chaos, a testament to Dr. King's direct involvement with these groups in 1966.

In the six days following Dr. King's death, Washington, D.C., experienced the most significant occupation and surge of social unrest since the Civil War. President Lyndon B. Johnson deployed approximately 13,600 federal troops, including 1,750 federalized D.C. National Guard troops, to assist the DC Metropolitan Police Department in safeguarding federal buildings and the White House. By Monday, around 1,200 buildings had been set on fire, including inner-city businesses that were reduced to rubble. This devastation crippled the inner-city economy, with many of the burned buildings remaining in ruins for decades.

Stokely Carmichael was in Washington, D.C., on the night following King's assassination in April 1968. He led a group through the streets, demanding businesses to close out of respect. However, when the marchers began to riot uncontrollably, the media blamed Carmichael for the violence. He was quoted as saying, "I think white America made its biggest mistake when she killed

Dr. King last night because when she killed Dr. King last night, she killed all reasonable hope."

One of the ironies in America's long, cynical history is the painful reality that the ideals expressed in The Declaration of Independence—"We hold these truths to be self-evident, that all men are created equal, that they are endowed by their Creator with certain unalienable Rights, that among these are Life, Liberty and the pursuit of Happiness"—weren't intended to be universally applicable.

Winston Churchill, a renowned Member of Parliament in Great Britain, once stated, "History is written by the victors." It's comforting to believe that our government would never deceive its citizens with a clandestine history of cover-ups and a complex web of distorted narratives. However, the grimmest chapters of American history are often glossed over or rationalized as the growing pains of a nascent nation, implying that the result justifies brutal means. The genocide perpetrated against America's Native population, the ruthless exploitation of people of African heritage, and the vast amounts of drugs smuggled into America's poorest communities with the protection of various government agencies are harsh realities that lurk beneath the surface of our history.

Reverend Jeremiah Wright, former pastor of the Trinity United Church of Christ, gained national attention during the U.S. Presidential election in 2008 when the media scrutinized excerpts from two of his previous sermons. In a sermon titled "The Day of Jerusalem's Fall," delivered shortly after the September 11 attacks in 2001, Wright stated:

"I heard Ambassador Peck in an interview yesterday. Did anybody else see him or hear him? He was on Fox News. This is a white man, and he was upsetting the Fox News commentators to no end. He pointed out - did you see him, John? - a white man, he pointed out, ambassador, that what Malcolm X said when he got silenced by Elijah Muhammad was, in fact, true: America's chickens are coming home to roost.

We took this country, by terror, away from the Sioux, the Apache, the Arawak, the Comanche, the Arapaho, the Navajo. Terrorism - we took Africans from their country to build our way of ease and kept them enslaved and living in fear. Terrorism. We bombed Grenada and killed innocent civilians - babies and non-military personnel. We bombed the black civilian community of Panama with stealth bombers and killed unarmed teenagers, toddlers, pregnant mothers, and hardworking fathers. We bombed Gaddafi, his home, and killed his child. Blessed be they who bash your children's heads against the rocks.

We bombed Iraq; we killed unarmed civilians trying to make a living. We bombed the plant in Sudan to pay back for the attack on our embassy - killed hundreds of hard-working people - mothers and fathers, who left home to go that day, not knowing they'd never get back home. We bombed Hiroshima, we bombed Nagasaki, and we nuked far more than the thousands in New York and the Pentagon, and we never blinked an eye. Kids playing in the playground, mothers picking up children after school - civilians, not soldiers...

America's chickens are coming home to roost. Violence begets violence. Hatred begets hatred, and terrorism begets terrorism. A white ambassador said that, y'all, not a black militant."

U.S. Presidential candidate Barack Obama found himself in the midst of controversy when segments from Pastor Wright's sermon titled "Confusing God and Government," delivered in March 2008, were aired on ABC's Good Morning America, Fox News, and other media outlets. The phrase that garnered the most attention was "God damn America" for its ill-treatment of people of color. Here are segments of Reverend Jeremiah Wright's sermon:

"If you were to ask the average Christian, 'did Jesus' cry?' almost every Christian would quote for you that John 11:35 verse, which most Bible students call the shortest verse in the Bible: 'Jesus wept'…"

"Prior to Abraham Lincoln, the Government in this country said it was legal to hold Africans in slavery in perpetuity… When Lincoln got in office, the government changed."

"Prior to the passing of the 13th, 14th, and 15th amendments to the Constitution, the government defined Africans as enslaved people, as property – property! – people with no rights to be respected by any Whites anywhere… but I stopped by to tell you tonight that Governments change!"

"Where governments change – write this down, Malachi 3:6 – 'thus says the Lord:' – repeat after me – 'for I am the Lord, and I change not.' That's the King James version. The New Revised says, 'For I the Lord do not change.' In other words, where Governments change, God does not change."

"Governments fail. The government in this text comprised Caesar, Cornelius, and Pontius Pilate, but the Roman government failed. The British government… failed. The Russian government failed. The Japanese government failed. The German government failed. And the United States of America government, when it came to treating her citizens of Indigenous descent fairly, she failed."

"She put them in chains. The government put them in slave quarters, put them on auction blocks, put them in cotton fields, put them in inferior schools, put them in substandard housing, put them in scientific experiments, put them in the lowest paying jobs, put them outside the equal protection of the law, kept them out of their racist bastions of higher education and locked them into positions of hopelessness and helplessness."

"The government gives them the drugs, builds bigger prisons, passes a three-strike law, and then wants us to sing 'God Bless

America.' No, no, no. Not 'God Bless America;' God Damn America! That's in the Bible, for killing innocent people. God Damn America for treating her citizens as less than human. God Damn America as long as she keeps trying to act like she is God and she is supreme!"

The conspiracy is indeed an intricate game of deceit. In June 1971, President Richard Nixon declared drug abuse to be "public enemy number one" to the U.S. Congress. After his election, Nixon significantly expanded the scope and presence of federal drug control agencies and officially declared a "war on drugs" that would focus on eradication, interdiction, and incarceration. The Drug Policy Alliance (DPA), a non-profit organization, estimates that the United States government spends $51 billion annually on the "War on Drugs." According to Human Rights Watch, this "war on drugs" has led to skyrocketing incarceration rates, with African Americans disproportionately targeted and affected.

John Ehrlichman, Richard Nixon's domestic policy chief, admitted in a Harper's Magazine article that the "war on drugs" declared in 1971 was a strategic move to criminalize and denigrate black people and the antiwar left. In a 1994 interview, Ehrlichman stated:

"The Nixon campaign in 1968, and the Nixon White House after that, had two enemies: the antiwar left and black people. Do you understand what I'm saying? We knew we couldn't make it illegal to be either against the war or black, but by getting the public to associate the hippies with marijuana and blacks with heroin and then criminalizing both heavily, we could disrupt those communities. We could arrest their leaders, raid their homes, break up their meetings, and vilify them night after night on the evening news. Did we know we were lying about the drugs? Of course, we did."

While Richard Nixon first declared the "war on drugs" in 1971, it was Ronald Reagan who, eleven years later, declared illicit drugs to be a threat to U.S. national security. African Americans are far more likely than whites to be arrested and receive harsher sentences for selling or possessing drugs. This war on drugs has set the nation on a violent and counterproductive path, particularly in black communities, reminiscent of the struggles faced during the Reconstruction era. Post-slavery, African Americans found themselves ensnared in a flawed legal system designed to perpetuate involuntary servitude for the benefit of the white race.

In a February 8, 2002 interview with Week Online, MIT professor Noam Chomsky responded to a series of paid advertisements run by the drug czar's office that attempted to link drug use with the "war on terrorism." The ads claimed that drug use supported terrorism. Chomsky responded:

"Terrorism is now being used and has been used pretty much the same way communism was used. If you want to press some agenda, you play the terrorism card... That is absolutely infantile, especially when you consider that much of the history of the drug trade trails right behind the CIA and other US intervention programs. Going back to the end of the Second World War, you see — and this is not controversial, it is well-documented — the US allying itself with the French Mafia, resulting in the French Connection, which dominated the heroin trade through the 1960s. The same thing took place with opium in the Golden Triangle during the Vietnam War and again in Afghanistan during the war against the Russians."

Shadow Wars: The Covert Nexus of Drugs and Politics

There have been widespread allegations of government agencies, including the CIA, importing cocaine to curry favor with drug lords during the Cold War. It's argued that the American people, especially the poor and black communities, paid a terrible price as a result. During the Reagan Administration, the federal government took the lead in the war on drugs, coinciding with a new influx of crack cocaine hitting the streets of our inner cities. Crack cocaine provided a cheap high for low-income citizens who couldn't afford the more expensive high of powder cocaine. However, the justice system imposed harsher sentencing guidelines for crack cocaine offenses.

In the mid-1980s, the Reagan administration created twelve new regional task forces, employing hundreds of government agents and prosecutors to combat the rise in drug offenses.

Reagan quietly began sending aid to the Nicaraguan Revolutionary Democratic Alliance, also known as the Contras, shortly after his inauguration. These were former Somoza national guardsmen fighting against the Sandinistas to restore Somoza to power in Nicaragua. The CIA officers actively fought alongside the Contras to overthrow the new Sandinista government. When Congress cut funding due to numerous reported human rights violations by the Contras, the CIA allowed them to engage in drug trade in the United States to finance their military operations. Thus, the Contras resorted to drug smuggling to the United States to fund their anti-Sandinista activities.

On July 17, 1980, Klaus Barbie, a Nazi fugitive working as a Bolivian intelligence officer, orchestrated plans for an Argentine-backed military coup in Bolivia. The coup was led by Colonel Luis Arce-Gomez, the cousin of cocaine kingpin Roberto Suarez, and resulted in the installation of General Luis Garcia Meza as Bolivia's new president. Argentine intelligence personnel supported the uprising, recruiting neo-fascist terrorists such as the Italian Stefano Della Chiaie, who had been collaborating with Argentine death squads.

The coup earned the nickname "Cocaine Coup" due to its financing by six of Bolivia's most notorious cocaine traffickers, who collaborated with the military conspirators. The conspirators stormed the national labor headquarters and arrested former military dictator Hugo Banzer on corruption charges. The ensuing violence was brutal, with government buildings and prisons invaded, employees tortured and killed, drug traffickers released, and female captives gang-raped as part of their torture. As undercover DEA agent Michael Levine noted, "Death was very much a way of life in Argentina."

Despite the geopolitical atmosphere that seemed to favor the CIA, Levine and his DEA field agents were pursuing some of the conspirators for drug crimes. To Levine, it was clear that protecting and controlling Bolivia's cocaine industry was a primary goal of the revolution. In May 1980, the DEA in Miami seized 854 pounds of cocaine base and arrested two top Bolivian traffickers. However, one of the suspects, Jose Roberto Gasser, was almost instantly released from custody by the Miami U.S. attorney's office, Levine wrote. The other defendant's bail was reduced, allowing him to escape the United States. According to Levine, Arce-Gomez boasted to a top trafficker: "We will flood America's borders with cocaine." This was a boast that the coup-makers made good on.

Indeed, Bolivia emerged as the primary supplier of cocaine base to the nascent Colombian cartels, making it the key source of cocaine to the United States. As Levine noted, "And it could not have been done without the unspoken help of DEA and the active, covert help of the CIA."

Instead of taking decisive action to reduce drug trafficking, such as increasing the DEA presence in the country and leveraging the foreign aid the United States was providing to Honduras, the United States shut down its DEA office in Tegucigalpa and seemed to ignore the issue. This indicates a severe discrepancy between the public stance against drugs and the covert actions that indirectly facilitated the drug trade.

By late 1981, the palpable connection to cocaine was straining U.S.-Bolivian relations. The pioneers of the Cocaine Coup soon found themselves evading justice. Interior Minister Arce-Gomez was eventually extradited to Miami and is serving a 30-year sentence for drug trafficking. Roberto Suarez received a 15-year prison sentence. General Garcia Meza became a fugitive, hiding from a 30-year sentence imposed on him in Bolivia for abuse of power, corruption, and murder. Barbie was extradited to France to serve a life sentence for war crimes. He died in 1992.

The Hitz report revealed a cable to CIA headquarters stating that a July 1981 drug delivery had occurred from Honduras to Miami. The cable included the names of those involved and referred to it as "an initial trial run" by members of the Nicaraguan Revolutionary Democratic Alliance. An earlier cable mentioned that the rebels felt they were "being forced to stoop to criminal activities in order to feed and clothe their cadre." Under the guise of the War on Drugs, the Reagan Administration was able to selectively apply pressure to covertly fund right-wing Latin American guerrillas, which were killing thousands of civilians and burning entire villages.

Gary Webb, a determined investigator reporter for the San Jose Mercury News, kicked off a riveting series of exposés on August 18, 1996. His target? Unveiling the shadowy involvement of the CIA in the cocaine trade that swept through Los Angeles in the 80s:

"For the better part of a decade, a Bay Area drug ring sold tons of cocaine to the Crips and Bloods street gangs of Los Angeles and funneled millions in drug profits to a Latin American guerrilla army run by the US Central Intelligence Agency, a Mercury News investigation has found. This drug ring "opened the first pipeline between Colombia's cocaine cartels and the black neighborhoods of Los Angeles" and, as a result, "The cocaine that flooded in helped spark a crack explosion in urban America - and provided the cash and connections needed for L.A.'s gangs to buy weapons."

In April 1986, Senators John Kerry and Christopher Dodd, a Democrat from Connecticut, proposed hearings to investigate allegations of Contra involvement in cocaine and marijuana trafficking. The resulting Kerry Committee report was the final report of an investigation by the Senate Foreign Relations Committee's Subcommittee on Terrorism, Narcotics, and International Operations into the potential involvement of the Nicaraguan Contras in drug trafficking. Senator Richard Lugar of Indiana, the Republican chairman of the committee, agreed to oversee the hearings.

A CIA internal investigation found that agents had worked with drug traffickers to support the Contra program, and a Contra leader was being paid by Colombian traffickers for help with cocaine shipments, with the money being used 'for the cause' of fighting the Nicaraguan government.

The Kerry Committee report also found that "the Contra drug links included that the U.S. State Department, authorized by the Congress, paid over $806,000 to known drug traffickers to carry humanitarian assistance to the Contras." The Senate report concluded that Honduras became an important way station for northbound cocaine shipments and that "elements of the Honduran military were involved ... in the protection of drug traffickers from 1980 on."

In her 1986 sworn testimony before Sen. John Kerry's Senate Subcommittee on Narcotics and International Terrorism, Martha Palacio, a former airline employee whose cocaine trafficking career spanned two years, acknowledged that she could not prove the CIA was conducting the drug exchange operation. However, she added, "What I saw raised many questions about the source of the U.S. weapons I know Ochoa has obtained." As an FBI operative, Palacio would later realize the extent of the damage done to the United States government by the guns-for-drugs exchanges that permeated the hemisphere during the early 1980s. "To my great regret," she said in her statement, "the bureau has told me that some of the people I identified as being involved in drug smuggling are present or past agents of the Central Intelligence Agency."

According to Miami-based John Mattes, a former federal public defender, and Iran-Contra investigator for John Kerry, "What we investigated, which is on the record as part of the Kerry committee report, is evidence that narcotics traffickers associated with the Contra leaders were allowed to smuggle over a ton of cocaine into the United States."

Gary Webb's investigative journalism, particularly his "Dark Alliance" series, sheds light on the murky underworld of governmental offenses and scandals. The series aimed to unveil the social impacts of the crack cocaine trade, noting its disproportionate effects on African-Americans in the justice system, the role of the Contras in the drug trade, and the CIA's knowledge of drug activities by the Contras. The series exposed the crimes of individuals concealed or protected from prosecution.

According to the "Dark Alliance" narrative: "Meneses - who ran the drug ring from his homes in the Bay Area - is listed in the DEA's computers as a major international drug smuggler and was implicated in 45 separate federal investigations. Yet he and his cocaine-dealing relatives lived quite openly in the Bay Area for years, buying homes, bars, restaurants, car lots, and factories... But records and interviews revealed that a number of those probes were foiled not by the elusive Meneses but by agencies of the U.S. government."

Webb's articles in the San Jose Mercury News revealed a drug triangle during the 1980s that linked CIA officials in Central America, a San Francisco drug ring, and a Los Angeles drug dealer. According to his report, the CIA and its operatives used profit of crack cocaine, sold primarily in the Los Angeles black community, to raise millions to support the agency's covert operations in South and Central America. Webb alleged that the Reagan Administration had been involved in the exchange of illegal drugs in inner cities through the use of a kingpin named Freeway Ricky Ross.

Celerino "Cele" Castillo III, a former DEA agent, alleged that during the 1980s, the Ilopango Air Force Base in El Salvador was used by Nicaraguan Contras for smuggling narcotics into the United States, with the collaboration of the CIA and the National Security Council, under Lt. Col. Oliver North's direction.

U.S. Congresswoman Maxine Waters, a U.S. Representative from California's 43rd district, referenced Webb's articles as evidence of a calculated plot to destroy inner-city black America. The New York Times, Los Angeles Times, and Washington Post criticized Webb's credibility, and Webb was eventually forced out of his job. There were four investigations into the matter of the CIA, Contras, and the crack cocaine explosion: two by Congress, one by the Justice Department, and one by the CIA's Inspector General, Frederick Hitz.

On October 5, 1986, a CK123 Cargo plane carrying weapons and CIA employees crashed in Nicaragua. The sole survivor of the crash was Eugene Hasenfus. Residents of Mena, Arkansas, reported that former Marine Lt. Colonel Oliver North and Eugene Hasenfus were frequent visitors during the 1980s, often seen renting cargo vehicles in town. Hasenfus eventually confessed to being part of an illegal operation to arm and resupply the Contra forces from the Mena airport. This revelation led to the eruption of the Iran-Contra scandal.

After the Iran-Contra scandal broke, allegations emerged that the same planes used to carry weapons to Nicaragua were transporting cocaine back to the United States for sale. Despite then-Governor Bill Clinton's public statement that he was fully investigating the allegations of CIA drug running at Mena, an independent group of researchers in Arkansas accused him of covering up an airport used by the CIA and major cocaine smugglers in a remote corner of the Ozark mountains.

According to Deborah Robinson, a journalist with 'In These Times - a progressive magazine focusing on politics, labor, and culture, has reported that the Inter-Mountain Regional Airport in Mena, Arkansas, was allegedly a central point for prominent figures such as the late cocaine mogul Barry Seal, and for clandestine government operations tied to arms and drug trafficking. Robinson further states that Clinton seemingly disregarded this issue until the onset of his presidential campaign, when he pledged financial support for a state-led inquiry into the Mena airport. However, Robinson asserts that Clinton's team never carried through with this promised investigation.

Barry Seal, son of a KKK member and employed by the Medellin Drug Cartel as a pilot, was indicted on conspiracy of money laundering and smuggling Quaalude into Florida in 1984. Seal offered to cooperate with the DEA as an undercover informant during a sting operation targeting Pablo Escobar and other high-ranking members of the Colombian Medellin Cartel and the Marxist Sandinista government in Nicaragua. As a result of his cooperation, the judge in Seal's Florida case reduced his sentence from 10 years to six months' probation.

In December 1984, Seal was arrested in Louisiana for flying in a cargo of marijuana. U.S. District Judge Frank Polozola was bound by the Florida plea agreement and sentenced Seal to six months of supervised probation, which he was to serve at the Salvation Army halfway house facility. On February 19, 1986, Barry Seal was shot to death in front of the Salvation Army halfway house in Baton Rouge. On the same night, Seal's mistress, "Barbara," was also murdered in Miami, along with three other top lieutenants of the Medellin Cartel in Colombia.

The FBI seized all of Barry Seal's personal property from the Louisiana State Police forensics lab but inadvertently left behind a piece of paper in his briefcase containing Vice President George H. W. Bush's personal phone number. George H. W. Bush's connection with the CIA dates back to January 1976, when President Gerald Ford appointed him director of the Central Intelligence Agency.

On March 27, a state grand jury in Baton Rouge indicted three Colombians, Miguel Velez, Bernardo Antonio Vasquez, and Luis Quintero, for the murder of Barry Seal. In May of 1987, all three men were found guilty of first-degree murder and sentenced to life in prison without parole. A fourth assailant, Renteria-Campo, was extradited to Miami to be tried on federal weapons charges. The three assassins claimed that once inside the US, they received directions from a US military official, who was later identified as Lieutenant Colonel Oliver North of the National Security Council, using the alias "John Cathey."

In the 1980s, the US government sold arms to Iran, which was under an arms embargo, to free seven American hostages held in Lebanon. Simultaneously, the CIA was illegally supporting the Nicaraguan Contras by smuggling billions of dollars' worth of drugs into the United States. This became known as the Iran-Contra scandal or Iran Gate. However, the CIA was using gang members as pawns to sell drugs in their own neighborhoods and to suppress black activists who opposed drugs and black-on-black crime. The Reagan/Bush Administration and Iran Contras paved the way to the bloodiest era in America's inner-city history.

While America's elite benefited from the illegal drug trade, violence erupted in most of America's major cities. Michael

Ruppert, an investigative journalist and former Los Angeles Police narcotics detective, wrote extensively about the government's involvement in drug trafficking globally. Ruppert believed that the CIA, the US military, and the LAPD were all involved in illegal drug operations that devastated poor neighborhoods of Los Angeles as well as New Orleans. He resigned from the L.A. Police Department in November 1978. Ruppert stated that politics isn't the only motive: "The control of the cash from the drug trade is of vital importance to Wall Street because drug profits are laundered under corporations and banks net profits."

CHAPTER EIGHT

Drugs, Deception, and the Dirty Wars: Political Tools of Control

"The greatest purveyor of violence in the world: My own Government, I cannot be silent."

————

Martin Luther King Jr.

Imam Abdul Alim Musa, a major drug dealer in Oakland, California, who later converted to Islam after serving time in prison, stated: "So the government wanted to stop the black movement in its tracks? Technically, they used us, drug dealers; it gave us high-quality heroin and cocaine to pump into our own neighborhood, and then we sold it to our own people to break the back of the revolution."

While George H. W. Bush was CIA director, the United States' allies in Central America engaged in "dirty wars" that targeted, tortured, and killed political activists or anyone associated with socialism or communism. In the mid-1970s and early 1980s, the military units, security forces, and death squads of the Argentina

Anticommunist Alliance (Triple A) were trained and armed by the United States and rebranded as counter-revolutionaries or "contras." The United States feared that Soviet Union victories and the establishment of pro-Soviet communist governments in the region would threaten the Panama Canal and isolate the rest of South and Central America from the United States.

El Salvador and Honduras participated in both Operation Condor and the "dirty wars," also known as the Process of National Reorganization. Argentina's new rulers began abducting dissidents off the streets, sending them to torture camps, and subsequently killing them. Many women "disappeared," their children kidnapped by groups acting for the dictatorship before being taken on "death flights." Typically, these victims were drugged, stripped naked, loaded onto aircraft, and thrown alive from military planes and helicopters over the Río de la Plata or the Atlantic Ocean to drown. The Argentina Anticommunist Alliance (contras) was responsible for approximately 30,000 deaths or disappearances during Argentina's last military dictatorship between 1976 and 1983. According to human rights groups and judicial investigations, there were 2,758 death flights in Argentina between 1976 and 1978.

In 1975, Operation Condor was implemented to eliminate communist or Soviet influence associated with the Cold War. Condor coordinated terrorist plots against political opponents, union and peasant leaders, priests and nuns, students and teachers, scholars, and suspected rebels in the Southern Cone of South America. One reporter wrote, "Subversion has grown to include nearly anyone who opposes government policy. In countries where everyone knows that subversives can wind up dead or tortured, educated people have an understandable concern about the boundaries of dissent."

The officials who ran "Operation Condor" were trained at the notorious School of the Americas (SOA), a training center for

Latin American and Caribbean military and police officers originally located in Panama but later moved to Fort Benning in Columbus, Georgia. Operation Condor rounded up thousands of people suspected of affiliation with radical leftist movements under the guise of "fighting terrorism." It involved the intelligence services of Argentina, Bolivia, Brazil, Chile, and Paraguay, which shared information to secretly arrest, torture, and interrogate suspects, followed by executions and secret disposal of bodies through cremation or in mass graves. Rumors swirl that the US government didn't just stand by and watch. Allegedly, through the powerhouse that is the Central Intelligence Agency, they rolled up their sleeves and jumped in, offering technical assistance and even funneling military aid to those involved.

Death squads were dispatched to abduct social activists and relatives of activists and political refugees. Following the military coup in Argentina, these squads carried out violent assassinations of major exile leaders. On July 2, 1976, declassified CIA reports mentioned that six governments convened in Santiago in June and agreed to coordinate operations in Argentina. The report cited a joint operation involving security officers from Chile and Uruguay to raid a human rights office in Buenos Aires and seize records of refugees. The report also mentioned that the leftist leader Edgardo Enriquez, leader of the Chilean MIR (Movement of the Revolutionary Left), was arrested, "subsequently turned over to the Chileans, and is now dead."

CIA officials met with their counterparts at the State Department and informed them that Operation Condor was more than a mere exchange of terrorist intelligence. This report confirmed that Condor had evolved into an international assassination organization involved in "locating and 'hitting' guerrilla leaders," extending its reach beyond the Southern Cone countries to places as far away as Paris and London. By the time Operation Condor ended in the early 1980s, an estimated 60,000 people had been killed and 400,000 arrested or imprisoned.

The Global Ripple Effects of Cold War Interventions

Violent conflicts, known as La Matanza (the Massacre), broke out in Argentina, Chile, Nicaragua, El Salvador, Honduras, Guatemala, and various places in Central America. During the 1970s and 80s, the United States conducted large military exercises in Honduras and hosted bases for the Nicaraguan Contras. The Contras, armed and financed by the United States, targeted anyone they suspected of supporting social and economic reform, including unionists, clergy, independent farmers, and university officials. The violence manifested in an endless cycle of murders, kidnappings, and coups, with the Contras attacking schools, health centers, and the majority of the rural population sympathetic to the Sandinistas or the Socialist Party.

In September 1980, the five major leftist revolutionary organizations merged to form the Sandinista National Liberation Front (FMLN) to oppose the right-wing paramilitary forces. During President Jimmy Carter's administration, four American churchwomen were raped and murdered by paramilitary forces, leading to Carter cutting off aid to El Salvador. However, when Ronald Reagan was elected president, he saw the Salvadoran Dictatorship and the Contras government as allies and a barrier against communist expansion in Central America during the Cold War era.

By December 1981, units from the U.S. began assisting in the formation of the Atlacatl Rapid Deployment Infantry Battalion, aimed at counterinsurgency warfare. They provided significant military aid and advisors. President Ronald Reagan defended his support of the Contras, stating, "What we see in El Salvador is an attempt to destabilize the entire region and eventually move chaos and anarchy to the American border." From 1980 to 1992, approximately 75,000 Salvadorans were killed by government forces during the civil war in El Salvador.

Throughout the 1980s, the civil war between the Contras, paramilitary forces, and Sandinista rebels continued to produce systematic human rights abuses, bloodshed, and terror across Central America. The Sandinistas Liberation Front, known as a democratic socialist political party, fought to give Central Americans a voice in the new revolutionary government and promote democratic ideas. The Contras carried out more than 1,300 terrorist attacks against the Nicaraguan government, seeking to unify the Contra forces fighting the Sandinista rebels. However, they failed to win widespread popularity or military victories within Nicaragua, with a majority of the U.S. public opinion not supportive of the Contras.

The Central Intelligence Agency (CIA) carried out acts of sabotage against the Sandinista government without approval from Congress. The Boland Amendment was passed by Congress, cutting off appropriated funding for the anti-Sandinista rebels known as the Contras. Despite this ban, the Reagan Administration secretly continued to train, equip, and arm the Contras to oppose the left-wing governments in Latin America and oppose its ties to Cuba and the Soviet Union. The support for the Contras came at the expense of large shipments of drugs to poor neighborhoods back in the United States.

On January 4, 1982, Reagan signed the top-secret National Security Decision Directive 17 (NSDD-17), giving the CIA the authority to recruit and support the Contras with $19 million in military aid. The CIA trained teams to sabotage two bridges in Nicaragua and mine the harbor of Managua, the capital city of Nicaragua, and two other harbors to spark a full-scale uprising against the leftist Sandinistas. The mining was an attempt "to severely disrupt the flow of shipping essential to Nicaraguan trade during the peak export period." The CIA's mining operation finally came to the attention of the Senate Select Committee on Intelligence, turning into an international scandal.

Reagan sought to redefine U.S. foreign policy toward Russia and used his signature "war on drugs" as a justification to target Communist leaders in Central and South America. The Boland Amendment prohibited the federal government from providing military support "for the purpose of overthrowing the Government of Nicaragua" and aimed to prevent the CIA and Defense Department from spending money to assist the Contras in overthrowing the Nicaraguan government - a law that the Reagan administration flagrantly ignored. The Reagan Administration became an avid supporter of the Contras and pro-U.S. regimes in El Salvador and Guatemala.

Throughout the 1970s and 1980s, Panama's General Manuel Noriega was a vital ally in Central America, a region that was becoming politically hostile to U.S. interests in the wake of the Cuban Revolution. Noriega was recruited as a CIA informant as early as the 1950s. As head of G-2, Panama's military intelligence command, Noriega was the second most powerful man in Panama and provided critical support for the Contras in Nicaragua and against the FMLN guerrillas in El Salvador. Noriega was a major cocaine trafficker with ties to the notorious Colombian drug lord Pablo Escobar, a key member of the Medellín Cartel. The U.S. intelligence community was aware of his involvement in drug trafficking and corruption for years but chose to ignore it. Noriega allegedly played a role in the Iran-Contra affair, which involved smuggling weapons and drugs for the CIA in an effort to aid the Contras opposing the Sandinistas in Nicaragua.

On July 31, 1981, Colonel Omar Torrijos, the dictator of Panama who signed a treaty during the Carter Administration returning the Panama Canal zone to Panamanian control, was mysteriously killed in a plane crash. For the next two years, Panama was unable to form a unified opposition, leading to an outbreak of strikes and public demonstrations and leaving a power vacuum. Dr. Hugo Spadafora, a well-known Panamanian physician and combat doctor for the Contras in Costa Rica, became a critic of the Panamanian military regime and publicly accused Noriega of protecting drug traffickers, money laundering, and corruption.

Before returning to Panama, Spadafora told friends that he had gathered the evidence needed to implicate Noriega in drug dealing and money laundering. In September 1985, Spadafora was apprehended by Noriega's defense forces while traveling from Costa Rica to Panama. He had been carrying documents revealing Noriega's involvement in cocaine trafficking. Dr. Hugo Spadafora was subsequently tortured and killed. His decapitated body was found dumped under a bridge in a U.S. mail sack on the Costa Rica-Panama border.

Shortly before Spadafora's death, he had befriended two of Noriega's closest allies, Floyd Carlton Caceres and Alfredo Caballero. Floyd Carlton Caceres was a Panamanian who served as General Manuel Noriega's personal pilot, and Alfredo Caballero, a drug trafficker and arms smuggler, had been hired to deliver humanitarian aid to the Contras by the State Department. Noriega provided security for drug shipments by allowing flights from Colombia to land on Panamanian-controlled airstrips. Spadafora started sharing information he received from the two men with the DEA's office in San Jose and the Costa Rican authorities. This news was swiftly relayed back to Panama, and rumors circulated that Noriega had said, "I want Spadafora's head."

After Spadafora's murder, public outrage forced President Nicolás Ardito Barletta to order an immediate investigation.

However, General Noriega's power compelled Barletta to resign before any real progress could be made. Spadafora's brutal death ignited widespread protests; thousands flooded the streets of Panama City, demanding justice. It wasn't until the 1993 administration of President Guillermo Endara that Noriega was finally convicted in absentia for orchestrating Spadafora's assassination.

Washington's propaganda efforts failed to salvage Noriega's image. Even after Spadafora's murder, the Reagan Administration continued supporting Noriega, providing an additional $200 million in foreign aid. However, the National Security Council advised the Administration to distance itself from the embattled dictator.

On December 20, 1989, the United States invaded Panama in Operation Just Cause, aiming to depose General Manuel Antonio Noriega. He faced trial for drug trafficking, indicted in both Tampa and Miami, and for undermining Panamanian democracy.

At his trial, Floyd Carlton testified that Noriega demanded at least $100,000 for every planeload of Colombian cocaine transiting through Panama. Carlton also alleged that he had previously reported Noriega's crimes to U.S. law enforcement, only to be dismissed by the DEA and Embassy officials. He stated, "I asked only for protection for my family and myself. At the time, I had faith in the American justice system."

Throughout the 1980s, the Soviet-Afghanistan War played a significant role in bringing the Cold War era to an end. The early 1990s saw much of the Eastern Bloc disintegrate, leaving a vacuum in the governance of the Soviet Union. By the end of 1991, the Soviet Union ceased to exist, and Mikhail Gorbachev had no country to govern. Boris Yeltsin established a new Commonwealth of Independent States after Gorbachev's resignation and became the most powerful political figure in Russia. On February 1, 1992, President George H. W. Bush and Boris Yeltsin of Russia formally declared an end to the Cold War.

With the Cold War's end, Central and South America had to re-structure without significant superpower support. The U.S.-Russia rivalry had pressured governments worldwide to address racial inequality for black and brown populations. Latin America's black communities faced similar oppression as their counterparts in the U.S. and globally. The colonial-era caste system, favoring those of European descent, kept indigenous peoples and those of African heritage economically marginalized.

Dr. Martin Luther King, Jr. urged young Americans to challenge imperialism, the Vietnam War, and the exploitation of Asia, Africa, and South America by Western capitalists. He called for a values revolution to highlight wealth disparities and unjust alliances with Latin America's elite. The collapse of Eastern European communism and the USSR's 1989 fall contributed to apartheid's end. The white South Africa's apartheid government, backed by the U.S. and Great Britain, had used anti-communism to justify oppression. Apartheid maintained a capitalist system for whites and suppressed blacks.

In February 1990, President F.W de Klerk, the last head of state of South Africa under apartheid, lifted the bans on the African National Congress (ANC) and the Communist Party of South Africa and released Nelson Mandela and other political prisoners. De Klerk stated that communism and socialism had been thoroughly discredited worldwide and were no longer a serious option. He concluded that South Africa's interests "could be best secured by accepting negotiations rather than by committing itself to a long and ruinous civil war."

In the chilling throes of the Cold War, Africa became a grand chessboard for the superpowers, their contest for influence driven largely by the continent's rich natural resources. These resources inadvertently fanned the flames of conflicts that would last for generations.

The colonial overlords, in their pursuit of control, masterfully divided the diverse ethnic groups of Africa. This strategy, ingeniously crafted, was exploited generation after generation to perpetuate Eurocentric dominance across the continent.

The Anglo-White power structure, however, showed little to no interest in nurturing the development of Africa's infrastructure. Instead, the focus was on using the continent as a means to bolster European power structures that had taken root in Africa. Resources were either used to feed this power structure or shipped out of the continent, destined for the bustling markets of Europe or America.

In essence, Africa's wealth was plundered, its potential stifled, and its people left grappling with the consequences of a system that was designed to exploit rather than empower.

The Formation and Impact of the European Union

Today, some conspiracy theorists assert that the European Union (EU) signifies the rise of a totalitarian global government. They envision a world ruled by powerful elites through a so-called New World Order. In reality, the European Union has brought about significant shifts in political and economic power. By consolidating the majority of EU members under a single European Central Banking System and adopting the Euro as its currency, the EU has transformed the landscape of power. The 27 member states are subject to binding laws rooted in a complex system of treaties and must cede a portion of their sovereignty to the EU for policy and foreign affairs decisions. The primary objective of the EU is to stimulate monetary growth and build a robust infrastructure to support an expanding employment system. As the world's largest trading bloc, the EU and its member states account for a quarter of the global economy.

The Treaty of Rome, signed on March 25, 1957, established the European Economic Community, now known as the European Union (EU). Its aim was to ensure that the coal and steel industries would not be used to manufacture weapons of war against neighboring countries. This measure was intended to unite Western European countries, fostering enduring peace and economic growth amongst its members based on democratic principles. It sought to eliminate the brutal chaos and bloodshed of previous conflicts. In 1957, the European Union (EU) was established by six foundational states: Belgium, France, Italy, Luxembourg, the Netherlands, and West Germany. Over the years, the EU expanded to encompass 28 European countries. The UK is the only sovereign nation-state to have left the European Union, reducing the number of member states to 27.

The European Union's governance is divided into three bodies: the European Commission, the Council of the European Union, and the European Parliament. The European Commission is the EU's executive branch, representing the interests of the Union as a whole, not individual countries. It proposes legislation, manages daily operations and budgets, enforces rules, and negotiates international trade agreements on behalf of the EU. The Council of the European Union, in conjunction with the Parliament, adopts laws, coordinates economic policies, and develops foreign and security policies with EU members and other countries or international organizations.

The European Parliament, often referred to as the 'Voice of European Citizens,' is comprised of 785 representatives elected by the citizens of the EU for five-year terms. The Parliament is responsible for approving the membership of the EU Commission and the EU budget in cooperation.

According to Daniel's prophecy, the fourth and final world power, the Roman Empire, has already risen and fallen. In the famous dream, King Nebuchadnezzar saw a grand statue with a golden head, silver chest and arms, bronze torso and thighs, iron legs, and feet of iron and clay. Daniel interpreted the statue as representing successive empires. The golden head symbolized Babylon, the first kingdom and initial "antichrist" system. The silver chest represented the second kingdom, the Medo-Persian Empire. The bronze belly and thighs signified the third kingdom, the Greek Empire under Alexander the Great.

The fourth kingdom, represented by the statue's feet and toes of iron mixed with clay, symbolizes the divided Western and Eastern powers seeking global dominance. This mirrors the fourth and fifth beast systems. The entity, likely the European Union and its allies, extends the Roman Empire's influence, wielding similar economic and military power. However, the iron-clay composition suggests significant internal weaknesses, possibly related to racial issues. Most scholars interpret Daniel's prophecy as referring to the Roman Empire as the final kingdom, which split into Western (Rome) and Eastern (Constantinople) halves.

In 312 AD, Emperor Constantine defeated Maxentius at the Mulvian Bridge on the Tiber River, seizing control of the Western Roman Empire and ending the persecution of Christians. Christianity, a growing religion, spread rapidly throughout Rome and, later, the Byzantine Empire. The following year, Constantine and Licinius, the Eastern Roman Emperor, signed the Edict of Milan in 313. This edict granted the freedom of worship to all religions, regardless of deity, and marked the end of the Age of Martyrs. During this period, thousands of Christians were tortured for refusing to worship Roman deities or the emperor. Around 250 AD, Emperor Decius ordered the execution of all Christians as a sacrifice to the Roman gods, forcing them to choose between their faith and their lives.

Christianity was first recognized as a religious sect in Rome in 64 A.D., when the catastrophic Great Fire of Rome broke out, lasting six days and seven nights. Emperor Nero blamed the Christian community for the disaster, marking the onset of the first mass persecution of Christians. Christians were hunted down, and Nero ordered them to be fed to lions during events in the city's arena. It was during Nero's reign that Peter and Paul, along with other apostles of Jesus Christ, were martyred in Rome by being beheaded.

The imperial spirits, Sol Invictus (Unconquered Sun), and the religious cult of Mithras were all Roman sects. Christianity, with its monotheistic belief in one God, emerged as a rival to the polytheistic religions that the Romans relied on for protection. In 274 AD, Emperor Aurelian established Sol Invictus as the official sun god of Rome and erected a circular temple for worship. December 25th became the dedication date of the temple and a day of celebration. The Roman festival of Dies Natalis Solis Invicti (Birthday of the Unconquered Sun) became a public holiday and later merged with Christmas.

In 324 A.D., after unifying the Roman Empire, Constantine attended the Council of Bishops and the Council of Nicaea in 325 to resolve the controversies plaguing the Christian Church. The central issue was the relationship and nature of Jesus Christ as the Son, God the Father's divinity, and the Holy Spirit's power. Following the council, most Christian leaders agreed that Jesus and God were both truly divine and of the same substance. However, Arius, a priest from Alexandria, Egypt, argued that Jesus, though the Son of God, was of a different substance or essence than the Father and thus inferior. Arius and the five bishops who refused to sign the creed were subsequently exiled.

Nonetheless, Constantine continued to observe pagan rituals and allowed many pagan temples in Byzantium, the new capital of Eastern Rome, to be restored. These temples were often used by local residents as safe havens to store gold, ivory, artwork, and other valuables. Constantine plundered these treasures to fund his extensive renovation of Byzantium into a Christian imperial city.

In 321, Constantine decreed that Christians and non-Christians should unite in observing the venerable day of the sun. This made Sunday the official day of rest in the Roman Empire, a day that Aurelian had previously established as an official cult in reference to sun worship. Constantine lived in a time when it was customary to serve countless deities, which was essential for the preservation of Rome's political and social structure.

After Constantine's death, the Christian Church emerged as Europe's new unifying force, supplanting the Roman Empire. The Latin-speaking Western Empire was led by the Pope, and the Church evolved into the Roman Catholic Church, Western Europe's most powerful institution. As the bishop of Rome, the Pope wielded significant authority within the Western Roman Empire. In contrast, the Greek-speaking Eastern Empire adhered to the Eastern Orthodox Church. Over time, the Eastern Empire flourished as the Western Empire declined, its military weakened by the population's greater loyalty to the Church than the emperor. Despite the Western Roman Empire's fall in 476 A.D., the Eastern Empire endured for centuries as the Byzantine Empire.

The Roman Empire's legacy would resurface as Eurocentric nations competed for global control of economic and religious systems. According to Daniel's prophecy, an Antichrist beast system – symbolized by the statue's feet and ten toes – would arise from Rome's ashes and rule through European nations seeking world domination. This prophecy seemed to find fulfillment in the Brussels Treaty, also known as the Second Treaty of Rome, signed on April 8, 1965. The treaty unified the executive bodies of the European Coal and Steel Community, the European Atomic Energy Community, and the European Economic Community into a single authoritative structure.

During Daniel's era, who practiced the religion of the beast? Many religious leaders falsely attribute this force opposing Almighty God to Western culture to Nimrod or Kush. However, a closer look at Greco-Roman mythology reveals a more likely candidate. Jupiter, the god of the sky and thunder, would shroud himself in clouds to hide his mistresses, but his wife, the goddess Juno, could peel back the clouds to reveal his infidelity. As an ancient Roman goddess, Juno was Jupiter's wife and sister, Saturn's daughter, and Mars' mother, serving as a guardian of Rome. The names of all planets, except Earth, derive from Greco-Roman mythology. Unique among them, "Earth" stems from Old English and Germanic origins, not from a Greek or Roman deity.

Western culture has deeply incorporated the mythology and philosophy of ancient Rome and Greece into the arts, literature, poetry, science, history, and religion. Many celestial objects bear names inspired by Roman mythology, reflecting the rituals devised to communicate with the gods' spiritual realm. While the Greco-Romans practiced polytheistic religions with a pantheon of gods, mythology played a vital role in bridging Old Europe with Western culture. These Old-World myths personified significant relationships, creating brief allusions that connected Western history to ancient Greco-Roman culture. Even today, Western culture often employs mythological designs and names to reconnect with these ancient stories.

The U.S. Apollo Space Program, designed to take humans to the moon, was named after Apollo, the god of the sun, light, knowledge, medicine, and truth. In Greek mythology, Apollo was a formidable god who once had his divine powers stripped by Zeus and was forced to live on earth for a year. According to the Director of Space Flight Operations, Dr. Abe Silverstein, he proposed the name Apollo because an image he saw in a book on mythology caught his attention. He said the image of "Apollo riding his chariot across the sun was appropriate to the grand scale of the proposed program."

In today's news the Artemis program, named after the goddess of the hunt, is a groundbreaking initiative by NASA. Its mission: to take humans back to the Moon, and then even further into space. This ambitious endeavor aims to reestablish human presence on the lunar surface, a feat not achieved since the Apollo 17 mission in 1972.

The program consists of several key components. First, a powerful rocket will propel astronauts beyond Earth's orbit. The Orion Spacecraft, specifically designed for crewed missions, will transport astronauts to and from the Moon. The Lunar Gateway, a space station in lunar orbit, will serve as a staging point for lunar exploration.

Two missions are pivotal to the program's success. Artemis 2, scheduled for no earlier than September 2025, will use the second launch of the Space Launch System (SLS) to fly astronauts around the Moon. Artemis 3 aims to land a crew near the Moon's south pole, potentially in September 2026 or later. Notably, this mission will include the first woman to set foot on the lunar surface.

But the Artemis program won't stop at the Moon. NASA's long-term vision involves sending astronauts to Mars, marking a monumental leap in human space exploration. With the Artemis program, space travelers will be stepping into a future where the boundaries of human reach extend far beyond our home planet.

Further evidence suggests that future Babylon would again be influenced by myths of supremacy, sorcery, and an evil realm of polytheistic religions related to the gods of the outer world. In

Eurocentric culture, mythology played a pivotal role in shaping future structures aimed at controlling material wealth through the targeting of natural resources, often resulting in genocide, slavery, and oppression. The Sea People invaded Israel in the 12th century BC and captured five major cities in Canaan along the northern and southern coasts. The Bible collectively refers to these groups of Indo-European settlers as the Philistines.

Historically, the Sea People left Southern Europe during the late Bronze Age, sailing eastward toward the Mediterranean. Their unsuccessful attempt to invade Egypt led them toward Canaan. According to legend, the Sea People worshipped the Hindu goddess Danu and brought the story of Atlantis to the Mediterranean. Some references refer to her as Dana, considered one of the most ancient Celtic deities. She is known as a Triple Goddess, embodying the essence of the earth, air, and water. She is also known as the Divine Lady and the cosmic energy of universal wisdom. In Hinduism, Danu is identified as a demonic serpent slain by Indra, the god of war and thunder.

In Western culture, the legend of Atlantis tells of a vast area in the Atlantic Ocean, considerably larger than the combined size of Libya and Asia Minor. This utopian island, where peace and justice reigned, eventually fell out of favor with the gods and dramatically disappeared beneath the sea west of the Mediterranean.

The citizens of Atlantis came into conflict with Athens and Egypt, only for the island to be submerged in a single day by celestial powers. Yet, could this vision of a magnificent land, abundant in beauty, often referred to as Atlantis, be a metaphorical and allegorical representation of the genocide and oppression initiated by the Sea People of Old Europe following a natural disaster in ancient Crete?

The legend of Atlantis owes its birth to the ancient and awe-inspiring civilization of Crete, also known as the Minoans. Picture it: around 1500 BC, Santorini, an island known as Kalliste back then, experienced a volcanic eruption of such magnitude that it sent tidal waves towering almost 300 feet high. The tsunami wreaked havoc from 70 miles away, reducing the grand Minoan cities to ruins and claiming the lives of around 40,000 people.

Now, the Minoans weren't just any ordinary people. They were pioneers, way ahead of their contemporaries. With their peaceful ways and the astonishing practice of treating women as equals to men - a rarity in a world where women were often seen as mere possessions - they stood out. Their influence was far-reaching, with established trade connections that spanned from Spain to the coasts of Africa, including Egypt and Ethiopia.

These early Minoans were fearless seafarers and architectural marvels. They demonstrated that early humans could brave the deep waters with boats or rafts, reaching as far as the Greek Island of Crete. It's widely believed that the Minoans themselves journeyed from North Africa to Crete on rafts. And so, the tale of the Minoans, their grandeur, and their tragic end continues to captivate us to this day.

Indeed, the Minoans were extraordinary. They were the first in Europe to introduce farming, domesticated animals, and build a palace, no less. And oh, what palaces they built! They were lavish, filled with towering columns and walls decorated with intricate hieroglyphic murals.

Their capital, Knossos, was a sight to behold. It was the jewel of the Mediterranean - grander and more beautiful than any city in the region. A city ahead of its time, Knossos boasted luxurious baths, a sophisticated primary drainage system, and even underground sewage beneath its paved roads.

The Minoans didn't just survive; they thrived. They rose to a position of political and economic power, their society prospering.

But then, tragedy struck. A catastrophic event brought their flourishing society to its knees. And before they could even begin to rebuild, invaders descended upon Crete.

Indo-European groups, including the Aeolians, Dorians, Ionians, and Sabines, established new settlements on the Aegean Sea islands, such as Crete. This laid the groundwork for the rise of the Greek city-states. These city-states, along with Roman colonies, expanded their reach extensively, conquering Crete and much of the Mediterranean. Consequently, Greco-Roman culture permeated throughout Europe.

Despite this, the legacy of the Minoans, those trailblazing pioneers, refused to be silenced. It resonated, echoing through the pages of history.

World peace and a utopian society - these lofty ideals may not have been achieved by the great empires of the past, nor were they seemingly on their agenda. Western culture, too, doesn't confine itself to the geographic boundaries of Europe or the nations of the European Union.

It's a culture that's been shaped by waves of European migration, the far-reaching effects of colonization, and the impactful influence of religious ideas. Together, these forces have left indelible marks on regions far removed from Europe, such as the United States of America.

At the heart of Western civilization lies Ancient Greek culture, often hailed as its birthplace. It emerged around 4,000 years ago, following the Indo-Europeans' conquest of Crete. In the grand tapestry of history, the threads of the Minoans, the Greeks, and the Romans intertwine, creating a rich narrative of human civilization.

Thales of Miletus, a figure of great significance, is often hailed as the pioneer of human reason in the Western world. He brought with him a wealth of knowledge from Babylonia and Egypt to

Greece, spanning navigational techniques, mathematical break-throughs, and the seeds of scientific thought.

Yet, it's essential to remember that these Western philosophers, Thales included, were standing on the shoulders of the giants that came before them. They were the inheritors of the great civilizations that had laid the groundwork, most notably the Minoans of Crete - a civilization they had conquered.

These philosophers sought to unravel the mysteries of the world not through the lens of the supernatural, myths, or superstitious beliefs but through nature itself. Thales was a trailblazer in this regard, setting a precedent that would profoundly shape the minds of other Greek thinkers.

His influence didn't stop at Greece's borders. It rippled outwards, shaping Western society in ways that continue to be felt today. Thales of Miletus, an inheritor of the Minoan's artistic engineering and a philosopher guided by reason and nature, left an indelible mark on the annals of human thought.

CHAPTER NINE

Parallel Pasts: Daniel, Diaspora, and the Struggles of Identity

"History, despite its wrenching pain, cannot be unlived, but if faced with courage, need not be lived again."

———

Maya Angelou

The story of the Prophet Daniel and the Jewish community bears a striking resemblance to the harrowing experience of Africans during the Middle Passage. Both groups were subjected to the brutalities of slavery, the crushing weight of oppression, and the heartbreak of being torn away from their homelands.

And just like the Africans, Daniel and his fellow Jewish citizens were stripped of their names, a deliberate attempt to erase their true identities. This shared experience of dehumanization and identity theft is a chilling reminder of the cruel tactics used to subjugate and control.

In his prophecies, Daniel paints a picture of a society riddled with systemic racism. He talks about the final beast system and the feet and toes - symbols that represent the precarious nations that emerged from the fragmentation of the Roman Empire.

This beast, with its half-clay and half-iron makeup, signifies the division within the empire itself. Daniel's prophetic vision holds a mirror up to the instability and disunity that plagued the empire and continues to resonate with societies today.

In the annals of biblical history, the tale of Daniel and his three friends - Shadrach, Meshach, and Abednego - is a powerful testament to faith and resilience. These four Hebrews were uprooted from their home in Jerusalem during one of Nebuchadnezzar's raids, the first siege of Judah, and taken captive by the Babylonians.

Yet, despite their status as captives, they rose to prominence, entrusted with overseeing the affairs of the Babylonian province. However, their position did not shield them from controversy. They were denounced by some of the kingdom's wise men for refusing to worship the golden image erected by the king.

The citizens of Babylon were forced to bow before this golden image, their worship signaled by the sound of music. But Shadrach, Meshach, and Abednego stood firm in their faith, refusing to bow down. Their defiance was brought to the king's attention, with the wise men declaring, "O king, these men, whom you have placed in charge, have not paid due regard to you. They serve not your gods nor worship the image you've set up."

Nebuchadnezzar, seething with rage, summoned Shadrach, Meshach, and Abednego. Yet, they remained persistent in their defiant. They declared, "O Nebuchadnezzar, we need not defend ourselves before you. If it be so, our God whom we serve is able to deliver us from the fiery furnace, and he will deliver us from your hand, O king. But even if he does not, let it be known to you, O king, that we will not serve your gods, nor worship the image you have set up" (Daniel 3:14-16).

Their unwavering faith in the face of danger stands as a beacon of courage and devotion, a testament to their resolve to stay true to their beliefs, even under the most trying circumstances.

Babylon stands as a historical symbol of polytheism (the worship of many gods), mythology, and rebellion against the singular Creator God. The name "Babylon" itself translates to "confusion" and signifies the "Gateway of the gods" - a portal through which fallen angels entered to mislead humanity. The foundation of Babylon was built on delusion, deception, and oppression.

Structures of Power and Worship in Ancient Babylon

One of the most prominent structures in Babylon was the ziggurat, designed to serve as a bridge between Heaven and Earth. It was a hotspot for occult worship and communication with lower deities who defied the Almighty God. People of the ancient world believed in the power of astrological communication with the cosmos, hoping to harness the positive influence of the stars and gain insight into the veneration of celestial beings or divine forces of nature.

However, most pagan religions drifted towards idol worship, with symbolic statues representing various gods. The tale of the false god Tammuz, referred to as "the good, young one" in the book of Ezekiel, was widespread not only in Jerusalem but across the known world. Even nude statues of significant deities were often exhibited in public spaces.

The underlying theme throughout these practices was the cosmic battle between the spirit of light and the malicious spirit of darkness. According to these beliefs, the cosmos is populated with both good and evil entities from the potent spiritual world. This opposition symbolizes the eternal struggle between good and evil, light and darkness, that pervades spiritual and religious narratives across various cultures.

In the narratives of the Old Testament, Babylon is a potent symbol of human defiance, a seductive force drawing people away from their Creator. The city of Babylon, in all its grandeur, represents political and religious unity. Yet, it's a unity built on a foundation of oppression, making this formidable city-state a symbol of power misused, and authority abused.

In the book of Revelation, specifically chapter 17, the symbolic mantle of "Babylon" is passed to Rome. Rome is depicted as a major religious, economic, and political system that has surrendered its power to the Antichrist, serving as a tool for his dominion.

Babylon, in this depiction, is seen as a spiritual prostitute serving Satan's purposes. It's associated with a false religious system, a system that has built its infrastructure on the suffering and persecution of God's Covenant People. This portrayal of Babylon as an entity that betrays the faithful and aligns itself with dark forces underscores its role as an enduring symbol of rebellion and corruption in biblical narratives.

The chronicles of history have witnessed cycles of invasions and persecutions inflicted upon Jewish and African nations. Assyrians, Persians, Babylonians, Greeks, and Romans have all played their part in this relentless onslaught. In more recent history, the baton of oppression was passed to Eurocentric nations, who introduced their own brand of devastation in the form of genocide, slavery, colonialism, and apartheid across the globe.

Fueled by an insatiable thirst for wealth, European powers exploited indigenous populations, plundering their resources without remorse. They enacted mass murder and oppression as a means to seize lands and resources, spreading their ideologies while immorally amassing riches from the territories they conquered.

In the Americas, a system heavily favoring the White-Anglo-Saxon population was implemented. This led to the decimation of millions of Native Americans, a tragic consequence of systemic discrimination and exploitation. Europe and America shared a similar blueprint for nation-building, a blueprint that hinged on the forced labor of enslaved Black Africans. This mirrored the practices of ancient Greece and Imperial Rome, creating a chilling parallel between the past and the recent history.

Thus, the cycle of exploitation and oppression, deeply rooted in the pursuit of wealth and power, continued to perpetuate, leaving in its wake a legacy of pain and injustice that is still being grappled with today.

Wealth and Power in Modern America

In contemporary America, the wealth disparity is stark. The uppermost one-tenth of 1 percent possesses nearly as much wealth as the lower 90 percent, while the middle class continues to diminish. Despite being the wealthiest nation in the world's history, the United States has been grappling with the largest wealth gap between the affluent and the working poor since the time of the Great Depression.

Unfortunately, many right-wing politicians advocate for policies that favor the rich as supposed solutions to this wealth gap. Some of the wealthiest individuals, while benefiting from corporate welfare and exploiting tax loopholes that allow them to pay a significantly lower tax rate than average Americans, audaciously blame the poor for their predicament.

An Oxfam report published in January 2017 puts the global wealth disparity into perspective, stating that the world's eight richest people possess more wealth than half the world's population, with a combined net worth of around $426 billion.

Elon Musk, CEO of SpaceX and Tesla, owner of X (formerly Twitter), and founder of Neuralink, which has implanted devices in human brains, is on track to become the world's first trillionaire. His vast empire encompasses electric vehicles, social media, space rockets, and neurotechnology. Despite his father Errol's wealth – "We had so much money at times we couldn't even close our safe" – Musk claims to have accepted no inheritance. On Twitter, he stated, "I don't have an 'emerald mine,' nor was I given free money from anyone, inheritance or otherwise."

In a 2017 Rolling Stone interview, Musk described his father as "a terrible human being" with a "carefully thought-out plan of evil," alleging, "Almost every crime you can possibly think of, he has done." Musk left South Africa to avoid mandatory military service, saying, "Suppressing Black people just didn't seem like a really good way to spend time." Despite his billionaire status, Elon Musk has been one of the biggest recipients of corporate welfare.

Three billionaires have donated a staggering $220 million to support Donald Trump's re-election bid in the campaign's final months. Elon Musk, Miriam Adelson, and Dick Uihlein have emerged as Trump's biggest benefactors, donating unprecedented sums that could reshape the election landscape.

Musk, the world's wealthiest individual, contributed nearly $75 million to his pro-Trump PAC between July and September, according to Federal Election Commission filings. Adelson and Uihlein have also donated tens of millions to groups supporting Trump's re-election. These substantial donations have given Trump a war chest that dwarfs what most politicians could raise.

This late-stage influx of cash has the potential to upend the election's dynamics. With these vast fortunes, Trump can mount an unprecedented advertising blitz, mobilize volunteers, and fund get-out-the-vote efforts on a massive scale. The question is: how will this money shape the race's outcome? Will Trump's billionaire backers propel him to victory, or can Vice President Kamala Harris overcome the financial disadvantage? As the campaign concludes, all eyes will be on how these fortunes are spent and their impact on the electorate.

In his summer 2002 newsletter, Representative Bernie Sanders aptly described the moral decay in corporate America:

"A cancer named 'greed' is gnawing at the heart of corporate America. It's becoming glaringly clear that many large corporations will stop at nothing, legal or not, to boost the already hefty compensation packages of their CEOs. They've falsified financial statements, evaded taxes, scaled back employee pensions and health benefits, and laid off dedicated workers, shifting their plants to China. Concurrently, they've queued up for billions in corporate welfare from the federal government... The 'greed culture' pervading corporate America today is spiraling out of control."

The concept of a trickle-down tax overhaul, which involves reducing taxes on businesses and the wealthy in society as a means to stimulate business investment in the short term and benefit society at large in the long term, has been a subject of much debate among economists.

In particular, critics argue that such tax policies can exacerbate income inequality by disproportionately benefiting the wealthy, while offering little to the middle class. Furthermore, these tax cuts can lead to increased budget deficits, which could potentially result in cuts to public services that often hurt those in the lower income brackets.

In essence, while the initial benefits of the tax overhaul may seem promising, it's important to consider the potential long-term implications, particularly for the middle class and the overall health of the economy.

In the biblical book of Revelation 17:7, the reference to the woman and the beast with seven heads and ten horns is indeed suggestive of the future Babylon, supported by the Antichrist, being an extension of the ten kingdoms of the Roman Empire. The prophecy indicates that Satan, who initially aligns with Babylon, will eventually turn against it, and God will not step in to save Mysterious Babylon from its downfall.

The woman riding the beast is a powerful symbol of her vast influence over global leaders. From the central realms of Mysterious Babylon, the beast's capital, she executes the orders of the Antichrist, wielding her power worldwide.

When we turn to the historical context of European conquest in the Americas, we see a tragic parallel. Indigenous communities were subjected to brutal coercion to convert to Christianity or face death. Unfortunately, this fate was not exclusive to the indigenous peoples of the Americas. Jews, whether in Europe, Israel, or America, were similar.

The Americas have historically been a melting pot of various faiths, with immigrants bringing their religious beliefs, including Judaism, Protestantism, and Islam, to the New World. However, Catholicism, with its elaborate rituals and reverence for saint statues, emerged as the dominant religion, becoming a symbol of cultural pride.

In a dark chapter of history, the Christian Church, interpreting slavery as divine retribution for sin, became one of the largest slaveholders. This position underscored the misuse of religious interpretation to justify inhumane practices.

In the present day, the governance of the Catholic Church remains under the purview of a European Pope. American Protestantism, on the other hand, has largely severed ties with European control, with congregations aligning with specific local denominations.

Contrary to popular belief, the pursuit of the "American Dream" has been primarily driven by economic motivations rather than religious values. The promise of economic prosperity and upward mobility has often been a more potent pull factor for immigrants than the freedom to practice their religious beliefs. This underlines the complex interplay of economic, social, and religious factors in shaping the history and development of the Americas.

Slavery, indeed, played a significant role in catapulting Euro-America to global economic dominance. The brutal system of the transatlantic slave trade, where countless enslaved Africans were forcibly transported to the New World for exploitation, fueled the economic machinery of the European conquest. Slaves who revolted against this oppressive system faced severe punishments, often culminating in public dismemberment as a gruesome warning to others. With slaves considered mere property, insurance companies even offered coverage to slave owners to ensure their profits from forced labor remained uninterrupted. This period marked a time of immense wealth accumulation built on the backs of the enslaved.

The late 1800s brought another dark chapter in American history during the Gold Rush. California reportedly spent over a million dollars on hunting and scalping Native Americans. White settlers, empowered by the lack of consequences, could abduct Indigenous women and children at will.

The indigenous communities faced immense hardships from violent assaults, intimidation, and the spread of infectious diseases. These diseases, particularly devastating to children, led many to seek help from missions. However, their pleas for help were met with further oppression: their children were taken away, and adults were subjected to hard labor.

In the face of such atrocities, the indigenous communities revolted, but this led to a tragic reduction in their population. From an initial population of approximately 300,000 before the arrival of European settlers, the indigenous population dwindled to around 34,000, a devastating outcome of what is now known as the California Genocide. This period stands as a stark reminder of the immense human cost of colonial expansion and economic ambition.

Across America, thousands are protesting police brutality, injustice, and discrimination. Peaceful marches, organized by churches, individuals, and Black Lives Matter supporters, respond to police shootings and inner-city violence that threaten national unity. The fatal shootings of Alton Sterling and Philando Castile, with Castile's final moments going viral, exemplify the acts of brutality eroding the American dream. On August 12, 2017, a Charlottesville rally saw white nationalists, neo-Nazis, and Klan members met with counter-protests. The event turned tragic when a far-right activist drove into a crowd, killing one and injuring 19. Two police officers also died in a helicopter crash. A former Klan leader vowed to "take our country back," echoing Donald Trump's rhetoric.

In 2024, police violence still plagues Black America. Bodycam footage shows the chaotic moment Deputy Grayson fatally shot Sonya Massey, who had called 911 about a suspected intruder. Inside her home, deputies seemed exasperated as Massey sat on her couch, searching her purse for identification. The tension escalated when Grayson spotted a pot on the stove with a flame underneath.

"We don't need a fire while we're here," he said.

Massey quickly got up and moved the pot to the sink. She and Grayson seemed to share a laugh over her pan of "steaming hot water" before she unexpectedly said, "I rebuke you in the name of Jesus." Then, Sangamon County Sheriff's Deputy Sean Grayson began aggressively yelling at Sonya Massey to put the pot of boiling water that she had removed from the stove.

"You better not, or I swear to God, I'll shoot you in your face." Grayson then pulled his 9mm pistol and demanded she drop the pot.

Massey said, "OK, I'm sorry." In Grayson's body camera footage, he pointed his weapon at her. She ducked and raised her hands.

After Grayson shot her, he discouraged his partner from grabbing a medical kit to save her.

"You can go get it, but that's a headshot. Goddamn it, Fuck. There's nothing you can do, man."

He added: "What else do we do? I'm not taking fucking boiling water to the fucking head."

Noting that Massey was still breathing, he relented and said he would get his kit, too. The other deputy said, "We can at least try to stop the bleeding." In less than thirty minutes after the 911 call, Sonya Massey, a 36-year-old Black mother, was shot and killed by a sheriff's deputy in her own Illinois home. Now, her family is demanding answers. They want to know how this deputy, with a troubling history of working at six different law enforcement agencies in just four years and two DUI charges, was ever hired in the first place.

Sonya's tragic death echoes the shocking killing of Breonna Taylor, the 26-year-old emergency medical technician shot by plainclothes police officers in her Louisville apartment. Like Sonya, Breonna was killed in her own home, a place where she should have been safe. The "no-knock" warrant that led to Breonna's death sparked outrage across the country, with protesters demanding justice for Breonna and an end to the racial disparities that fuel police violence against unarmed Black Americans.

Breonna's name, along with George Floyd's, became a rallying cry for a global movement. People took to the streets, calling for the officers involved to be held accountable and for systemic changes to address the deep-seated racism in our policing system. The protests led to real change, with some states banning "no-knock" warrants and others implementing reforms to increase police accountability.

Social media played a powerful role in amplifying Breonna's story and the calls for justice. It connected people across the country, allowing them to organize and demand change. But social media is a double-edged sword. While it can shine a light on injustices and mobilize movements, it can also spread misinformation and deepen divisions.

As we move forward, we must harness the power of social media to create a more just world. We must use these platforms to hold those in power accountable, to lift up the voices of those who have been marginalized, and to demand real change. The memories of Breonna, George, and Sonya demand nothing less.

School Massacres: The Deadly Toll of Social Media Radicalization

Imagine this: a young person, fueled by an extremist ideology spread through social media, walks into a school with a gun, intent on slaughter. This isn't the opening of a horror movie - it's a terrifying reality that's becoming all too common in America.

The mass shootings that have rocked our schools in recent years are a form of domestic terrorism, plain and simple. The perpetrators, often self-radicalized through online platforms, display a chilling willingness to die for their twisted beliefs, much like suicide terrorists. Their private messages and public posts on social media offer a disturbing glimpse into their minds, a trail of digital breadcrumbs that too often lead to bloodshed.

Take the Uvalde tragedy. On May 24, 2022, a gunman stormed Robb Elementary School, claiming the lives of 19 children and two adults in the deadliest school shooting in Texas history. The most haunting messages from the killer were sent privately via social media, a stark reminder of the role these platforms play in the lead-up to such atrocities.

Or consider the Nashville horror. On March 27, 2023, Aiden Hale, a 28-year-old transgender man and former student, fatally shot three 9-year-old children and three adults at The Covenant School, a Presbyterian elementary school. Hale's rampage, which ended only when police shot him dead, is now the deadliest mass shooting in Tennessee's history. Like the Uvalde shooter, Hale left behind a digital footprint that has investigators scouring his social media history for clues.

And then there's the Iowa school shooting, where a chilling TikTok video is believed to have been posted by the gunman just before he killed a sixth grader and wounded seven others. On the morning Dylan Butler opened fire, a TikTok post believed to be from the shooter shows him inside a school bathroom posing with a blue duffel bag, captioned: "Now we wait." This was posted on the short-form video platform TikTok.

The song "Stray Bullet" by a German band accompanies the post, which was used to signal an act of unspeakable violence.

In Winder, a Suburb east of Atlanta, Georgia a 14-year-old Colt Gray a Apalachee High School student and his father, who are charged in connection with a shooting left two students and two teachers dead appeared in court, both declining to enter a plea to the charges against them. Colt Gray made his initial court appearance on a Friday September 6th 2024 following the Apalachee High School shooting in Barrow County, Georgia. Under Georgia law, a juvenile aged 13 to 17 who commits a serious crime is automatically tried as an adult. Colin Gray was also charged alleged that he gave his son a firearm "with knowledge he was a threat to himself and others."

Colt Gray's father, Colin Gray, 54, was arraigned on four counts of involuntary manslaughter, two counts of second-degree murder and eight counts of cruelty to children. The tragedy has left the small community grieving, marking the 45th school shooting in the United States this year.

These cases, and others like them, paint a grim picture of a pattern: young people absorbing extremist ideologies online, their minds warped by hate and intolerance, until they unleash horror on their former schools. Social media, while a powerful tool for good, has a dark side - it's a breeding ground for the radicalization that fuels domestic terrorism in all its forms, including the school massacres that have shattered communities nationwide.

As a society, we must confront this reality head-on. It means demanding more from social media companies to detect and prevent radicalizing content, improving mental health resources for young people, and addressing the root causes of extremism. Our schools should be safe havens of learning, not hunting grounds for those driven to violence by online hate. The time to act is now, before the next devastating attack.

Global Conflicts and Humanitarian Crises

In the Israel-Palestine conflict, more than 41,000 people have tragically lost their lives, including over 15,000 children, in the Gaza Strip. Additionally, many civilians in both Gaza and Israel have suffered from severe humanitarian crises, including displacement and lack of access to basic necessities like food, shelter, and healthcare.

The Israel-Palestine conflict is deeply rooted in historical and political issues, including disputes over territory, sovereignty, and the rights of Palestinians and Israelis. In contrast, the Sudan conflict is characterized by a power struggle between rival military factions, specifically the Sudanese Armed Forces (SAF) and the Rapid Support Forces (RSF), both vying for control of the government.

While the Israel-Palestine conflict often receives significant international attention and media coverage due to its longstanding nature and geopolitical implications, the Sudan conflict may garner comparatively less global attention. This could be attributed to various factors, including the complexity of the situation and competing global crises.

Israel has refused calls for a ceasefire in the Israel-Palestine conflict and instead opted for temporary pauses in its assault on Gaza. Israel's demands include the surrender of the Hamas militant group or its defeat.

Similarly, the situation in Sudan may require international efforts to negotiate a ceasefire and address the root causes of the conflict. Both conflicts have resulted in significant human suffering and displacement, each with its distinct root causes and dynamics. While the Israel-Palestine conflict often garners more international attention, the Sudan conflict is equally devastating, particularly for children and civilians, and urgently requires humanitarian assistance and a path to resolution.

The Sudan conflict has displaced over 6 million people from their homes, with nearly 4.8 million internally displaced and 1.2 million, predominantly women and girls, seeking refuge in Chad. This crisis has led to the largest child displacement crisis worldwide, with more than 3 million children forced to flee their homes. Moreover, over 70 percent of Sudan's healthcare facilities have been forced to close due to the conflict, further exacerbating the humanitarian crisis.

The U.S. Treasury Department has revealed that the Russian mercenary group Wagner Group is supplying surface-to-air missiles to one of the factions involved in Sudan's ongoing conflict.

This action is exacerbating the conflict and causing instability in the region. Sanctions have been imposed on a Wagner commander in response to this revelation.

Conditions in the capital city of Khartoum have deteriorated significantly due to Sudan's civil war, leading to hardship for many residents. However, even those who managed to escape the city in its early days are now struggling to survive.

Wagner Group's involvement in Sudan is part of its expanding presence in Africa, with the aim of undermining U.S. and French influence while profiting from the mining wealth and gold resources of African countries. The proceeds from these activities are believed to be supporting Russia's war in Ukraine.

Wagner Group, a powerful Russian mercenary outfit, has played a prominent role in Moscow's foreign military campaigns, particularly in Ukraine, and has faced accusations of committing atrocities. In Africa, it has bolstered Moscow's growing influence and resource exploitation efforts.

Reports from Sudanese and regional diplomatic sources suggest that Wagner has been supplying Sudan's Rapid Support Forces (RSF) with surface-to-air missiles to support their conflict against the country's army. These missiles have significantly strengthened RSF paramilitary fighters and their leader, Mohamed Hamdan Dagalo, in their power struggle with Gen. Abdel Fattah al-Burhan, Sudan's military ruler and head of its armed forces.

Satellite imagery in neighboring Libya, where Wagner supports rogue general Khalifa Haftar, indicates increased activity at Wagner bases, reinforcing these claims.

Sudan's strategic significance extends beyond its vast size as the third-largest country in Africa. It lies within an unstable and geopolitically vital region, straddling the Nile River, which has far-reaching implications for downstream Egypt and upstream

Ethiopia, with its ambitious hydroelectric plans affecting the river's flow. Sudan shares borders with seven countries, each with its own security challenges linked to Khartoum's politics.

Furthermore, suspicions of gold smuggling involving Russia's Wagner group have arisen, adding to the complexity of their dealings. The U.S. Treasury has accused the Wagner Group of exploiting Sudan's natural resources for personal gain and exerting negative influence.

Russia's interests in Sudan and the broader region extend to the possibility of establishing a military base in Port Sudan along the Red Sea. Such a base would provide Moscow access to and influence over one of the world's busiest and most contested sea lanes. Negotiations regarding this base have been ongoing between Russia and Sudan's military government, which came to power in a coup in 2021.

The delegation to Russia, led by Mohamad Hamdan Dagalo, also known as Hemeti, includes Sudan's Sovereign Council Deputy Chairman and the leader of the powerful paramilitary group, the Rapid Support Forces (RSF). Hemeti has established close ties with Russia through Wagner, relying on him as a key source of gold since the ousting of al-Bashir in April 2019. While gold has helped Russia mitigate the impact of Western sanctions due to its Ukraine invasion, it has also brought increased scrutiny to the RSF.

Ukraine has been implicated in drone strikes and a ground operation against a Wagner-backed militia near Sudan's capital. A CNN investigation suggests Ukrainian special services were likely behind these attacks, targeting the RSF, which is believed to receive support from Wagner in its struggle against the Sudanese army for control of the country. The use of Ukrainian-style drone attacks and the involvement of commercially available drones commonly used by Ukrainians have raised concerns. These covert actions in Sudan mark a significant expansion of Ukraine's conflict with Moscow, extending beyond eastern and southern Ukraine.

Russia's invasion of Ukraine is significantly impacting African economies and governments. African countries are grappling with challenges in the supply of grain, fertilizer, and fuel, as well as the absence of Russian investment, particularly in mining projects. Moscow and Western countries are actively engaging African nations to align with their respective positions.

Adding complexity to this situation is Sudan's reliance on Russia and Ukraine for over a third of its wheat supply. The ongoing war has disrupted wheat imports from both countries. The World Food Programme (WFP) has recently warned that due to the halt in international funding to Sudan since the coup, coupled with poor harvests and the Ukraine conflict, 20 million Sudanese, or half the population, will face food shortages this year.

Survivors of Sudan's Ethnic Cleansing Campaign Speak Out

Hamza Abubakar still remembers the day his life changed forever. The 30-year-old was living peacefully in the village of Misteri in West Darfur until Arab militants, backed by the Rapid Support Forces, launched a brutal attack at dawn in late May. As Hamza and his neighbors fled for their lives, the militants chased them down, wielding AK-47s and other weapons from horseback, camels, and cars. Hamza was hit in the arm, but managed to escape. His brother and sister weren't so lucky – they died in the street from their injuries. "They had no reason to start killing us," Hamza said, still recovering from his wounds.

Hamza's story is just one of many. Naima, a 48-year-old from a Black ethnic group, has lost everything to the violence. Her home has been burned down four times in the past 20 years, and her husband was murdered by the Janjaweed Arab militia nine years ago. "I've lost count of how many relatives I've lost," she said, her voice heavy with grief.

Mariam Adam Yaya was forced to flee her village, leaving seven of her children behind, after "heavily armed" men attacked. "What we went through in Ardamata is horrifying. The Rapid Support Forces killed elderly people and children indiscriminately," she said, still traumatized by the violence.

Amira Khamis, a 46-year-old mother, was targeted because of her Masalit ethnicity. She's lost five of her children and is still recovering from her injuries. "They systematically kill all the people of dark black color," she said, her eyes welling up with tears.

Mahamat Nouredine, a 19-year-old who lost four relatives in the violence, said the RSF mercilessly targeted the Masalit community. "A group of RSF followed us to a hospital and tried to kill everyone... they laid us on the ground in groups of 20 and fired at us," he said, nursing a fractured arm. "Their unspoken goal is to kill people due to their skin color."

The violence has torn families apart and spread like wildfire across Sudan, fueled by a deep-seated desire for ethnic cleansing. The country's Arab leadership has long targeted Black ethnic groups, seeking to drive them out of the region. The conflict has its roots in a twisted ideology of racial supremacy, with lighter-skinned Arabs seeking to dominate and destroy darker-skinned Black groups.

The international community has been slow to respond to the crisis. Despite the growing evidence of ethnic cleansing, Western powers have been reluctant to intervene. The United States has even deepened its military ties with the (UAE) United Arab Emirates, a key backer of the Rapid Support Forces, despite criticism from human rights groups.

As the violence continues to escalate, the people of Sudan are left to suffer. Families have been torn apart, communities destroyed, and countless lives lost. The survivors are left to pick up the pieces, struggling to rebuild their lives in the face of unimaginable trauma.

The world cannot turn a blind eye to the ethnic cleansing taking place in Sudan. It's time for Western powers to take action, to impose sanctions, to support a UN peacekeeping mission, and to hold those responsible for these atrocities accountable. The people of Sudan deserve justice, and they deserve it now.

The Protest Movement

The Roman Catholic Church significantly altered Rome's governance structure, but it was the Protestant Movement that delivered the final blow. In parallel to Rome, America wasn't established through peaceful means or laws but via genocidal violence. The United States shares numerous similarities with ancient Rome. Both Rome and America originated as small agricultural societies. Rome emerged from the Greek Empire, while America gained independence from the British Empire. Each evolved into a democratic republic, requiring laws to pass through two legislative bodies. However, inequality and injustice have driven social unrest, dividing ethnic groups against one another.

During the Civil Rights Movement, one of the initial actions of the Ku Klux Klan was to infiltrate police departments. This allowed them to perpetrate violent acts, including murder and terrorism, against Black Americans. With KKK members becoming part of law enforcement, their acts of savagery were exempt from scrutiny. White violence was often justified as a patriotic act.

The criminalization of Black identity and the legitimization of white violence under the guise of patriotism have been longstanding issues. Police violence against young Black men can be traced back to years of white supremacists associating crime and violence with the Black community.

Today's events serve as indications of a significant shift in the age we know. Many biblical scholars argue that the United States is not mentioned in scripture. However, based on my study of the Holy Bible and historical texts, the British Empire is portrayed as the seventh beast. Therefore, the power structure of the United States, originating from Great Britain, could be interpreted as the eighth beast.

The United States of America, recognized as the most powerful nation in history, shares the emblem of the eagle with Rome. Given that the Roman Empire, once the world's most dominant nation, eventually fell, it's natural to question the enduring power of the United States.

In the apocalyptic Revelation of John, Rome is depicted as the sixth beastly kingdom. After Rome's fall, England inherited a substantial portion of the Roman Empire, allowing Great Britain to rule over the Seven Seas.

John the Prophet was exiled from Rome to the Greek Island of Patmos by Roman Emperor Domitian due to anti-Christian persecution. The division of the Roman Empire is described in Revelation 17:9-11.

"Here is the mind which has wisdom: The seven heads are seven mountains on which the woman sits. There are seven kings. Five have fallen, one is, and the other has not yet come. And when he comes, he must continue for a short time. The beast that was, and is not, is himself also the eighth, and is of the seven, and is going to perdition."

In the past, Rome's reliance on slavery and oppression created economic turmoil, rendering many of its lower-class citizens dependent on the government or forced to work harder for the affluent. Similarly, the United States, with the assistance of its wealthiest elites, has established a status quo reminiscent of Rome, leading to widespread poverty and depriving many of opportunities by placing barriers to the American Dream. To exacerbate the situation, illegal drugs were funneled into impoverished inner-city neighborhoods.

Systemic Inequality and Divine Judgment

Our ghettos are not an accident. The Federal Housing Administration created "residential security maps" to determine the level of security required to provide guaranteed loans at lower interest rates to banks. These funds were then used to build suburban neighborhoods, with the stipulation that no homes be sold to Black families. These biased zoning restrictions forced racial and ethnic minorities into specific geographic areas, either directly or through selective price increases. When realtors or bankers agreed to sell properties to minorities, these homes were often vandalized or even burned down.

The National Housing Act of 1934 established the Federal Housing Administration, which, with the aid of state and local governments, created ghettos and public housing. This was achieved through "redlining," a practice of outlining areas on a map where banks would not invest, leading to the creation of inner-city slums. Redlining is essentially the invisible force behind concentrated poverty and escalating violence in inner cities. Richard Rothstein, a research associate at the Economic Policy Institute, said, "It was an explicit, racially purposeful policy that was pursued at all levels of government, and that's the reason we have these ghettos today, and we are reaping the fruits of those policies."

One of the remarkable aspects of divine wrath, as depicted in Revelation, is that each era of judgment comes with a warning and a call to repentance. On the Island of Patmos, John was enraptured by the Spirit, hearing an angel proclaim, "Woe, woe, woe to the inhabitants of the earth, due to the remaining blasts of the trumpet of the three angels who are about to sound!" Although the first four angels had already sounded their trumpets, prompting a flash of lightning, thunder, and a severe earthquake on Earth, the angel's proclamation signaled those three more judgments, each triggering a series of disasters, were still to occur.

In the sixth chapter of Revelation, John's vision propels him into the future age of the Apocalypse, where angels and demons are actively involved in human affairs. John witnesses Jesus Christ, referred to as Lord (Yeshua Ha'Mashiach in Hebrew), unsealing the first seal. This is followed by the appearance of a rider on a white horse, the first of the four horsemen of the Apocalypse: "And I looked, and behold, a white horse. He who sat on it had a bow and a crown was given to him, and he went out conquering and to conquer" (Revelation 6:2).

The rider on the white horse is often interpreted as symbolizing the great deceiver, also known as the lawless one, who will preside over a period of injustice and deception during the early days of the Tribulation. This figure is referenced in 2 Thessalonians 2:3-4, which warns, "Let no one deceive you by any means; for that Day will not come unless the falling away comes first... who exalts himself above all that is called God or that is worshiped, so that he sits as God."

When Christ, the Lamb of God, opened the second seal, John heard another living creature say, "Come and see." In response, the rider of the fiery red horse emerged. This rider was granted a great sword, symbolizing the power to remove peace from the earth and wage war worldwide, unleashing terror and atrocities on a global scale.

When the third seal was opened, John saw the rider of the black horse carrying a pair of balance scales. While scales typically symbolize commerce and trade, in this apocalyptic context, they ominously signify famine. According to the biblical narrative, the presence of scales indicates a scarcity of vital food, suggesting a time of great economic hardship where even basic necessities become exorbitantly priced. The arrival of this rider marks the onset of widespread hunger and desperation, further intensifying the trials of the Tribulation period.

"So, I looked and behold a black horse, and he who sat on it had a pair of scales in his hand. And I heard a voice in the midst of the four living creatures saying, 'A quart of wheat for a denarius, and three quarts of barely for a denarius; and do not harm the oil and the wine'" (Rev. 6:5-6).

Upon the opening of the fourth seal, John witnessed the last rider of the four horsemen. He saw a pale horse, and the name of its rider was Death, with Hades following closely behind. They were given power over a fourth of the earth to kill with the sword, hunger, death, and by the beasts of the earth (Revelation 6:8).

Before the final Judgment, the cries of the souls of those who had been slain for God's word and for righteousness were heard. John heard the voices of these martyrs from beneath the Altar, questioning, "How long, O Lord, holy and true until You judge and avenge our blood on those who dwell on the earth?"

In the Book of Matthew, the disciples privately asked Jesus on the Mount of Olives about the signs of His Second Coming and the end of the age. Jesus replied:

"Take heed that no one deceives you. For many will come in My name, saying 'I am the Christ,' and will deceive many. And you will hear of wars and rumors of wars. See that you are not troubled, for all these things must come to pass, but the end is not yet.

For nation will rise against nation and kingdom against kingdom. And there will be famines, pestilences, and earthquakes in various places. All these are the beginning of sorrows.

Then they will deliver you up to tribulation and kill you, and you will be hated by all nations for My name's sake" (Matthew 24:4-9).

CHAPTER TEN

Hunger, Power, and Global Struggles

"To a man with an empty stomach, food is God."

———

Mahatma Gandhi

The World Food Program, a prominent defender against global hunger, states that a staggering 795 million people, or one in every nine individuals on earth, don't have enough food for a healthy lifestyle. The struggle for food is not just about hunger but also about power. Throughout history, food has been used as a weapon in conflicts, with nations withholding or destroying resources to gain the upper hand. It's a ruthless game of chess where the pawns are the innocent people in war-torn regions of Asia, Africa, and the Middle East. Sadly, it's always the working poor who bear the brunt, unable to stockpile food or access their food sources in times of crisis.

Let's take a trip back to 1806, right in the middle of the Haitian Revolution. The U.S. Congress, in league with Great Britain, France, and Spain, slapped a crippling embargo on Haiti. The brave locals were fighting tooth and nail against their oppressors. The embargo, backed by the grim threat of re-enslavement, stripped the white plantation owners of their access to the island's resources. This was the aftermath of the French army's defeat, an army sent by none other than Napoleon himself with the grim intention of re-enslaving Haiti's Black populace. The U.S. and European powers were not fans of Haitian independence and used diplomatic isolation as punishment, pushing Haiti into a cycle of poverty that lasts to this day.

In recent times, nations like Syria, Yemen, Libya, Sudan, and Palestine have seen a large chunk of their people displaced due to unending conflicts and migration. Millions of refugees, driven by the relentless horrors of violence, have embarked on perilous journeys seeking sanctuary. They have found themselves knocking on the doors of neighboring countries and even venturing into far-flung regions of Europe in their quest for safety and a chance at a peaceful life. The situation in Syria is particularly grim. Since March 2011, close to a million people, including many women and children, have lost their lives. The UN has accused all parties involved of war crimes, including denying people access to basic necessities like food, water, and healthcare. In the first two years of battle against the ISIS militia, the U.S. coalition, led by General Sean MacFarland, reports that nearly 45,000 jihadists have been killed in Iraq and Syria.

The Human Cost of Conflict in Syria, Yemen, and Sudan

In the heart of Syria, as the United Nations High Commissioner for Refugees (UNHCR) diligently tracks, a staggering 4.8 million individuals had been forced to abandon their homes by July 2016. This immense number represents a striking 22% of the country's pre-war population. Yet, the turmoil doesn't stop there. A further 8.7 million people — over half of Syria's contemporary population — have had to relocate within the country, leaving behind their homes and livelihoods.

The drama of displacement in Yemen is just as heart-wrenching as elsewhere. The BBC News adds depth to this tale of human tragedy that has gripped Yemen since the war's inception in March 2015. An astounding 3.3 million people were forced out of their homes and into uncertainty. By January 2017, the crisis hadn't subsided, with over 2 million people still living in displacement. This figure marked a staggering six-fold increase from the numbers registered at the end of 2014. The story of Yemen is a poignant testament to the chaos and displacement that war brings.

But it's not just about displacement. The war has triggered a cascade of humanitarian crises: cholera outbreaks spread fear and disease, medicine shortages undermine health efforts, and the specter of famine looms large. The human toll of the war is devastating, with over 4 million people displaced from their homes.

In Sudan, the narrative is hauntingly familiar. The International Organization for Migration Displacement Tracking Matrix (IOM DTM) reports that conflicts within the country have uprooted approximately 4.57 million people. These displaced individuals have found temporary homes in different locations, covering every single one of Sudan's 18 states.

In a world where food is often a bargaining chip in power struggles, the fight against hunger is not just about feeding the starving, but also about challenging the systems that allow such injustices to persist.

The Great Tribulation, a period detailed by Christ, is characterized by catastrophic events, including the transformation of oceans into blood red and the subsequent death of sea life. This period of supernatural disaster is prophesied to occur globally.

In the Book of Daniel, the Prophet envisions a 'Seventy Weeks' era, with each week symbolizing a seven-year period at the end of the age.

In the final seven weeks, or the 62nd week of history, the Messiah will appear but will be 'cut off' by a "people of the prince who is to come" (Daniel 9:26). This will be a period that religious leaders will construct a stronghold through deception that incites war, famine, and greed, ushering in a period of global suffering. This phase of the Great Tribulation is also referred to as "the time of Jacob's trouble," primarily focusing on the dispersion of Israel (Jeremiah 30:7). According to the New Testament, the Great Tribulation, as mentioned by Christ in the Olivet Prophecy, signifies an era "such as has not been since the beginning of the world until this time, no, nor ever shall be" (Matthew 24:21).

"Then the seventh angel sounded: And there were loud voices in heaven, saying, 'The kingdoms of this world have become the kingdoms of our lord and of his Christ, and he shall reign forever and ever."

–Revelation 11:15

"Then I heard a loud voice saying in heaven, 'Now salvation, and strength, and the kingdom of our God, and the power of His Christ have come, for the accuser of our brethren, who accused them before our God, day and night, has been cast down. And they overcame him by the blood of the lamb."

–Revelation 12:10–11

The great conflict between Michael and his angels and Satan with his demonic forces is vividly depicted in Revelation. John describes the escalating scene, "and another sign appeared in heaven: behold, a great, fiery red dragon having seven heads and tens horns, and seven diadems on his heads. His tail drew a third of the stars of heaven and threw them to the earth" (Revelation 12:3-4).

"So, the great dragon was cast out, that serpent of old, called the Devil and Satan, who deceives the whole world; he was cast to the earth, and his angels were cast out with him."

—Revelation 12:9

God's servants triumphed over the devil by the blood of the Lamb, their faithful testimonies, and some through martyrdom. Others found refuge in the wilderness when the Antichrist's armies advanced upon Israel.

"Therefore, rejoice, O heavens, and you who dwell in them! Woe to the inhabitants of the earth and the sea! For the devil has come down to you, having great wrath, because he knows that he has a short time."

—Revelation 12:12

In the final victory before Christ's return, a massive earthquake kills seven thousand people. Yet, the remaining city dwellers were filled with fear and gave glory to God. Revelation 14:14 states, "The second woe is past. Behold, the third woe is coming quickly."

Historically, Europe's struggle for control over Africa and its vast wealth justified the enslavement and colonization of millions and sparked wars to control their abundant natural resources. Africa has played a vital role in the industrial development of European societies, and the continent's incredible wealth was a significant trigger for both World Wars.

China and Russia have been strengthening their ties to counter the United States, notably over the South China Sea. China supports Russia's backing of Pyongyang and North Korea against the United States and South Korea. China has even commenced the construction of its first overseas military facility in Djibouti and revealed plans for Chinese banks to operate in the Horn of Africa. Many African nations have become crucial to this rising Eastern superpower as Africa seeks funding to improve infrastructure, including roads, railways, dams, seaports, and airports. China's increasing interest in Africa for its strategic value and access to natural resources, paired with its position as Africa's largest trading partner, could signal the end of European control and make a third world war imminent.

Michael Collins, the deputy assistant director of the CIA's East Asia Mission Center, stated during a session on the rise of China at the Aspen Security Forum that Chinese President Xi Jinping and his regime are waging a cold war against the US. The goal of China's global influence operations is to replace the United States as the world's leading superpower.

The Role of BRICS and Apocalyptic Visions

The rise of the BRICS countries aligns with the concept of the ascension of the South, resonating with Daniel's prophecy and the Apocalypse of Revelation. "The South" is frequently used as a metaphor for the developing nations, predominantly those in the southern hemisphere. Initially, the term BRICS was not just a geographical reference, but it encapsulated the broad spectrum of emerging and soon-to-be industrialized nations from the Global South, including Russia in the Northern Hemisphere and China in the Eastern Hemisphere. The term BRICS was first coined within the sphere of foreign investment strategies, as detailed in the 2001 publication Building Better Global Economic BRICs by Jim O'Neill, the then-chairman of Goldman Sachs Asset Management.

These countries established the BRICS group in 2006 to encourage cooperation and dialogue on a variety of global matters, especially in the realms of economics, politics, and security. The first summit, attended by the founding nations Brazil, Russia, India, and China, took place in Yekaterinburg. South Africa joined the coalition in 2010, followed by Egypt, Ethiopia, Iran, Saudi Arabia, and the United Arab Emirates, who became members on January 1, 2024. The BRICS nations collectively make up around 30% of the world's landmass and 45% of the global populace. Brazil, Russia, India, and China are among the world's ten most populous countries. As of January 1, 2024, the BRICS organization broadened its membership to include 15 nations.

In prophecy, the dramatic conclusion of Western dominance arrives with a fierce east wind bringing the final temporal judgments. The temple in heaven is opened, and John observes seven angels dressed in pure bright linen, their chests girded with golden bands. One of the four living creatures' hands each of the seven angels a golden bowl containing the wrath of God. The temple fills with smoke from God's radiance, brilliance, and mighty power, and no one can enter the sanctuary until the seven plagues are complete.

"I saw something like a sea of glass mingled with fire, and those who have the victory over the beast, over his image and over the mark and over the number of his name, standing on the sea of glass, having the harps of God."

—Revelation 15:2

A loud voice from the temple commanded the seven angels to pour out the first bowl upon the earth, targeting all those who worship the beast and his image. Consequently, all those who bore the mark of the beast and his image broke out in dreadful and painful sores.

Next, the second angel poured out his bowl into the sea, turning the ocean into the blood of corpses. Every living creature in the sea died as a result.

The third bowl was poured out on rivers and springs, turning all the water into blood. Following these events, John heard a voice cry out from the altar. This voice was destined to say:

"You are righteous, O Lord, The One who is and who was and who is to be, Because You have judged these things. For they have shed the blood of the saints and prophets, and You have given them blood to drink. For it is their just due." Another angel cries out from the altar, saying, "Even so, Lord God Almighty, true and righteous are Your judgments."

—Revelation 16:5-7

The fourth angel poured his bowl upon the sun, causing a scorching heatwave that burned the earth with intense heat. Yet, even as they suffered immensely, the people remained devoted to Satan's charm, refusing to repent of their sins. Those afflicted by these horrific plagues would not change their ways or give glory to God Almighty.

The fifth angel poured his bowl upon the throne of the beast, and its kingdom was plunged into darkness. This plague struck at the very heart of the beast's power. The people gnawed their tongues in agony, tormented by unbearable pain and suffering. Yet, they still refused to repent of their wicked ways.

The sixth angel poured his bowl upon the great river Euphrates, and its waters dried up. This plague cleared the path for the armies of the east to march towards the Battle of Armageddon. John saw three unclean spirits emerge, taking the form of frogs, leaping from the mouths of the dragon, the beast, and the false prophet. These were the demonic spirits of Satan, summoned to gather the nations of the earth and incite a global war.

"Then the seventh angel poured out his bowl into the air, and a loud voice came out of the temple of heaven, from the throne, saying, 'It is done!'"

A massive earthquake, unlike any in recorded history, shook the earth. This cataclysmic quake, punctuated by flashes of lightning and deafening thunder, marked the end of human history as we knew it.

The catastrophic earthquake was felt worldwide, shattering the great city of Babylon—magnificent capital of the ancient empire—into three parts. If the theory holds true, that America is the prophesied Babylon, the eighth beast of scripture, then perhaps this cataclysmic quake would rend Washington, D.C., the U.S. capital, into three parts.

Scripture hints that God will grant the righteous and the oppressed a brief respite from the coming devastation, a chance to flee Babylon (America). Yet, swiftly, God pronounces judgment on Mysterious Babylon, for it is written, "Vengeance is mine; I will repay," says the Lord (Romans 12:19).

John hears a voice from heaven saying, "Come out of her, my people, lest you share in her sins and lest you receive of her plagues. For her sins have reached heaven, and God has remembered her iniquities."

"Render to her just as she rendered to you, and repay her double according to her works; in the cup which she has mixed, mix double for her.

Babylon's pride is so immense that she glorifies herself and lives in luxury, exploiting the poor. The rulers or elites of the earth, who have profited from her trade and financial transactions, will weep and mourn when they see the smoke and flames of her destruction.

"In the measure that she glorified herself and lived luxuriously, in the same measure give her torment and sorrow; for she says in her heart, 'I sit as a queen, and am no widow, and will not see sorrow.' Therefore, her plagues will come in one day—death and, mourning and famine. And she will be utterly burned with fire, for strong is the Lord God who judges her" (Revelation 18:7-8).

Her economy, built on oppression, will face a double dose of vengeance for her wickedness. The rulers and elites who indulged in her immorality and luxuriated in the suffering of martyrs will face sudden financial ruin. Heaven's hosts, the apostles, and the prophets are summoned to rejoice at Babylon's fall, for God has exacted vengeance.

A mighty angel hurled a massive millstone into the sea, proclaiming, "With such violence will Babylon the great be thrown down, never to be found again...In her was found the blood of prophets, saints, and all slain-on earth" (Revelation 18:21-24).

John heard loud voices of a multitude in heaven exclaiming, "Alleluia! Salvation, glory, honor, and power belong to the Lord our God! For His judgments are true and righteous. He has judged the great harlot who corrupted the earth with her fornication, and He has avenged on her the blood of His servants shed by her" (Revelation 19:1-2).

Following this, John heard the voices say, "Alleluia! Her smoke rises up forever and ever!" The twenty-four elders and the four living creatures fell down and worshipped God, who sat on the throne, saying, "Amen! Alleluia!" Then, a voice from the throne said, "Praise our God, all you, His servants, and those who fear Him, both small and great!"

This praise was followed by a grand chorus of a great multitude from heaven, reminiscent of the sound of ocean waves crashing onto the shore and the booming of thunder, exclaiming, "Alleluia! For the Lord God Omnipotent reigns! Let us be glad and rejoice and give Him glory, for the marriage of the Lamb has come" (Revelation 19: 2-7). John was commanded to record this vision.

Overwhelmed with emotion, John fell at the feet of the angel to worship, only to be swiftly rebuked. The angel said, "See that you do not do that! I am your fellow servant, and of your brethren who have the testimony of Christ. Worship God! For the testimony of Christ is the spirit of prophecy."

—Revelation 19:10

Suddenly, the heavens opened, and a white horse appeared. The moment of truth had arrived, and the time had come for Almighty God to judge the world.

John saw Christ seated on the white horse, many crowns on His head. His eyes were like flames of fire, and He wore a robe dipped in blood. He was known as "The Word of God." At this time, the Lord Christ was referred to as 'Faithful and True,' ready to bring vengeance to the world in holy righteousness. He bore a name on His forehead that no one understood except Himself (Revelation 19:12).

Christ rode forth, trailed by the armies of heaven, clad in pristine white linen, mounted on white steeds. From His mouth flashed a sharp sword, poised to smite the nations with God's fierce wrath. Inscribed on His robe and thigh: KING OF KINGS AND LORD OF LORDS.

In the New Testament, Christ is often depicted as the bridegroom, with the Church as His bride. This symbolizes the spiritual union through faith in Christ and God's love. However, it's crucial to distinguish the Church or religion from the holy city of New Jerusalem.

The Bible proclaims that God is building a great holy city for the chosen inhabitants of New Jerusalem. The ritualistic and man-made religious system of Babylon will be destroyed with the return of the Messiah. It is a promise of a new spiritual order that transcends human institutions and religious practices, centered solely on God's divine presence and the rule of the Messiah.

"Now I saw a new heaven and a new earth, for the first heaven and the first earth had passed away. Also, there was no more sea. Then I, John, saw the holy city, New Jerusalem, coming down out of heaven from God, prepared as a bride adorned for her husband. And I heard a loud voice from heaven saying, 'Behold, the tabernacle of God is with men, and He will dwell with them, and they shall be His people."

–Rev. 21:1–3

The Legacy of Yeshua and the Struggle for Justice

During Jesus Christ's (Yeshua Ha'Mashiach in Hebrew) life on earth, a revolution was growing in Judea, threatening to tear the nation apart. Freedom fighters had taken up arms to rebel against Roman rule. The story of Christ emphasizes the concept of a kingdom far greater than Rome, a message perceived by the Romans as a political threat. Yeshua's teachings appealed directly to the poor, and by divine validation, salvation became available to all, including the Gentiles.

Yeshua's family hailed from Nazareth in Galilee; a stronghold of the Jewish militant sect known as the Zealots. The Zealots were prominent in political affairs and fought, albeit unsuccessfully, with the Edomites, who also sought to rebel against Roman occupation or Eurocentric domination during Yeshua's time on earth. Yeshua broke family traditions and initiated a new messianic movement focused on loving Yahweh (the One true God) with all one's heart and soul and demonstrating a universal love for all humanity.

Many Israelites and Jewish extremists were anticipating a Messiah who would descend from the clouds to lead a Jewish revolt. However, Yeshua came spreading peace and salvation, teaching a subliminal message that this new movement, which the disciples simply called 'The Way,' would ultimately consume the Roman Empire from within.

Following the crucifixion of the Lord Christ, a new religion began to emerge around the Mediterranean region, known as the Good News or simply the Gospel. The ethnic and cultural ties between the Jewish people and African society have always been intertwined, and any historical representation of Jesus Christ was intentionally altered to coexist with European dominance. During His time on earth, Jesus was called "Yeshua," which translates to "Salvation." Additionally, the title of Messiah (Ha'Mashiach), which signifies the Savior of the world, originates from the Hebrew language and means "Anointed One" to serve YHVH, pronounced Yahweh.

In many ways, the chaos and oppression experienced by the Israelites during the era of Jesus Christ mirror the pain and suffering of people of African heritage. This close and peculiar relation to systematic racism has manifested in the daily lives of people of color around the globe. However, there are indications that this wild and evil power that has ensnared people of African heritage worldwide has come through the gateway of the primordial powers of Satan and his unholy fallen angels, who have been cast out of the highest heavenly realms. John 12:31 refers to Satan as the ruler of this world.

Both the Old and New Testaments warn that a counterfeit Christ or Antichrist will manifest in the everyday world by exerting control over the global economy through ten nations that were once part of the Roman Empire. However, there is also the ever-present supernatural power that will be poured out on the earth in the latter days.

In 1 Timothy says that, "in the latter times some will depart from faith, giving heed to deceiving spirits and doctrines of demons, speaking lies in hypocrisy."

Unsurprisingly, the history of Ethiopia is deeply intertwined with that of Israel and Egypt. Early interpreters of the Bible, referring to Greek translations, have suggested that the term "sun burned faces" used to describe the Jews may also refer to all Ethiopians or Kushites, given that the geography of Africa, the Middle East, and southern Asia was dominated by dark-skinned people during that era.

Indeed, Ethiopia is frequently mentioned in the Bible, often as the land of the sons of Cush, who was one of Noah's grandsons. The creation story in Genesis even sets the Garden of Eden in this region.

The rise of European dominance coincided with growing hypocrisy and greed, which, in turn, gave birth to supremacy. This power, characterized by Eurocentric dominance, played a central role in creating negative stereotypes of people of African descent, which persist today through systemic and individual racism. This biased concept permeates our institutions and social structures and is deeply ingrained within the fabric of our society.

Religious allegiances and nationalists reinforced these biases by adopting policies that favored people of European heritage. Archbishop Desmond Tutu, a social rights activist and African Anglican bishop during the apartheid era in South Africa said, "If you are neutral in situations of injustice, you have chosen the side of the oppressor. If an elephant has its foot on the tail of a mouse and you say that you are neutral, the mouse will not appreciate your neutrality."

This bias was evident in the 1887 Supreme Court decision in Dred Scott v. Sandford, where Chief Justice Roger Taney claimed that the Constitution regarded blacks as "so far inferior that they had no rights which the white man was bound to respect, and that the negro might justly and lawfully be reduced to slavery for his benefit."

In Revelation, the Lord gives a final warning in letters to the seven churches in each city of the Roman prefectures of Asia Minor. The Lord Jesus Christ (Yeshua Ha'Mashiach) instructed the Apostle John to record what he was about to witness in his vision leading up to the Messiah's return. The message was given to seven specific congregations in seven cities located along the great circular route of the Roman Empire's most influential territories.

"The mystery of the seven stars which you saw in My right hand, and the seven golden lampstands: The seven stars are the angels of the seven churches, and the seven lampstands which you saw are the seven churches" (Revelation 1:20).

John's vision continues with a message to the Church of Ephesus: "I know your works, your labor, your patience, and that you cannot bear those who are evil. And you have tested those who say they are apostles and are not, and have found them, liars...Nevertheless, I have this against you, that you have left your first love. Remember therefore from where you have fallen; repent and do the first works, or else I will come to you quickly and remove your lampstand from its place unless you repent" (Revelation 2:1-4).

John's vision further includes a message for the historical city of Smyrna, situated on the Aegean coast of Anatolia. The church there held a deep spiritual love of God but was suffering under the persecution of the Roman authorities because of its prehistoric roots. Smyrna, calling itself "the first city of Asia," believed to be the first settlers of ancient Crete before the Greco-Roman era, thought to have migrated from North Africa and considered themselves the indigenous people of Asia Minor. Similar persecution was happening in Judea, Carthage, Numidia, and other coastal cities of North Africa and Asia Minor.

The letter to Smyrna implies that the oppressed Indigenous people, persecuted by the Romans, may have been of Jewish descent. Similarly, many African Americans and those from the African Diaspora, who suffered under European oppression, are believed to be direct descendants of ancient Israel's original Hebrews. The Indigenous Smyrnaeans attempted to placate the Romans by erecting a pagan temple for Emperor Tiberius in 23 BC.

"And to the angel of the church in Smyrna write, 'These things say the First and the Last, who was dead, and came to life: "I know your works, tribulation, and poverty (but you are rich); and I know the blasphemy of those who say they are Jews and are not, but are a synagogue of Satan. Do not fear any of those things which you are about to suffer. Indeed, the devil is about to throw some of you into prison, that you may be tested, and you will have tribulation in ten days. Be faithful until death, and I will give you the crown of life. He who has an ear, let him hear what the Spirit says to the churches. He who overcomes shall not be hurt by the second death'" (Revelation 2:8-11).

Revelations and Repentance

Each message from the Lord Jesus Christ (Yeshua) to the churches unveils the historical significance of particular congregations. However, judgment begins at the house of God. The seven visions, given to John on the Isle of Patmos while he was "in the spirit," lay out prophetic messages for mankind's future through signs and allegories.

The third letter targets the church in Pergamos, a hub of paganism with three temples dedicated to Roman emperors and the famed Altar of Zeus. As a center of Hellenistic culture and learning, Pergamos was deeply loyal to Rome. Christ sternly warned the church, "I know your deeds and where you reside, where Satan's throne sits."

Prior to Christ's birth, the Roman Republic successfully campaigned against Asia Minor's Greek city-states and Africa's coastal regions. When Numidian commander Jugurtha defied the Roman army, the Senate declared war on his kingdom, Numidia, in North Africa. With Bocchus I of Mauretania's help, Jugurtha was captured, brought to Rome in chains, and paraded naked through the city. Stripped of his finery, he was imprisoned in the Tullianum, where he starved to death.

Many leaders from Africa and Asia Minor, such as Hannibal, the Carthaginian general who famously crossed the Alps to bring the fight to the walls of Rome, waged significant battles. Another notable figure was Mithradates, the king of Pontus, who fought the Roman Empire for five years in an attempt to prevent Rome from conquering Greek cities in Asia. Despite his efforts, which included the slaughter of about 80,000 Romans in a single day, he failed to stop Rome, and the conflict ended in a Roman victory in 85 BC. Consequently, the fertile and resource-rich region of Carthage became the Roman province of Africa, and Pergamum became the capital of the Roman province of Asia Minor.

Once more, the Apostle John was divinely inspired to deliver a message, this time to Thyatira. Though the smallest of the seven cities, Thyatira thrived as a manufacturing and trade hub, strategically located on the route from Pergamos in western Asia Minor. It was here that Paul encountered Lydia, a Philippi businesswoman who aided his mission. Yet, despite its prosperity, Thyatira grappled with paganism and immorality.

The church of Thyatira, while faithful and loving, was the most corrupt of the seven churches of Asia. John was instructed to write a message to them:

"To the angel of the church in Thyatira write, 'These things say the Son of God, who has eyes like a flame of fire, and His feet like fine brass: I know your works, love, service, faith, and your patience; and as for your works, the last are more than the first. Nevertheless, I have a few things against you because you allowed that woman Jezebel, who calls herself a prophetess, to teach and seduce My servants to commit sexual immorality, and she did not repent. Indeed, I will cast her into a sickbed, and those who commit adultery with her into great tribulation, unless they repent of their deeds'" (Revelation 2:18-22).

Yet, those who steadfastly reject Satan's doctrine and pagan sacrifices will be glorified when the Lord Jesus Christ (Yeshua) returns.

"Now to you I say, and to the rest in Thyatira, as many as do not have this doctrine, who have not known the depths of Satan, as they say, I will put on you no other burden. But hold fast what you have till I come" (Revelation 2:24-25).

John's visions proceeded with a message for Sardis, an Asia Minor city boasting the immense Temple of Artemis, with altars to Artemis, Zeus, and the Imperial family. Notably, a Christian refuge existed within the temple grounds. Yet, beneath its façade of vibrancy, the Sardis church was spiritually bankrupt, riddled with hypocrisy.

"To the angel of the church in Sardis, write, 'These things say He who has the seven stars: I know your works, that you have a name, and that you are alive, but you are dead. Be watchful, and strengthen the things which remain, that are ready to die, for I have not found your works perfect before God...Therefore, if you do not watch, I will come upon you as a thief, and you will not know what hour I will come upon you" (Revelation 3:1-3).

The church of Sardis was founded on repentance, but it had become lifeless over time. However, the glorified Christ assured those who remained faithful and committed, "He who overcomes shall be clothed in white garments, and I will not blot out his name from the Book of Life; but I will confess his name before my Father and before His angels" (Revelation 3:5).

Sardis, renowned for its precious metals and coinage, was a significant hub in the Roman Empire. Historians credit it with inventing minting and pioneering coin-based trade. Post-Carthage, Rome controlled Asia Minor's Mediterranean region, structuring provinces into its initial prefectures.

All nations will succumb to Satan's godless allure. The Antichrist will command global commerce, enriching the elite and embodying Babylon's might. As Mysterious Babylon amasses wealth, much of the world will struggle to feed its people.

The Antichrist's plagues unleashed poverty, starvation, and disease upon the world. Though many institutions deny systemic racism, Western Europe and America built their prosperity on slavery and segregation. Some scholars liken America's culture and arrogance to Babylon's in Revelation, with both powers amassing fortunes through human trafficking and slave labor.

However, a sudden change is imminent! "He who has an ear, let him hear what the Spirit says to the churches."

"To the angel of the church in Philadelphia write, 'These things say He who is holy, He who is true, "He who has the key of David, He who opens and no one shuts and shuts, and no one opens." I will make those of the synagogue of Satan, who say they are Jews and are not, but lie – indeed, I will make them come and worship before your feet, and to know that I have loved you. Because you have kept My command to persevere, I also will keep you from the hour of trial which shall come upon the whole world, to test those who dwell on the earth..." "He who overcomes, I will make him a pillar in the temple of My God, and he shall go out no more. I will write on him the name of My God and the name of the city of My God, the New Jerusalem, which comes down out of heaven from My God. And I will write on him My new name'" (Revelation 3:6-12).

John was instructed to address the lukewarm church of Laodicea. This immensely wealthy city, though lacking a natural water supply, engineered aqueducts to bring in lukewarm water from distant hot springs. When a 60 AD earthquake razed Laodicea, Hierapolis, and Colossae, Laodicea rebuilt independently, declining Rome's financial aid.

The Lord Jesus Christ (Yeshua Ha'Mashiach) delivers a stern message to the lukewarm church of Laodicea, describing them as spiritually blind:

"These things say, the Faithful and True Witness, the Beginning of the creation of God: I know your works, that you are neither cold nor hot. I could wish you were cold or hot. So then, because you are lukewarm and neither cold nor hot, I will vomit you out of My mouth. Because you say, 'I am rich, have become wealthy, and have need of nothing' — and do not know that you are wretched, miserable, poor, blind, and naked" (Revelation 3:14-17).

Interestingly, some scholars propose that Asia Minor's initial settlers migrated from Africa circa 7,000 years ago via primitive sea vessels. The region prospered until the southern Sea People's assault out of Balkans (Old Europe), followed by devastating incursions from Persia, Greece, and Rome, radically transforming their lifestyle. Apostle Paul later evangelized in Asia Minor, establishing several churches.

Through an angel, the Lord Jesus Christ affirms the indigenous people's true historical identity: "I will make those of Satan's synagogue, who claim to be Jews but lie, come and worship at your feet, so they will know I have loved you" (Revelation 3:9).

In the letter to Philadelphia, Christ praises the church's faithfulness and loyalty, ensuring their crown remains secure: "I know your works. Behold, I have set an open door before you, none can shut it, for you possess little strength, yet upheld My word and confessed My name" (Revelation 3:8).

The Holy Father readies vengeance against Satan's worldly system. Christ does not remain silent on the racial identity of Asia Minor's indigenous people, urging them to stand for truth. These dark-skinned Jews, a cohesive people with a rich culture and Yahweh-guided future, face a global political force opposing God's kingdom. There is a political thread running throughout the world that works against the kingdom of God, favoring a corrupt systematic system while many watchmen remain silent on the matter.

In today's America, the core values fought for during the equality struggle appear to be publicly disregarded, dividing people much like the atmosphere the Apostle Paul faced in Asia Minor.

In Lystra, Apostle Paul was stoned and left for dead. Similarly, Asia Minor's Aboriginal people faced persecution, oppression, or forced relocation to the mountainous regions above their coastal cities. Some indigenous groups sought refuge in Africa, abandoning the brilliant civilization they had spent centuries building.

In her New Yorker essay "Mourning for Whiteness," Pulitzer laureate Toni Morrison reflects on Donald Trump's election: "The choices made by white men, who are prepared to abandon their humanity out of fear of black men and women, suggest the true horror of lost status."

Morrison further explains that many whites see Donald Trump as a savior who will secure white supremacy: "This is a serious project. All immigrants to the United States know (and know) that if they want to become real, authentic Americans, they must reduce their fealty to their native country and regard it as secondary, subordinate in order to emphasize their whiteness.

Unlike any nation in Europe, the United States holds whiteness as the unifying force. Here, for many people, the definition of 'Americanness' is color."

Toni Morrison's depiction of the extreme lengths some individuals are willing to go to maintain the illusion of white superiority is a searing indictment of racial hatred. Her words paint a stark picture of the willingness to commit heinous acts of violence, even against innocent children and churchgoers, all to perpetuate a sense of racial dominance. Such actions, carried out under the guise of patriotism and hidden behind masks, deny the perpetrators the dignity of face-to-face confrontation.

This lawless behavior, as Morrison describes, bears a stark resemblance to the ascent of the lawless one, who has taken his place on the elegant throne of mysterious Babylon. It's a chilling reminder of the persistent and deeply rooted issues of racial inequality and systemic racism that plague societies, not just in America but around the world. It's a call to action for all of us to confront these issues head-on, to commit to dismantling racist structures, and to strive for a world where all individuals are valued equally, regardless of the color of their skin.

Conclusion

In conclusion, our journey through this content has been both eye-opening and thought-provoking. We've explored the complex history of America, marked by government actions that have had far-reaching implications on social equality and peace, often disproportionately affecting marginalized groups. From the dark history of slavery and its profound impact on the nation's economic growth to revelations about government involvement in drug trafficking and the devastating crack epidemic, we've seen how these actions have shaped America's socio-political landscape.

The narrative of America's past, with its roots in white supremacy and a caste-like system, serves as a stark reminder of the challenges the nation has faced in achieving true equality. The Civil War, born out of these societal structures, testifies to the deep-seated divisions that once tore the country apart.

Yet, amidst this history of oppression and injustice, there is hope. The notion that changes may be on the horizon, akin to a new era, beckons us to listen to the whispers of prophecy. Some scholars see a striking similarity between America's culture and the biblically depicted grandeur of Mysterious Babylon in Revelation. Just like Babylon, the U.S. has grown wealthy from the dark history of human trafficking and exploiting free labor. If America really reflects Babylon, then those in charge might not be celebrating for long. We could be on the verge of a major historic shift, a moment of reckoning for a nation striving for equality and justice.

Throughout our journey, we've also delved into the timeless themes of racism and discrimination, which have persisted throughout history. While racism may continue to persist, there is a call to be better and to reject societal standards that perpetuate inequality based on social class or skin color. The stories of individuals from diverse racial and religious backgrounds who opposed the evils of oppression stand as a testament to the power of kindness and compassion in the face of adversity.

In essence, this journey has been a profound exploration of history, scripture, and the human condition. It has shed light on the origins of discrimination and wrongdoings, urging us to use the knowledge gained from this exploration to make a positive impact on our society. As we come to the end of this book, I want to express my gratitude to you, the reader, for joining me on this enlightening journey. Let us all strive to be agents of change, promoting kindness and equality in our society. Cheers to a brighter future.

Bibliography

Archives.gov. (1979). *National Archives*. Retrieved November 7, 2015, from JFK Assassination Records: www.archives.gov/research/jfk/select-committee-report/part-2-king-findings.html

BBC . (2011, December 11). *Panama's General Manuel Noriega and his fall from grace*. Retrieved February 8, 2016, from BBC News: http://www.bbc.com/news/world-latin-america-15853540

Black Panther Party. (n.d.). Retrieved 7 17, 2015, from Wikipedia, the free encyclopedia: https://en.wikipedia.org/wiki/Black_Panther_Party

Bromwich, D. (2008, May 16). *AntiWar.com*. Retrieved July 7, 2015, from Martin Luther King's Speech Against the Vietnam War: http://antiwar.com/orig/bromwich.php?articleid=12844

CIA funnels drugs into poor US neighborhoods. (2011, January 11). Retrieved December 31, 2015, from Crime, Politics, Drugs, History, USA: https://www.rt.com/usa/usa-cia-drugs-poor-americas/

Daily Mail Reporter. (2010, December 13). *Revealed: Richard Nixon's slurs on blacks, Jews, Italians, and the Irish*. Retrieved April 30, 2016, from Daily Mail: http://www.dailymail.co.uk/news/article-1338217/New-tape-recordings-reveal-Richard-Nixons-racist-rants-resigning-Watergate-scandal.html

DeBerry, J. N. (2014, January 16). *Martin Luther King Jr.'s opposition to Vietnam enraged even some allies*. Retrieved July 7, 2015, from The Times-Picayune : http://www.nola.com/opinions/index.ssf/2014/01/martin_luther_king_jrs_opposit.html

Delaval, C. (1995-2014). *cocaine, conspiracy theories and the cia in central america*. Retrieved December 17, 2015, from FRONTLINE · pbs online · wgbh: http://www.pbs.org/wgbh/pages/frontline/shows/drugs/special/cia.html

Delegation of the European Union to the United States. (n.d.). Retrieved July 4th, 2016, from How do the EU Works: http://www.euintheus.org/who-we-are/how-the-eu-works/

DeRienzo, P. (n.d.). *ARKANSAS GOVERNOR BILL CLINTON PRESIDENT GEORGE BUSH CIA DRUGS FOR GUNS CONNECTION.* Retrieved December 20, 2015, from Civil Intelligence Association Defense Oversight Group: http://www.ncoic.com/clinton.htm

Dinges, J. (n.d.). *Columbia University.* Retrieved February 5, 2016, from Operation Condor: http://www.latinamericanstudies.org/chile/operation-condor.htm

Ecyclopedia of World Biography. (n.d.). *Manuel Noriega Biography.* Retrieved February 8, 2016, from Ecyclopedia of World Biography: http://www.notablebiographies.com/Ni-Pe/Noriega-Manuel.html

Equal Justice Iniaative . (2014). *Harper's: Legalize It All: How to Win the War on Drugs.* Retrieved 03 28, 2016, from Nixon Adviser Admits War on Drugs Was Designed to Criminalize Black People: http://www.eji.org/node/1240

FettMann. (2003, July 31). *THE BEST KIND OF BIGOT – HARRY TRUMAN AND HIS HATREDS.* Retrieved April 28, 2016, from New York Post: http://nypost.com/2003/07/31/the-best-kind-of-bigot-harry-truman-and-his-hatreds/

Fogelman, J. S. (2003). *http://jdstone.org.* Retrieved July 15, 2016, from CONVERT TO CHRISTIANITY OR DIE: http://jdstone.org/cr/files/converttochristianityordie.html

Gjohnsit. (2008, August 14). *The OB Rag.* Retrieved July 19, 2016, from The Great California Genocide: http://obrag.org

Holmes, M. S. (2009 , February). *The Freedom Riders, Then and Now.* Retrieved October 31, 2015, from Smithsonian Magazine: http://www.smithsonianmag.com/history/the-freedom-riders-then-and-now-45351758/

Huffton Post. (2013, 3 11). *The Reagan Era:Turning Back Racial Equality Gains.* Retrieved 04 24, 2016, from HuffPost Black Voices: http://www.huffingtonpost.com/dedrick-muhammad/the-reagan-eraturning-bac_b_2838625.html

Hutchinson, E. O. (203, December 17). *The Nixon Tapes, Racism and The Republicans.* Retrieved April 30, 2016, from News & Politics: http://www.alternet.org/story/17422/the_nixon_tapes,_racism_and_the_republicans

Jones, B. (2009, January 19). *Socialistworker.org*. Retrieved July 9, 2015, from The King they won't celebrate: http://socialistworker.org

Jr., M. L. (1968, April 3). *American Rhectoric Top 100 Speeches* . Retrieved November 1, 2015, from I've Been to the Mountaintop: http://www.americanrhetoric.com/speeches/mlkivebeentothemountaintop.htm

Kane, M. (2002, December). *The El Salvadoran Civil War*. Retrieved February 5, 2016, from http://novaonline.nvcc.edu/eli/evans/his135/events/elsalvador80/salvador80.html

Kerry Committee report. (2006, April). Retrieved December 17, 2015, from Wikipedia, the free encyclopedia: https://en.wikipedia.org/wiki/Kerry_Committee_report

King, M. L. (1967, April 4). *Beyond Vietnam -- A Time to Break Silence*. Retrieved August 29, 2015, from American Rhetoric Online Speech Bank: http://www.americanrhetoric.com/speeches/mlkatimetobreaksilence.htm

King, M. L. (1967, August 16). *Martin Luther King, Jr. and the global freedom struggle*. Retrieved August 30, 2015, from Where do we go from here?: http://kingencyclopedia.stanford.edu/encyclopedia/documentsentry/where_do_we_go_from_here_delivered_at_the_11th_annual_sclc_convention/

King, M. L. (1967, August 16). *Martin Luther King, Jr. and the global freedom struggle*. Retrieved August 30, 2015, from Where Do We Go From Here?: http://kingencyclopedia.stanford.edu/encyclopedia/documentsentry/where_do_we_go_from_here_delivered_at_the_11th_annual_sclc_convention/

King, M. L. (2006, April 30). *The Pacifica Radio/UC Berkeley*. Retrieved August 30, 2015, from Why I Am Opposed to the War in Vietnam: http://www.lib.berkeley.edu/MRC/pacificaviet/riversidetranscript.html

Knight, D. B. (n.d.). *The CIA, the Contras and Crack Cocaine* . Retrieved December 21, 2015, from Albion Monitor : http://www.albionmonitor.com/9612a/ciacontra.html

Martin Luther King, J. (1968, February 4). *Martin Luther King< Jr. And The Global Freedom Struggle*. Retrieved October 30, 2015, from The Drum Major Instinct: http://kingencyclopedia.stanford.edu/encyclopedia/documentsentry/doc_the_drum_major_instinct/

Morrison, T. (2016, November 21). *Making America White Again*. Retrieved December 11, 2016, from The New Yorker: http://www.newyorker.com/magazine/2016/11/21/making-america-white-again

Morrow, R. (2013, Thursday, April 4). *Jeb Bush and the Murder of CIA Drug Smuggler Barry Seal in 1986*. Retrieved December 31, 2015, from Did Jeb Bush, VP George Herbert Walker Bush and Oliver North Murder CIA Drug Smuggler Barry Seal in February, 1986?: http://barrysealmurder-1986jebbusholivernorth.blogspot.com/2013/04/jeb-bush-and-murder-of-cia-drug.html

Nessen, S. (2015 , Feb 4). *Remembering Malcolm X: Rare Interviews and Audio*. Retrieved September 21, 2015, from WNYC News : http://www.wnyc.org/story/87636-remembering-malcolm-x-rare-interviews-and-audio/

NOI.org. (n.d.). *Nation of Islam*. Retrieved November 2, 2015, from Dr. Martin Luther King not a 'Dreamer': http://www.noi.org/dr_king_not_dreamer/

O'Callaghan, J. (2016, 7 5). *NASA's Juno Mission Involves A Scientific Joke That Took 400 Years To Set Up*. Retrieved 7 5, 2016, from IFLScience: http://www.iflscience.com/space/nasas-juno-mission-to-jupiter-has-awkward-mythological-origins-in-mistresses-and-infidelity/

Parry, R. (1997). *Dark Side of Rev. Moon (Cont.): Drug Allies*. Retrieved December 17, 2015, from The Consortium : https://www.consortiumnews.com/archive/moon6.html

Quora. (2015, September 12). *Why were the moon missions named after the sun god, Apollo, rather than the moon goddess, Diana?* Retrieved 7 6, 2016, from Quora: www.quora.com

Sanders, B. (Summer 2002). *Sanders Scoop newsletter*. Retrieved july 14, 2016, from Third World Traveler : http://www.thirdworldtraveler.com/Political/Greed_MoreGreed_Sanders.html

Scanlon, J. (1999). *Jo freeman.com*. Retrieved November 7, 2015, from The Death of Dr. Martin Luther King, Jr.: http://www.jofreeman.com/photos/Kingfuneral.html

Severo, R. (2003, June 26). *New York Times* . Retrieved November 7, 2015, from Lester Maddox, Segregationist and Georgia Governor, Dies at 87: http://www.nytimes.com/2003/06/26/obituaries/26MADD.html

Sitkoff, H. (1981). *The Struggle for Black Equality, 1954-1992*. New York : Hill and Wang .

Smith, P. (2015, May 14). *Historian Says Don't 'Sanitize' How Our Government Created Ghettos*. Retrieved July 22, 2016, from Race: http://www.npr.org

South African History Online. (22-Mar-2011, March 11). *South African History Online*. Retrieved June 5, 2016, from The impact of the collapse of the USSR in 1989 : http://www.sahistory.org.za/article/impact-collapse-ussr-south-africa-grade-12

Soylent Communications. (2015). *NNDB tracking the entire world*. Retrieved December 31, 2015, from Barry Seal : http://www.nndb.com/people/140/000129750/

Stokely Carmichae Biography. (2015). Retrieved 7 Jul, 2015, from http://www.biography.com/people/stokely-carmichael-9238629.

Stokely Carmichael. (n.d.). Retrieved Jul 17, 2015, from Wikipedia, the free encyclopedia: https://en.wikipedia.org/wiki/Stokely_Carmichael

The Center for Justice & Accountability . (n.d.). *Bringing Human Rights Abusers To Justices*. Retrieved February 15, 2016, from El Salvador 12 Years of Civil War: http://www.cja.org/article.php

The Influence of The Roman Empire. (n.d.). Retrieved 7 8, 2016, from danxner : http://www.danxner.com/extramaterials/art003/Final_Project/Influences.htm

The JBHE Foundation, Inc. (1999). *The Transformation of the Racial Views of Harry Truman*. Retrieved 04 25, 2016, from The Journal of Blacks in Higher Education: http://www.jstor.org/stable/2999133?seq=1#page_scan_tab_contents

The National Sercurity Archive. (2004, June 10). *LIFTING OF PINOCHET'S IMMUNITY RENEWS FOCUS ON OPERATION CONDOR*. Retrieved February 4, 2016, from The National Security Archive: http://nsarchive.gwu.edu/NSAEBB/NSAEBB125/

This Day in HIstory, Vietnam 1967. (n.d.). Retrieved July 7, 2015, from Martin Luther King, Jr., speaks out against the war: http://www.history.com/this-day-in-history/

Wachtler, M. (2014, April 17). *RIP Michael C Ruppert, the Cop that busted the CIA*. Retrieved December 31, 2015, from whitehouse Press: http://www.whiteoutpress.com/articles/2014/q2/rip-michael-c-ruppert-the-cop-that-busted-the-cia/

Washington Post and the New York Times. (1998, November Tuesday). *Name-Base index of the CIA report, Volume II, and repost of articles.* Retrieved December 20, 2015, from CIA Report on Contras and Cocaine: http://www.namebase.org/hitz.html

Webb, G. (1996, Aug 22). *Cocaine pipeline financed rebels* . Retrieved December 20, 2015, from The Dark Alliance: http://www.mega.nu/ampp/webb.html

Week Online. (2002, February 8). *DRCNet Interview: On the War on Drugs.* Retrieved December 12, 2015, from Noam Chomsky interviewed by Week Online: http://chomsky.info/20020208/

Wikepedia. (n.d.). *Jeremiah Wright controversy.* Retrieved November 28, 2015, from Wikipedia, the free encyclopedia: https://en.wikipedia.org/wiki/Jeremiah_Wright_controversy

Wikipedi. (1986-2015). *CIA involvement in Contra cocaine trafficking.* Retrieved December 17, 2015, from Wikipedia, the free encyclopedia: https://en.wikipedia.org/wiki/CIA_involvement_in_Contra_cocaine_trafficking

Wikipedia. (n.d.). *War on Drugs.* Retrieved December 3, 2015, from Wikipedia, the free encyclopedia: https://en.wikipedia.org/wiki/War_on_Drugs

Wikipedia. (n.d.). *Wikipedia, the free encyclopedia.* Retrieved November 7, 2015, from King assassination riots: https://en.wikipedia.org/wiki/King_assassination_riots

Wikipedia, the free encyclopedia. (n.d.). *Constantine the Great.* Retrieved August 6, 2016, from Byzantine Empire: https://en.wikipedia.org/wik/Constantine_the_Greati

Wikipedia, the free encyclopedia. (n.d.). *Poor People's Campaign.* Retrieved October 31, 2015, from https://en.wikipedia.org/wiki/Poor_People%27s_Campaign

Wikipedia, the free encyclopedia. (n.d.). *Racial Segregation* . Retrieved August 14, 2016, from Redlining: https://en.wikipedia.org/wiki/Redlining

Wikipedia, the free encyclopedia. (n.d.). *Thales of Miletus.* Retrieved 7 10, 2016, from Wikipedia, the free encyclopedia: https://en.wikipedia.org/wiki/Thales

Wikipedia.org. (n.d.). *Assassination of Martin Luther King, Jr.* Retrieved November 3, 2015, from Wikipedia, the free encyclopedia: https://en.wikipedia.org/wiki/Assassination_of_Martin_Luther_King,_Jr.

Wright, J. (2008, March 27). *The day of Jerusalem's fall.* Retrieved November 28, 2015, from The Guardian : http://www.theguardian.com/commentisfree/2008/mar/27/thedayofjerusalemsfall

Wright, R. j. (2003, April 13). *Confusing God and Government.* Retrieved November 15, 2015, from BlackPast.org: http://www.blackpast.org/2008-rev-jeremiah-wright-confusing-god-and-government

Yellin, E. (1998). *King's Last March* . Retrieved October Monday, 2015, from The Sanitation Strike, the Assassination and Memphis in 1968: http://americanradioworks.publicradio.org/features/king/yellin.html

www.ingramcontent.com/pod-product-compliance
Lightning Source LLC
Chambersburg PA
CBHW021223130626
46554CB00004B/1343